GW00645046

The Political Campaigning Handbook

Real life lessons from the front line

Lionel Zetter

Hh Harriman House Publishing

HARRIMAN HOUSE LTD

3A Penns Road
Petersfield
Hampshire
GU32 2EW
GREAT BRITAIN

Tel: +44 (0)1730 233870
Fax: +44 (0)1730 233880
Email: enquiries@harriman-house.com
Website: www.harriman-house.com

First published in Great Britain in 2007
Copyright © Harriman House Ltd

The right of Lionel Zetter to be identified as Author has been asserted
in accordance with the Copyright, Design and Patents Act 1988.

ISBN: 1-905641-34-6
ISBN 13: 978-1905641-34-5

British Library Cataloguing in Publication Data
A CIP catalogue record for this book can be obtained from the British Library.

All rights reserved; no part of this publication may be reproduced, stored in a retrieval
system, or transmitted in any form or by any means, electronic, mechanical,
photocopying, recording, or otherwise without the prior written permission of the
Publisher. This book may not be lent, resold, hired out or otherwise disposed of
by way of trade in any form of binding or cover other than that in which it is published
without the prior written consent of the Publisher.

Printed and bound by Biddles Ltd, Kings Lynn, Norfolk

No responsibility for loss occasioned to any person or corporate body
acting or refraining to act as a result of reading material in this book
can be accepted by the Publisher or by the Author.

About the author

Lionel Zetter went to Sussex University where he took a BA Hons in History and an MA in African Studies, writing his thesis on 'Strategic Security Concepts in Southern Africa'. He was Chairman of the University's Conservative Association and active in local Brighton politics.

After University he worked for a variety of research and security companies before starting the political research division of the Media Information Group. He founded his own company, Parliamentary Monitoring Services Ltd, in 1984, before selling it to Dods Parliamentary Communications Ltd in 2006. In 2007, he became Dods' non-executive Deputy Chairman. He is a member of the National Union of Journalists, and a member (and former Chairman) of the Government Affairs Group. He is a Fellow of the Chartered Institute of Public Relations (and its President in 2007) and a Fellow of the Royal Society of Arts.

The author has been involved in every election campaign (general, local, European and GLA) since 1979. He has also participated in many of the by-elections since that date. He has worked at Conservative Central Office and in the House of Commons, and he has been an Association Chairman, a Ward Chairman, and a general election agent. He has also stood for council, the GLA and the Westminster Parliament.

Lionel lives in Enfield with his wife Claire (a deputy head) and three teenage children. Apart from politics, his hobbies include tennis, rugby and martial arts.

LONDON BOROUGH OF REDBRIDGE	
HJ	27/05/2008
324.941	SW

Acknowledgements

Many people have helped me with my campaigns over the years, and many have helped me with this book. Some of them still work for the three main parties, and have asked not to be credited by name. The fact that they have been willing to contribute speaks much for their generosity of spirit, but also for the camaraderie of the 'poor bloody infantry' who slug it out toe to toe in our increasingly less infrequent elections. The spirit of the football game in no man's land lives on.

Those who are less shy include Francis Ingham, Douglas Smith, Peter Forrest, Jonathan French, Malcolm Tyndall, Henry Lamprecht and Mark Glover.

I would also like to thank my family for putting up with my many absences over the years, as I fought one hopeless campaign after another. However, the experiences which went into those campaigns have also gone into his book – so there has been some end product at least.

 I was Chairman of Enfield Southgate in 1997, when between us (and a huge national swing) we succeeded in losing Michael Portillo his seat. I was at the Labour Party conference later that year in a work capacity when Siôn Simon MP (a former client) introduced me to a group of activists at the bar as the Chairman of Enfield Southgate. Thinking that I was the Labour Chair, they cheered 'our' victory. When Siôn kindly pointed out that I was in fact the Tory chair the cheers were redoubled – and I didn't have to buy a drink all night!

So thanks to my wife of three decades Claire (and there ought to be a campaign medal in that), and my three teenage children Alec, Annie and Richard. Without their tolerance (and occasional help) I would have achieved even less than I ultimately did.

My thanks are also due to my publisher, Harriman House, and to Myles Hunt in particular. He saw the potential (and possibly the humour) in this most esoteric of subjects. Finally, my grateful thanks to my editor, Suzanne Anderson, who ironed out my worst literary excesses and kept me on the straight and narrow.

Contents

Preface

Who the book is for

This book is aimed at the many thousands of people who take part in election campaigns every year. Whether you are standing as a candidate, running a campaign, or simply helping out, this book has helpful hints and shortcuts to help you on your way.

The lessons in this book are applicable whether the campaign in question is a general election, by-election, European election, Assembly election or Council election. The scale and resources may vary enormously, but the principles are very much the same: identify your supporters during the course of the campaign, and get them out to vote on Polling Day.

So whether you are a veteran of the campaign trail or a campaign virgin, this book has something in it for you.

What the book covers

This book begins by looking at how the political parties run elections from the centre. Even if you are campaigning in a no-hope seat a hundred miles away from the party headquarters, it is important that you have some idea of their thinking, and some explanation for their actions – no matter how bizarre they may appear.

The main part of the book is a 'how to' guide to fighting elections on the ground. It starts with the hunt for a seat, and some hints as to how to get yourself selected. It then moves on to describe the resources and equipment which you will need to fight and win a campaign. Finally, and hopefully most usefully, it describes some of the techniques (drawn from many campaigns and many campaigners) needed to leaflet, canvass and campaign in an efficient and effective manner so as to give you the best possible chance of success.

How the book is structured

The book is divided into the strategic and the tactical. It starts off with the overview (the air war) so that the foot soldier can glean some idea of what the generals are thinking – and doing.

The book then moves on to the practicalities of fighting and winning an election campaign on the ground – what you will need to have, and what you will need to do. If you are short of time, or if you are fighting a purely local campaign, skip the first part and go straight to the campaigning meat of the book.

As with a campaign, the book ends with Polling Day – the climax (or, sadly, possibly anti-climax) of your campaign: what you need to do on that final fateful day, and how you should behave – whether you win or lose.

Supporting website

A website supporting this book can be found at:

www.harriman-house.com/campaigning

Introduction

Clausewitz described diplomacy as war by other means. So too are elections – a clash of rival clans and armies, ground out over familiar territories over a set timescale to fixed (but not immutable) rules. Usually – but not always – there is just one winner. If the result is in any way inconclusive, the chances are the whole process will have to be gone through once more before too long.

Not for nothing are elections called campaigns. At every stage there is a direct analogy with the military equivalent – and the language and vocabulary are often identical.

A general election campaign, like a military campaign, is usually planned in advance in the minutest detail. This planning is captured in a tome known – yes, you guessed it – as the War Book. The campaign is conducted in one giant open room known as the War Room. Party strategists discuss the danger of being outflanked on the left – or the right. The objective of every campaign is to seize – and hold – the centre ground. And in politics, just as in military history, the generals always seem to be re-fighting the last war.

Also like a military campaign, a general election campaign cannot be fought without money. Political parties need to build up reserves ahead of the anticipated campaign – and these reserves are kept in the war chest. As with any military campaign, if you run out of funds, you will quite simply be swept aside.

For all the planning and all of the optimism which goes into election campaigns it is very rare for a surgical strike or a Blitzkrieg to succeed. Most election campaigns end up like the Somme, with mud and blood all over the place, and nobody fully knowing what they – or the enemy – are doing in the thick fog of war.

This book is divided into two parts: the strategic, and the tactical. This can also be categorised as the air war (where intelligence is gathered, propaganda distributed, and the enemies strategic assets are degraded) and the ground war (where the poor bloody infantry slog it out in hand to hand conflict). Hopefully those who are solely engaged in just one aspect will still find the whole book of interest and some use.

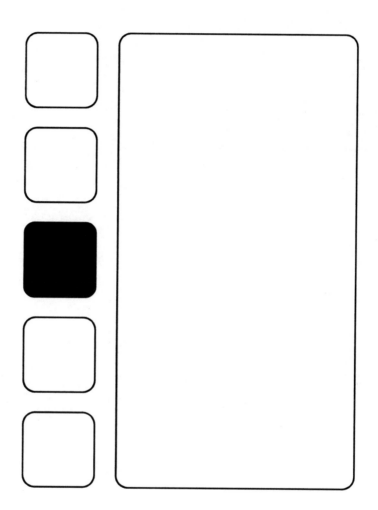

Part 1

Air War

Introduction

As with the two Iraq wars, the actual invasion and engagement of ground forces is preceded by weeks – or even months – of aerial warfare.

In the case of a military campaign the purpose is threefold.

Firstly, it is to gather military intelligence, which is not, as some wits are often prompted to opine, an oxymoron. Whether using high-flying reconnaissance aircraft, satellites, or agents on the ground, the objective is to build a precise picture of the disposition of the enemy's positions and assets. This would – broadly speaking – consist of strategic and tactical headquarters, ordnance depots, anti-aircraft batteries, tank formations, and concentrations of infantry units.

Having gathered as much intelligence as possible (because of course many military facilities are buried deep underground so as avoid surveillance), the secondary objective is to disrupt enemy communications and damage their morale. This can be accomplished by using specially adapted planes (in the case of the US military E3 AWACS or EA-6B Prowlers) to intercept or interdict the enemy's communications. Warplanes can also, of course, be used to drop leaflets in the enemy's own language urging them to desert or surrender and warning them of the campaign ('shock and awe') to come.

The third and final – and most important – aspect of the air war is to obtain air superiority (i.e. to deprive the enemy of the ability to deploy their own air force) and to interdict (i.e. destroy) or degrade (i.e. partially destroy) the enemy's key assets. This makes the life of the foot soldiers who will eventually have to be deployed a lot easier and a lot safer.

In electoral terms the principles are very similar.

The first job of the party's 'aviators' is to find out as much as possible about the enemy's personnel, policies and strategy. This can be done through overt means such as reading the papers or studying your opponent's press releases, policy statements and manifesto, or it can be done by covert means – including late night drunken conversations with HQ staffers or even infiltrating a spy into the enemy's camp.

In terms of morale the best tactic is to use the press – or the opinion polls – to convince the opposition that they are going to lose and there is therefore no real point in fighting – at least not to the death.

The enemy's key strategic assets – in electoral terms – are people and policies. Political parties tend to have only a handful of star players. These tend to reflect the great offices of state – the Prime Minister (or Prime

Minister in waiting), Chancellor (or Shadow Chancellor), Home Secretary (or Shadow Home Secretary) – and perhaps one or two others (Party Chairman, Defence Secretary, Health Secretary, etc). If a political party can seriously weaken the morale or credibility of its opponent's key personnel – or even leader – then they are half way home.

The same applies to policies. Manifestoes have to cover a huge range of issues, but generally speaking a political party – in order not to blur the message and confuse the public – will go into a general election with just a handful – five at most – of key policies or messages. If they can be forced to retreat from some or all of those, then again the battle is half won.

Phoney War

The UK is peculiar (but not unique) in that the Prime Minister can dictate the date of the general election and also (within reason) the duration of the campaign. Provided that a general election is called by the fifth anniversary date of the previous general election he or she has total flexibility as to when the general election is called – although the Monarch has to be asked to dissolve Parliament. In times of dire national emergency, with the agreement of both the Houses of Parliament and the Monarch, this term can be extended. This last occurred during the Second World War.

Political parties generally gear down in the period between general elections. This is because there is less for them to do, and less money with which to do it.

The HQ staffers will, generally speaking, take themselves off to get 'real' jobs such as in public relations or public affairs consultancies or polling companies. Some hire themselves out as 'mercenaries' to go and help in campaigns overseas – nearly always for the equivalent parties in those countries to their own party in the UK. Thus Tories will often go and work for the Republicans in the United States, whilst Labour supporters will go and work for the Democrats. This not only keeps them gainfully employed, but also enables them to pick up new techniques from what is by far the most sophisticated (and expensive) electoral system in the world.

Accordingly, between general election campaigns the political party headquarters content themselves with gathering intelligence about the enemy and firing off the odd speculative salvo for the purposes of demonstrating that they are still an effective fighting force – and keeping the morale of their own side up (especially in opposition). The public, however, will have almost no interest in the activities of political parties at this time – unless a prominent politician has been caught out in a sexual or financial scandal.

Skirmishes

Between general elections, which occur on average every four years or so, there are a number of minor wars or skirmishes.

These can be routine planned elections for local authorities, the European Parliament, the Scottish Parliament, the Welsh Assembly, the Northern Ireland Assembly, the Greater London Assembly or Mayoralties. These take place every four or five years according to a fixed timescale, and there are a wide variety of first-past-the-post and proportional representation systems in use.

Most years and in most areas there is therefore likely to be one election or another for one of these bodies. The parties fight them with different levels of intensity, depending on their own position within those bodies, the state of their finances, and the degree of importance which the leadership (and the rank and file) attach to them.

Perhaps it would be more accurate to describe the campaigns for the national and regional Parliaments and Assemblies as minor battles rather than skirmishes. However, the true skirmishes are the by-elections which occur periodically during the course of any Parliament.

By-elections can be called for many different reasons. The most common is the death of the sitting member. The next most common cause is the resignation of the sitting member, which is usually accomplished by them applying for the Chiltern Hundreds – a nominally paid post under the Crown which therefore conflicts with an MP's loyalty to Parliament. The real reason, however, is usually the offer of a job which creates a real conflict with the duties of an MP, such as an Ambassadorship or heading up an international organisation (NATO, WTO, etc). A recent example was Tony Blair's appointment as a peace envoy to the Middle East. The rarest cause of a by-election is where an MP changes Party, and feels honour-bound to put themselves up for re-election in order to secure a new mandate. This is always called for by the other parties, but the challenge is rarely taken up. The defection of Quentin Davies from the Conservatives to Labour is a recent example of a situation where a by-election was called for but the challenge (probably wisely) was not taken up.

For a by-election to be called there needs to be a Warrant from the Speaker of the House of Commons, a Writ, and a Motion on the floor of the House of Commons. The convention is that the timing of a by-election is dictated by the party which held the seat prior to the vacancy occurring.

I have included by-elections in this section of the book because although they are a local phenomenon affecting just one small area, they have strategic importance. The party headquarters attach great significance to the results, and the media regard them as a better test of the standing of the parties than opinion polls.

Funding arrangements for by-elections are much more generous than for individual seats in a general election – roughly five times the normal amount can be spent. This enables the political parties to deploy some of their HQ staffers for the duration, and also to spend more money on posters and advertising. They can also use their telephone call centres to blitz a constituency – sometimes to the point where the poor harassed electors are actually turned off the process or the party involved.

It used to be a general rule that the party in power loses by-elections. However, Labour have had a very good record at holding on to seats in by-elections since they came to power this time around in 1997. They have managed to keep the Tories totally at bay, and have only suffered a handful of losses to the Lib Dems (at Brent East in 2003, Leicester South in 2004 and Dunfermline and West Fife in 2006).

The Lib Dems have always had a formidable record in by-elections, often capturing seats with a twenty per cent plus swing against the incumbent party. There are a number of reasons for this. The Lib Dems have often been regarded by the electorate as the best receptacle in which to place their protest votes. Their members and activists are often highly dedicated and willing to travel and decamp for the duration of a by-election campaign. They also have a highly specialised by-election team within their party headquarters which are ready to roll out the minute a by-election has been called. Because they have a very good track record with by-elections, they are like an army which is used to winning – and that is often half the battle.

 I was leading a knocking up team on Polling Day at the Ealing Southall by-election. The conditions were positively monsoon-like, and everybody (including those with umbrellas) was soaked. At about five o'clock we decided to take a break and guiltily snuck into McDonalds for a coffee. Our guilt was somewhat assuaged when we walked in to find hordes of Labour and Lib Dem campaigners (including several MPs) also taking time off from the campaign to refuel, de-fuel and dry out!

Assassination

Between the skirmishes and battles the media and opposition parties conspire to bring about the resignation of a government minister. This is usually referred to as gaining a 'ministerial scalp' but it could also be categorised as a political assassination.

The reasons why a minister is forced to resign generally fall into a handful of categories. In days gone by ministers would resign over a question of principle, or as a matter of honour – such as Lord Carrington over the Falklands. In this era of professional politicians, ministers are much more loath to depart, and generally have to be hounded out of office by a concerted media and opposition campaign. This can be based on financial impropriety, as was the case with Peter Mandelson and his loan from Geoffrey Robinson. Alternatively, a ministerial departure can be prompted by a sex scandal – the most famous example being that of John Profumo, and a more recent one being David Mellor. Or it can simply be a matter of competence – or perceived lack of it – as with the more recent case of Charles Clarke.

Obviously the more senior the victim the greater the damage. If a party leader or Prime Minister can be brought down, the effect can be devastating. Generally speaking, however, this feat can only be accomplished by the leader or PM's own party. Both Margaret Thatcher and Tony Blair were forced out of 10 Downing Street not by the opposition or the electorate, but by their own parties.

Headquarters

Staff

Depending on the funds available, and the stage of the electoral cycle, a political party can employ anything from 100 to 200 people at its national headquarters. On top of this, they will also employ personnel at other national capitals in Edinburgh, Cardiff and Belfast – and possibly in key English regions as well. There are also, of course, the constituency agents, constituency organisers and organising secretaries – although they are engaged at the local tactical level.

Within the party headquarters, staff tend to be grouped into departments relating to a variety of functions. The fundraising department raises money for the day-to-day administration of the party, and also to fill that all-important war chest. The finance department administers payments for the staff, equipment and services needed.

The membership department uses marketing techniques to try and sign up new members. The subscriptions from these members will help to fill the party coffers – and come election time these new members might also be willing to help campaign on the ground.

The policy or research department will normally consist of one head and perhaps one or two deputies, plus individual desk officers responsible for specialist policy areas. They work closely with both the Parliamentary front benchers, and also with their colleagues in the press office.

There is also usually a rapid rebuttal unit, charged with speedily countering the other party's accusations. These units rely on extensive databases of speeches and press releases, and sophisticated search engines (the most famous being Excalibur), which can be used to identify occasions when the accusing party has said very much the same thing as the unit's party is being accused of saying.

Press officers can be attached to the Leader or senior front benchers, or they can specialise in a particular policy area. There will also be senior press officers who will specialise in the print and broadcast media, and who liaise with the all-important press gallery and lobby. There will also be a media monitoring unit, although this can be run by volunteers or contracted out to commercial firms.

Finally, there is the Leader's office and the offices of the senior front benchers. The Leader will have a staff of upwards of a dozen people, with constituency secretaries, diary secretaries, speechwriters, special advisers, at least one press officer and a chief of staff. Other senior opposition front benchers will likely have a staff of four to six, including a chief of staff, a press officer, and one or two researchers and secretaries.

Some of the people who work in the party headquarters are volunteers or interns – especially come general election time. It is great experience and looks very good on any job applicant's C.V. Professional staff are paid for out of party members' subscriptions, and from the proceeds of fundraising. There is also some state funding for opposition parties through 'Short Money', named after the former Leader of the House, Ted Short, who initiated the system. This gives opposition parties funding in a complicated ratio relating to the number of seats and the number of votes which they received at the last general election.

The party in power can afford to get by with fewer staff than the opposition because they have the might of the civil service behind them, doing ministers' bidding in all matters which are not directly party political. They also have 70-odd special advisers. These are party loyalists who are classed as temporary civil servants, but who are paid for by the taxpayer and who can indulge in party political work. They act as gatekeepers and sounding boards to their ministers, and they are supposed to insulate true civil servants from getting sucked in to party political activities. A senior minister might have two special advisers – one dealing with policy, and the other handling the media.

People go to work in party headquarters for a variety of reasons. For some it is just a job. For others, it is good experience, which will also look good on their C.V. Most staffers, however, are true believers. Certainly if they stay for more than one electoral cycle it will be belief which keeps them in place rather than ambition.

Buildings

At one stage all three political parties owned their own very lavish headquarters in Westminster.

The Lib Dems gained their very smart headquarters in Cowley Street after the break up of the old Liberal SDP Alliance, and they still have it. It is not ideal for a modern political party, but it is central and imposing, and it provides the party with a feel of continuity.

For many years the Conservatives were based at 32 Smith Square. After a series of defeats Michael Howard decided that the building should be sold. It had become associated with failure, and its many stairways and dark corridors provided an ideal environment for the incessant plotting which had become worse with every electoral setback. The party decamped to Victoria Street, and has since sold the freehold of Smith Square for a rumoured sum of £30.5m. It has now moved into Millbank Tower – ironically the location of the birth of New Labour.

Labour were for many years based in Transport House in Smith Square. However, the building was owned by the trade unions, and was reckoned to emphasise the dependence of the party on them. They moved first to Walworth Road, and then to Millbank Tower. When this lease ran out they moved to premises in Old Queen Street which were donated to them by the widow of Lord Hamlyn, but they have since had to sell these premises to cover their mounting debts and have moved into rented offices in Victoria Street.

Any army – or political party – has to have a headquarters. The actual location is largely irrelevant, but they have to be suitable for a war room to be constructed and for morale to be maintained. They also require suitable facilities to hold daily press conferences during a general election campaign, providing regular fodder to a hungry media in what is now a 24-hour news cycle.

Fundraising

I have already referred in passing to the role of fundraising and membership departments at party headquarters, and later in the book I will discuss fundraising activities at local level.

No campaign – political or military – can be fought without a war chest.

In the days when the Monarch and Parliament struggled for supremacy it was generally the case that the former led the country in to war and the latter were expected to pay for it. Only by refusing to part with the treasure – raised by taxation – which would be needed to fight wars could Parliament exert a measure of control over wayward and warlike Kings and Queens.

Fundraising is absolutely crucial to any political party aspiring to government. Whilst UK politics are still not as mercenary as in the United States, party machines are getting increasingly sophisticated, and more expensive. General elections have also been getting progressively more costly, although a cap on the total expenditure now seems likely to be imposed by the Electoral Commission.

In rough terms the Conservatives and Labour spend around £10m a year just running their party machine, with maybe a third of that (if they are in opposition) coming from Short Money. The Lib Dems spend about a third of the amount spent by the Conservatives and Labour.

At the 2005 general election Labour spent £17,939,617, the Conservatives £17,852,240, and the Lib Dems £4,324,574. Fundraising is much more sophisticated now, but most of it still revolves around personal contacts and the party leader. There is now, however, a piece of software called COMMITT, produced by the industry standard customer relations management company salesforce.com, which aims to broaden and professionalise political party fundraising.

It is not the case that the party with the most money will win and become the government. But there is certainly a correlation between money spent and votes gained. And, of course, donors are more inclined to be generous to parties which are either in power, or which are about to gain power.

From the very early days of party politics there have been scandals relating to fundraising. Since the time of Lloyd George the assumption has always been that substantial donations do not come without strings. The donor is reckoned to be seeking to change policy, curry favour – or perhaps gain an honour. In the UK, initiatives such as the instigation of the Committee on Standards in Public Life and the Electoral Commission, and the passing of the Political Parties, Elections and Referendums Act (PPERA) will hopefully ensure that British politics remains relatively clean. But the suspicion remains that donors (traditionally businessmen to the Tories and the trade unions to Labour) have their own self-interest at heart rather than the interests of democracy and the nation when they get their chequebooks out.

Apart from party headquarters and party staffers, here are the main areas in which political parties spend their funds.

Broadcasts

There are two main types of broadcasts: party political broadcasts, and party election broadcasts.

1 Party political broadcasts (PPBs) are normally aired after a major political event such as the Queen's Speech or the Budget. The objective is very simple: to convince the public that you have got it right, if you are the government, or that they have got it wrong, if you are the opposition.

2 Party election broadcasts (PEBs) take place during the course of an election campaign. They are provided free of charge to all political parties who field at least fifty candidates in a general election – and the number of broadcasts is in direct ratio to the number of candidates fielded.

In the past PEBs went out at the same time on all the channels – and this was the cue for a stampede to put the kettle on or use the toilet. Now, with satellite and cable TV, there is so much choice for viewers that there is no point in imposing a simultaneous airing, and PEBs are staggered throughout the evening. It is up to the parties to make the broadcasts sufficiently interesting or amusing to attract the viewer's attention.

PPBs and PEBs can feature celebrities or paid actors masquerading as members of the public. This, however, runs the risk that a newspaper might discover that the actor supports an opposing party. So sometimes party activists and candidates are used instead. Usually, however, parties use either their leader, a senior colleague, or a particularly well-known or telegenic front or back bencher – if they have one.

As I live and work in London, and have some broadcasting experience, I have been asked to appear in several PPBs and PEBs. On one Sunday morning I received a panicky early morning call asking if I could get to CCHQ in an hour – which I could. I ended up doing a local election PEB covering for a council leader who was (allegedly) too hungover to deliver his lines.

On another occasion, for a PEB for the European Parliament elections, I was filmed walking across Westminster Bridge with the Palace of Westminster to my left and the City of London looming to my right, delivering a message about the single currency. Anyone who has ever tried to walk and talk to camera will know that it is not an easy thing to do. What made it even harder in this instance was the fact that the camera was at the far end of the bridge and out of sight, so the dozens of commuters who passed me saw a man wandering across the bridge talking to himself about the euro – whilst making the odd gesture towards the Palace of Westminster and the City for good measure!

In the UK paid-for election broadcasts and advertisements on the television are banned. So if PPBs and PEBs serve no other purpose, they do save us from being bombarded with the negative TV ads and radio spots which feature so strongly in any US election campaign.

Whilst the actual broadcasting of PPBs and PEBs in the UK is free, the parties do have to pay for the production, and this can sometimes cost as much as a television advertisement for a commercial product.

Party conferences

Every year the parties hold an annual conference and usually there is a spring conference or forum as well. On top of this, the main UK parties also hold party conferences in Scotland and Wales.

There are four main reasons for party conferences:

1   To raise money

2   To showcase the party leaders and other senior figures

3   To boost the morale of party members

4   To help in the formulation of party policy, and to try and project those policies to the general public

Traditionally the main parties (Conservative, Labour and the Lib Dems) have always held their conferences at either Blackpool, Bournemouth or Brighton. However, the Lib Dems have in the past held theirs in Glasgow and Harrogate, and now Labour has broken ranks and held their annual conference in Manchester. Not to be outdone, the Tories have said that in future years they will hold their annual conference in Manchester and Birmingham.

By convention – no matter who is in power – the Lib Dems have their conference first (usually in the middle of September), Labour hold theirs next (at the end of September), and the Tories last (at the beginning of October). This arrangement seems to suit everyone – not least the conference towns, and the host of camp-followers and journalists who have to attend all three.

Parties make money from their conferences by charging delegates to attend. They also charge observers and even journalists if (as is often the case) they get their applications in after the deadline. They also charge companies and organisers for exhibition space, and allow them to sponsor items such as pass holders and lanyards or specific events such as the leader's dinner. They also charge for attendance at the big set-piece social events such as the Conference Dinner, the Leader's Dinner or the Gala Ball.

The main event at party conferences is invariably the leader's speech, which the leader and his or her team will have spent weeks preparing. Policies will be fleshed out, sound bites road-tested, and jokes refined and practiced. Even up until the morning of the speech last minute amendments will be made in order to improve the speech still further and to instil topicality. There are also usually one or two conference favourites who are rolled out every year. In the case of the Lib Dems it is usually a former leader such as Paddy Ashdown or Charles Kennedy. The Tories in the past have always enjoyed barnstorming speeches from Michael Heseltine or Michael Portillo, but now have speakers such as Ann Widdecombe or Boris Johnson. Labour have in recent years had policy-rich speeches from Gordon Brown, and music hall knockabout from John Prescott. Reputations can be made – or broken – by a party conference speech.

A good conference can do wonders for party morale. Sometimes this is achieved just by having one or two superb speeches. Sometimes it is more important to the rank and file simply that their leaders are presenting a united front. The opinion polls and the national newspapers can put a dampener on any party conference but sometimes it is something as basic as the weather which can dictate the general mood.

The Lib Dems are the only party whose rules dictate that – in theory at least – votes at the party conference can dictate policy. Labour also have votes at their party conference, although the casting of millions of votes by trade union leaders can create a somewhat surreal air to the whole affair. The Tories also have votes, but they are such a foregone conclusion that they make the old Soviet Congress appear democratic.

In truth, party conferences are not about the formulation of policy, but about the road-testing of policies among the membership, and the projection of policies through the media to the voting public. In this respect, fringe events are as important as the speeches and debates in the main conference hall. They give the parties, their ginger groups, and pressure groups the chance to 'fly kites' without any serious come-back if they crash and burn.

Party conferences have evolved over the years, but they still serve useful purposes, and are unlikely to be dropped any time soon. It would be a courageous party leader who was the first to scrap his or her party conference.

Party conferences are great fun, but they ought to come with a health warning. Vast amounts of alcohol are on offer, and drink is all too freely consumed. There used to be a tradition at the Conservative conference that some of the younger delegates would drink through the night in the conference hotel bar. One year myself and some colleagues had managed this feat, and we were still there when the technicians arrived to set up the lights and cameras for the breakfast TV interview. We waited to see who was going to be featured, and after a while a young journalist arrived, sat on the sofa, and was bibbed up in preparation for make-up. None of us recognised him, so one of our younger and more attractive female delegates went up and tapped him on the shoulder, and asked very politely "Excuse me, who are you?" The young presenter leaned back and very loudly and portentously exclaimed "I am Justin Webb." Thanking him politely the young lady then turned to the gathering at the bar and enquired very loudly "Who the f**k is Justin Webb?" The bar closed rapidly and we were encouraged to take our learned political discourses elsewhere.

Literature

Political parties are all about members, money and votes. Good quality literature can help to raise the numbers of all three.

Carefully targeted mail shots can help to get new members to join a political party. The targeting can be aimed at socio-economic groups, former voters or members, or members of single-issue pressure groups such as pro or anti hunting groups. However, most new members are simply walk-ins. They are people who have arrived in an area and want to join a political party, or those whose life situation has changed such as the kids leaving home or finding that retirement or redundancy offers more scope for external activities.

Another good source of new members is simply to have a stack of membership forms with you when you knock on doors. If somebody is particularly keen on voting for your party, you might just be able to persuade them to join it.

A carefully worded and scientifically targeted letter can sometimes yield a decent return in terms of donations. All three of the main political parties maintain their own list of potential donors, and they all employ marketing companies to help keep them topped up. It is also now possible to buy databases from marketing companies which contain vast amounts of data about the spending habits and circumstances of every household in the country. If you believe that organic pasta eating, real ale drinking Citroen C2 drivers are very likely to donate money or join your party the marketing companies can provide you with a list of every person who meets those criteria throughout the country. Just as military intelligence is vital in any war, marketing and demographic intelligence is essential to any political party and any election campaign.

But the main purpose of the literature produced by party headquarters is securing votes. With that in mind, they again employ targeted mailings of letters and leaflets to try and secure the electoral support of specific groups. These can be anything from car drivers to single mothers. Everybody belongs to a series of overlapping communities. The key, from the party headquarters point of view, is to identify those groups who would be most likely to support you come election time – and to start a conversation with them.

The most important piece of literature any political party produces is undoubtedly its general election manifesto. This is not because the general public is going to read it – very few people are that time-rich or, frankly, that sad.

When I was a general election candidate in 2005 I bought 20 copies of my party's manifesto at the start of the campaign in order to be able to respond to requests from the press, local interest groups, and the general public. At the end of the campaign I still had nearly half of them left.

The people who actually read manifestoes are:

- Your own **supporters** – which is preaching to the converted. They obviously want to know what they are fighting for, and need to be able to answer questions.

- Your **opponents** – who will never be converted. They are looking for any flaws in your argument, or any policies which they think will prove to be unpopular.

- The **print press** and **broadcast media**. Since very few people actually read manifestoes, the parties are reliant on the media to explain and publicise their manifestoes and policies for them.

It is very hard for policy wonks at party headquarters to actually get general election manifestoes right. If they are too long nobody (including the three groups above) will actually read them. If they are packed with policies covering every single area of public policy, you might be giving up a battalion of hostages to fortune, and you might offend a host of disparate pressure groups. It was Gerald Kaufman – a Labour MP – who described Michael Foot's 1983 general election manifesto as "the longest suicide note in history".

On the other hand, if your manifesto is too thin, you might be accused of being bereft of ideas. Even worse, you might be accused of having a hidden agenda which you are keeping from the electorate.

As a general rule, it is the party furthest away from power which produces the most detailed manifestoes. The Lib Dems – who have not seriously challenged for power (other than as part of a coalition) for close on a hundred years – produce policy-rich general election manifestoes. I have already referred to Labour's very long and detailed manifesto in 1983, a time when they were very far from power, but Margaret Thatcher's 1979 manifesto, produced at a time when Labour were in virtual meltdown, was thin to the point of anorexia. When you are within touching distance of power, the least said really is the soonest mended.

Advertising

The main reason why the political party headquarters have to raise huge sums of money to fight general election campaigns is advertising.

Local candidates have to raise their own funds to fight their own campaigns and this will be dealt with in the second part of the book. Party headquarters staff do increase enormously at election time, but some of these are volunteers, and generally this is only for a few weeks. Party leaders need to criss-cross the nation in their battle buses, helicopters and private executive jets but these are often donated by supporters. As mentioned, Party Election Broadcasts are free, and it is not possible to buy televised political advertising in the UK, so a very large chunk of the money accumulated in the war chests is used to buy advertising in either newspapers, magazines or on poster sites.

The advantage of advertising in newspapers and magazines is that your ads can, to a certain degree, be targeted. So if you wanted to highlight your policies for British business, you would probably place your ads in the *Financial Times* or *The Economist*. If, on the other hand, you wanted to explain your policies on social issues, you would probably run ads in the *Guardian* or *The Independent*. And if you just wanted impact, you would run the same ads in all the nationals, and link them to a co-ordinated poster campaign.

In theory at least poster campaigns are less targeted than newspaper ads. It is, after all, impossible to dictate who will pass a particular poster site whilst your ad is on display. Having said that, you can stipulate that your poster sites are concentrated in certain areas identified with specific socio-economic groups. And you can, of course, concentrate your spending (your fire power) on your target seats.

Over the years there have been few poster ads which really stick in the mind. The poster which propelled Saatchi & Saatchi to fame (and some would say Margaret Thatcher to power) was a long snaking line of people supposedly queuing up for unemployment benefit with the caption 'Labour Isn't Working'. This highlighted the fact that the rate of unemployment had at the time crashed through the psychologically significant one million mark. A Conservative poster which backfired badly was the infamous 'Demon Eyes', which sought to portray Tony Blair as some sort of devil with an equally diabolical agenda. A Labour poster which had a huge visual impact was one depicting William Hague in a Margaret Thatcher wig. This had the twin effect of ridiculing Hague, and portraying him as the heir to the then highly unpopular Thatcher.

Under Neil Kinnock, the Labour Party made huge strides in professionalising its operations. Realising that the Tory's had gained a big advantage by hiring top advertising agencies, they asked for volunteers amongst Labour supporters who worked in the industry. The result was the Shadow Communications Agency, which helped to counter the Tory's advantage in the field and helped Labour achieve a better result in the 1987 general election.

In the commercial world poster advertising is deemed – and proven – to be highly effective. There is strong evidence that it has a similar impact in election campaigns. It is, however, extremely expensive. One trick to avoid this expense is to simply design and hang a single poster, but to invite the media along to the unveiling – usually by a prominent figure within the party. Although you still have to dream up the poster and get the graphics done, if it is hard-hitting – or amusing – enough, it is possible to get substantial coverage in the newspapers and even on television. The parties – like companies – are also now increasingly experimenting with online advertising.

As in the world of commerce there are constant debates within party headquarters of the merits of spending scarce resources on advertising as opposed to marketing or public relations. However, it would be a courageous (in the 'Yes Minister' sense of the word) party which withdrew from the poster battle and conceded that territory to the enemy.

Another type of poster is the giant variety which is mounted on the back of a truck or van and used to tour up and down main roads. During the 2001 general election campaign the Labour Party got wind of the fact that William Hague was to make a major policy speech at One Whitehall Place. They had an ad-van ready to send out as a spoiler as soon as the time and location was verified. Amanda Platell ordered all members of the War Room to jump into their cars and try to head off the Labour ad-van. Within minutes the whole affair descended into a farce – resembling nothing more than an episode of the Keystone Cops.

Telephone call centres

All of the main parties now use telephone call centres. The Conservatives were the pioneers in this area. In 1999 the General Election Voluntary Agency (GENEVA) funded a bank of 32 screens and phones based at Conservative Central Office at 32 Smith Square. The Conservative call centre has always been based at CCO – or what is now called the Conservative Campaign Headquarters. Labour based their telephone call centre in the north east, where it is cheaper to employ professional telesales people. Trade union headquarters are also used as supplementary telephone call centres during general elections.

The original idea of call centres was, predictably, imported from the United States. They combine telesales software with postcode targeting. The idea is to target voters in a by-election, or to focus on target seats in a general election. The system automatically dials the number for the call centre operative, and if the call goes through the details of the electors in that household come up on the screen. The operative then talks through a script, which varies according to the responses received. The system filters out those electors who have previously been contacted during the course of the current campaign, as well as those who subscribe to the Telephone Preference Service (which means that they have opted out of receiving any unsolicited calls). The screen would also coach the operative through procedures for leaving answerphone messages, and recording when an elector had moved – or even passed away.

Initially the parties used activists and volunteers (often people on the candidates' lists) to make these calls. However, many of these volunteers have work, family and political commitments and were not able to offer their services on a regular basis. The parties therefore rapidly turned to employing students, or even professional call centre personnel. They would often be more efficient than the volunteers, who might waste time trying to convert respondents, instead of just ascertaining their voting intentions. Employing professionals – or at least students who had built up some expertise – also meant that the call centres could be used for other purposes, such as conducting surveys on policy issues, recruiting new members, or even fundraising.

I made the first ever call from the CCO GENEVA call centre. There had been a call for volunteers to road-test the project, and only half a dozen candidates turned up. I just happened to be the first to get through to a real live voter – it was a bit like being a latter day Alexander Graham Bell!

Voice blasting

A variation on the telephone call centre theme is another US import – voice blasting.

This procedure consists of recording a short message from the party leader urging the electorate to vote for his or her party. A stunned elector won't quite have time to work out whether this really is the party leader on the phone or not, before the message ends.

This technique is especially effective when the call is met with an answerphone. When the elector returns home he or she may well be convinced that the prime minister or leader of one of the opposition parties has telephoned and left a message. Consequently, these voice blasts are often timed to coincide with the maximum numbers of electors either being out or unavailable, such as during *Coronation Street* or a particularly vital football match.

New media

There is no definitive definition of 'new media' or 'social media' but basically the term encompasses all the new forms of communication which have exploded onto the scene in the last decade based around the web and the internet. In the United States the political parties have been using the new media to raise money, boost membership and harvest electoral pledges for the best part of a decade – witness the Howard Dean campaign. In the UK, however, the political parties are only just beginning to grasp the potential of this array of inexpensive and immediate means of communicating with the public.

Websites

Political parties in the UK have had their own websites for years. Originally the idea was to simply impart information to supporters and the media about party personnel and policies. Thus there would be a directory of the staffers within the party headquarters, plus details of the responsibilities of front benchers in Westminster and probably the European Parliament, Scottish Parliament, Welsh Assembly and perhaps allied parties in the Northern Ireland Assembly too. Press releases would also be posted onto the website for the benefit of members and the media.

These websites now have a great deal more functionality, including a search engine, and archived, searchable press releases. They might also have web-streaming of their PPBs or PEBs for members who missed them when they were originally aired. Good party websites now also allow people to join the party and donate online. Applications for party conferences can be downloaded, as well as forms to apply for seats.

So a party website nowadays is not just a place where you go to get fixed information. They should be about interacting with the public and the membership, and should offer facilities which save time and money.

Email

Email is not new but the ways in which this particular channel can be effectively used is constantly changing.

Political parties now routinely communicate with their elected representatives, their candidates and their members by email. The costs involved are minimal, and there can be a high degree of immediacy – especially where the recipient uses a PDA such as a Blackberry. Email can be used to communicate information, such as the line to take on particular issues, and to martial troops. In a fast-moving election campaign the ability to redeploy resources rapidly from one constituency to another can make the difference between victory and defeat.

Text messages

Since 85% of the population – hopefully including the vast majority of party members – now carry a mobile phone the ability to SMS them with details of a meeting or campaign is invaluable. Having a telephone conversation with members can be time consuming, and the message can be wrongly taken down. Texting them, especially via a group text, is fast and effective, albeit not without cost.

Text messaging complements emailing, and the technologies collide with PDAs, but what SMS text messages have largely replaced is pagers. Very few people want to carry a mobile and a pager, and the technology is now regarded as being outdated.

Blogs

Blogs (derived from the words 'WebLogs') can be a double-edged sword. They are undoubtedly a cost-effective way of communicating with your electorate, and certainly appeal to the younger generation (who are statistically far less likely to vote than middle-aged and older voters).

Having said that, there are a number of drawbacks and danger associated with them. Firstly, there is the pressure to update your blog on a frequent and regular basis. Failure to do so means that people will not bother to check for your latest comments and you could be criticised for entering into the project and not seeing it through. The alternative – getting somebody else to post for you – is fraught with dangers. Plus, if you get caught out, you will (quite rightly) be heavily criticised.

The other danger with blogs is posting a comment which is ill-thought through and ill-considered. The whole point about blogs is that they are supposed to be spontaneous – but spontaneity can be lethal for a politician. If nobody else reads your blog your opponents certainly will – and they will be looking for hostages to fortune.

Podcasts

Podcasting involves posting your thoughts in aural form on a website which can then be downloaded onto an Ipod (or other MP3 player) and listened to.

The technology is very current but not that complicated. Making podcasts available on your website is a low-cost way of showing that you are up to date and engaging with a younger audience.

Web TV

Now that most households in the UK have broadband Web TV is starting to come into its own.

It is much easier – and cheaper – to broadcast via the internet than via the airwaves. This has opened the door to a growing number of web-based TV channels. Some of these take advantage of the fact that internet based channels are not subject to the same strictures as satellite or terrestrial broadcast TV in terms of the requirement to provide political balance. This has opened the door to stations such as 18 Doughty Street, which goes out on the internet and adopts a largely pro-Conservative viewpoint (although it is now becoming much more all-party).

Other manifestations of this phenomenon include WebCameron, where the Tory leader delivers his homilies whilst doing the washing up in his kitchen.

Opinion polls

Political parties spend great amounts of money on opinion polls – both during election campaigns and between them.

Very often the results of these 'private polls' are never released to the media and the public. They are designed not just to gauge the popularity (or otherwise) of the party, but also of individual party figures, and actual or proposed policies. These opinion polls can be invaluable sources of intelligence, and as such they are kept strictly confidential and the results distributed to only a handful of key politicians and party functionaries. However, if the results are positive, they can be leaked to a tame journalist or supportive national newspaper.

Newspapers and broadcasters also regularly commission polls. These normally relate to the simple respective standing of the parties. As such they are closely studied by the parties, and any positive swing is eagerly seized upon. Equally, if the polls are bad, the party concerned will blithely dismiss their findings, often saying that the only poll which matters is the one on the actual polling day.

Focus groups

Focus groups are a variation – and refinement – of mass opinion polling. Where an opinion poll for a national newspaper would typically be based on a thousand respondents, focus groups are normally made up of less than a dozen individuals. They will have been carefully selected to represent a cross section of society in terms of age, ethnicity, gender and voting intention.

There are a number of advantages to focus groups. Firstly, because they are made up of stable groups, it is possible to track any change in voting intention. Secondly, because they are being paid and they have time to devote to the exercise, it is possible to ask them more sophisticated – and sometimes esoteric – questions. A favourite in the past has always been to ask the group to compare party leaders with a car, thereby discovering whether their image is elitist, flash, mainstream – or downmarket.

There are also problems associated with focus groups. If you chose the wrong group in the first place, and don't get your weighting right, your results can be permanently skewed. There is also a phenomenon whereby focus groups become institutionalised. They begin paying more attention to politics than the average voter, and cease to be representative of the public at large.

The big parties all retain their own in-house pollsters and psephologists to help them to interpret the external opinion polls and focus group surveys which they commission. The Labour Party under Tony Blair relied heavily on the services of Philip (now Lord) Gould, who remorselessly road-tested every policy proposal against focus groups designed to represent a cross-section of UK society.

Press conferences

In between elections parties rarely hold press conferences. This is partly because they do not have that much to say but mainly because the press are not interested enough to attend.

Between elections party press conferences would mainly be called to highlight changes in personnel (a front bench reshuffle), a change of policy or a full-scale policy review. They would also be called – albeit somewhat reluctantly – in order to face some media storm which had arisen and which could not be ignored – usually a scandal involving the two old favourites; sex or money.

During election campaigns, however, all three of the main political parties would usually aim to hold a press conference every day bar Sunday. A gentleman's agreement is usually hammered out as to the regular timings of these events, so that the press pack can attend all three. Over the last few elections the pattern has been that the Lib Dems hold theirs first, then the Conservatives, and then Labour.

The parties vie with each other to provide the best coffee and hot food for the attending journalists. They also hand out press releases with the day's agenda, and often an itinerary for the party's main players. The UK press are rarely, however, content to stick to the party's agenda – despite the free coffee and croissants. If the party wants to talk about welfare reform, but the press wants to discuss a senior party member thumping a member of the public, you can be sure that welfare reform will get scant attention!

The national press are allowed to support a particular party, and they are free to try and influence their readers in that direction. National radio and TV, however, have to maintain strict neutrality. The performance of a party's big hitters at these morning press conferences influences the media and through them the public. Consistently assured performances can help to build up an individual's and a party's standing with the press. On the other hand, a stumbling performance (such as Charles Kennedy's bleary-eyed early morning performance in the 2005 general election) can have a severely detrimental affect on the party's prospects.

Press releases

Although parties do not hold many press conferences between election campaigns, they do issue a large number of press releases.

In these days of electronic distribution it costs next to nothing to put out a press release, and the temptation (especially for opposition parties) is to produce a never-ending stream of them. This is pointless and often counterproductive.

Every time a minister makes even a minor mistake the opposition parties will often rush out a press release calling for their resignation. Every time the government announces a new policy or piece of legislation, the temptation is to condemn them. This kind of knee-jerk reaction makes the opposition look juvenile in the eyes of the press and the public. Moreover, every press release issued is automatically stored in a database by the other parties, and can be retrieved and quoted in the future when the party concerned issues a contradictory one.

The key to press releases is to issue them less frequently and more carefully. Once the opposition outgrows this incontinence phase, and starts to behave more like a government in waiting, then the press will actually start to approach them for comment, and also pay attention to the releases which are issued.

Spin doctors

The spin doctor is – to some extent at least – a mythical creature. The term, as with so many others, originated in the United States and its roots are reckoned to come from tennis, where players can impart different types of spin to a return ball at will.

The first real spin doctor was, by some reckoning, the youthful (and mercurial) George Stephanopoulos – who served Bill Clinton. However, many people would say that Joe Haines spun for Harold Wilson, and Bernard Ingham for Margaret Thatcher. The most famous spin doctor in the UK was undoubtedly Alastair Campbell, the former *Daily Mirror* journalist who was never far from Tony Blair's side from 1994 to 2003. The most notorious spin doctor ever to operate on these shores was probably Jo Moore, who infamously sent out an email following the 9/11 attacks in the US saying that the atrocity represented a 'great opportunity to bury bad news'.

However, despite the huge reputations which they have built up, the actual art of spin doctoring is itself much over-hyped. Any party press officer will try and portray every event in the best possible light for their employer – that is their job. The notoriety of the Stephanopouloses and Campbells of this world flows from the fact that they performed that function very ably – and the fact that they had unrivalled access to the ears (and minds) of their principals.

The Key Battleground

Due to the peculiarities of our first-past-the-post electoral system (at least for the Westminster Parliament), a huge number of votes in the vast majority of constituencies are wasted. The current system is inherently unfair (the Lib Dems generally poll about 20% of all votes but end up with about 10% of all seats), but generally achieves a decisive result. Hung parliaments and coalitions are rare – in fact you have to go back to February 1974 to find one. Meanwhile the other two parties pile up large majorities in their heartlands (generally speaking urban conurbations for Labour and the shire counties for the Tories). Even between the two main parties there is an unfair balance. With the trend to move out of city centres and into the suburbs, and the inevitable lag in the Boundary Commission correcting the resultant imbalances, it takes fewer votes to elect a Labour MP than a Conservative one. In the 2001 general election it needed an average of 92,554 votes to elect a Lib Dem MP, compared with 50,347 to elect a Tory, and just 26,031 to elect a Labour MP.

Generally, the primary objective of election campaigns is to maximise turnout by your own supporters. The overall effect of an energetic campaign is usually to increase turnout across the board. One exception to this general rule is where one party tries to deploy the 'Queensland Gambit'. This was invented by election guru Lynton Crosby, who (as the name implies) first used it in his native Australia. The idea is to let it be known that you are beaten, and that the result is a foregone conclusion. This (in theory at least) disproportionately depresses the turnout of the party that is in the lead at the polls. The Conservatives under Michael Howard used the Queensland Gambit in the 2005 general election, when their campaign was basically aimed at halting the long-term slide in the party's electoral fortunes.

In the last United States Presidential elections, the results all hung on a handful of battleground states – and ultimately on a minute majority in Ohio and a few thousand disputed votes in Florida. The Republicans and the Democrats had anticipated this, and threw all their efforts into them. At the end of the day an election for a country with a population of more than three hundred million came down to just a few thousand wavering voters in these swing states.

In the UK the same key battleground effect is apparent. Lib Dem strength is concentrated in the Celtic fringe in Scotland and Wales, and in the south-west. They also have a scattering of seats which they have gained in by-elections (very much a Lib Dem speciality), but then held onto through hard work and the natural incumbency effect which benefits the sitting MP. Labour, generally speaking, have their strength concentrated in Scotland,

Wales, the north of England and the big cities. The Conservatives are generally stronger in the rural and suburban areas, and the south of England. Close elections are generally won and lost in the Midlands. It is in belated recognition of this that the Conservatives are relocating their 2008-2011 conferences to Manchester and Birmingham.

At the next general election the Lib Dems will be looking to hold onto the seats they already have, and will then carefully target a further number of seats (certainly no more than twenty) where they are close enough to the incumbent (whether Labour or Conservative) to have a hope of victory. Their strategy is to gradually build up their number of MPs, but also to put themselves in a strong bargaining position if a hung parliament should come around.

Labour and the Conservatives, on the other hand, will both be looking for an outright victory; a majority over all the other parties put together. They will aim to achieve this by targeting the 75-80 key marginals in the key battleground areas – London, the Midlands and the north-west. This is where the majority of attention and resources will be focused: this is the key battleground in which the war will be won or lost.

Conclusion

As with any military campaign an election campaign is all about planning and co-ordination. The party headquarters must try to ensure that, whilst they hold the ground they already occupy, their forces are sufficiently focused to enable them to capture vulnerable enemy positions.

In order to achieve that, discipline is essential. Every candidate feels that his or her seat is vulnerable or winnable. It is up to the party HQ to make sure that this type of routine special pleading is ignored, and the focus remains firmly fixed on the key battleground seats.

As well as discipline, a winning army must also have high morale. If the troops feel that they are destined to lose, they will desert to the other side, go AWOL, or just go through the motions of fighting but without any passion. Even if a party knows they are going to lose, it is essential that they maintain the pretence that victory is achievable in order to minimise losses and make sure that they are in a stronger position to fight next time.

Battles and election campaigns are also about momentum – what the Americans call the 'big mo'. A party going into an election campaign behind in the polls but catching up fast can still win. Having a lead which is being rapidly eroded is bad for morale, and lack of belief in victory can be a self-fulfilling prophecy.

So that is the strategic view, the air war. It is now time to get down in the trenches with the poor bloody infantry.

Part 2

Ground War

Introduction

So all those extremely able, highly intelligent and well-paid people at party headquarters have spent months – if not years – planning this campaign. They have tested policies with focus groups, constructed a narrative, and worked out which of the party's leading lights are most likely to appeal to large sections of the electorate.

They will also have done the same – in reverse – against the opposition, identifying their policies with the least traction, and the leading figures most vulnerable to attack. They will also have worked out a negative narrative – a couple of sentences or phrases which denigrate the other parties' record in government or opposition.

The full force of your party's campaigning and communication capabilities – and the full content of their war chest – will have been brought to bear on the opposition nationwide. A huge aerial bombardment – shock and awe – will have been unleashed.

Now it is up to you to win the battle on the ground. To a large extent your success or failure will be decided by your party's national opinion poll rating, but there is such a thing as a personal vote – especially if you are the incumbent and have been a diligent constituency MP or councillor. Your local campaign really can make a difference. Indeed it can make all the difference.

At every election there are council seats which are won and lost by a handful of votes. Twice in Enfield in recent years council seats have been won by just three votes – and indeed one of those victorious councillors is still know as 'Tiny' as a tribute to his minute majority! In the case of Westminster Parliamentary seats, majorities of just a few hundred are not uncommon. So what you do in the time between being selected, when the election campaign begins, and the three and a half weeks of campaigning (especially the final thirty-six hours) really can make the difference between victory and defeat.

Getting Selected

Your role in the forthcoming battle will be dictated by whether or not you can get yourself selected. If you are not a member of the tactical headquarters staff (i.e. the chair or one of the officers), you have a choice between leading a campaign as the candidate or being a lowly non-commissioned officer or humble foot soldier. Election campaigns are interesting, exciting and fun – and they are all of those things in spades if you are the candidate.

There are currently 529 Parliamentary constituencies in England, 59 in Scotland, 40 in Wales and 18 in Northern Ireland. However, it should be noted that this does vary from one parliament to the next. The Parliamentary Boundary Commissions (there are four – one each for England, Scotland, Wales and Northern Ireland) are constantly reviewing seats with a view to making them all approximately equivalent in size. Accordingly, seats disappear or are created constantly with some being amalgamated, and others being split as their electorate grows too large.

The way in which the three main parties choose their candidates are all different, but certain basic principles are the same: You have to go through a selection procedure and be adopted onto a 'national list', 'national panel' or 'approved list' before you can be selected as a candidate for any position other than local councillor. All of the parties refine their selection criteria from time to time in order to try and address imbalances within their Parliamentary representation.

In 1997, Labour introduced all-women shortlists in some areas and as a result over one hundred female candidates were elected and became MPs. The party has persisted with this initiative, despite a succession of legal challenges. Another feature of Labour selections is that candidates must be nominated by at least two of the local branches within the Constituency Labour Party, and local trade unionists and affiliated organisations also have a say. All local selections have to be approved by the National Executive Committee, and there is a National Panel of pre-approved candidates.

Under David Cameron the Conservatives adopted a dual-track approach, with its standard Approved List and then a Priority or A List. The idea of the A List was to boost the party's relatively low number of female and ethnic minority candidates. After mixed results the system was adapted to one where female and minority candidates had to feature in the final selection, or alternatively where an open primary system opened up the process to local supporters who were not members. All candidates (whether on the priority A List or standard Approved List) have to pass muster with a local Candidate Selection Committee and then the Association's Executive Council before they can make it through to the final selection.

The Lib Dems have an election panel which chooses candidates for by-elections, and a Joint Candidates Committee which oversees selections nationwide. However, at constituency level the shortlist (which must include at least one male and one female candidate) is drawn up by the local party executive. It is then a simple one member one vote system with all local members entitled to attend and participate.

All three parties are trying to achieve the same objectives with their selection procedures. They want able candidates, capable of representing their constituents in Westminster, and they want to filter out candidates whose current or past activities could cause embarrassment to the party. In addition, their cadre of candidates should also look as representative of society as a whole as possible.

Intelligence Gathering And Reconnaissance

Some candidates spend a lot of time keeping tabs on older and frailer MPs. They are either – rather sinisterly and selfishly – hoping that this MP will die and a by-election could open the way for an early entry into Parliament, or, perhaps more kindly, they are simply looking out for MPs who are likely to stand down next time.

If you are lucky enough to have a strong line into a constituency which you know will become vacant and you have good personal connections with, that is great. However, you would be very unwise to assume that any seat is going to become yours as of right – even if you are the most obvious and strongest candidate. It is always a good idea to have other seats in mind.

If you don't have the advantage of a strong personal knowledge of the seat there are a number of ways you can find out about the area. Obviously the internet is a great place to start. Most of human knowledge is now there and most of it is free and easily accessible. You can check on the sitting member's contribution in Parliament, check out his or her website, and also visit the local council's website as well.

The other excellent source is the local newspapers (many areas have a paid for paper and at least one free paper). They will tell you all about the local issues, and the readers' letters will tell you a great deal about local views. You can either subscribe to these papers, or go through them in the local library. Alternatively, most newspaper offices will allow you to spend a couple of hours going through their archives. What is more, if they know you are interested in being a local candidate, the editor may even spare you some time to discuss local issues.

There are also some excellent directories available which will tell you all you need to know about a constituency. My own company, Dods, publishes highly detailed constituency guides, and the *Almanac of British Politics* also offers invaluable information.

Your final source of information is a member of the local party. Local agents and chairs are usually happy to brief potential candidates, as are some local councillors and activists. However, you would be well advised to treat anything they tell you with a degree of scepticism. They might be considering standing themselves, or they might have a preferred local candidate. Either way the information they give you could be fatally misleading, and cross-checking against other sources is advisable.

Finally, of course, there is no substitute for intelligence gathering on the ground. Drive around the constituency, and then walk through the main streets and shopping malls. Drink in the local pubs (a technique used by Lib Dem election guru Lord Chris Rennard), and find reasons to talk to local people. They're the ones who will ultimately form the electorate, and if they say something is an issue then it is!

Selection Processes

Westminster selection

Again, selection procedures vary to some degree between the three main parties. The basic principles, however, are very similar.

As with any job interview it is usually impossible to interview all of the applicants. Depending on the winnability of a seat and other factors (such as its proximity to London), anything from a dozen to a hundred or more approved candidates can apply for every seat. They are initially asked to send in a C.V. (based on a standard party template), which provides details of a candidate's education and any vocational qualifications. It may, depending on the party's prevailing philosophy and legislation, also ask for family details, age and perhaps a photograph. One very important section usually asks for any local connections through birth, family, education or work.

A selection panel is convened, consisting of officers and other senior local party members. They conduct a paper sift of the C.V.s, often allocating a mark out of ten for each one, and then eliminate the weaker candidates, to produce a list of maybe a dozen candidates to be interviewed.

Procedure at the interviews varies. Candidates can be asked to speak from five to ten minutes on a topic which they have had notice of or which has been sprung upon them. Typical topics include 'how I would win this seat' or 'how I would hold this seat'. They are then cross-examined on these speeches and their C.V.s. Whilst questions cannot be insulting or deeply personal, they can be extremely searching. The aim is to root out any dubious or unsuitable candidates at this stage.

If successful, candidates then go through to final selection. The number of finalists can vary from two to four. Some candidates drop out at the last minute, because a better opportunity has presented itself or because they have got cold feet, which is why four can be a safer bet. These final selection meetings are normally open to the entire membership of the local party. Occasionally they are also thrown open to local supporters who are not members.

If you make it through to the final, your appearance and demeanour can be as important as what you have to say. Communication is just as much about gesture and posture as it is about words. You should aim to look smart but not flash. You should aim to appear confident but not brash. You should aim to come across as a good communicator, which means somebody who can listen as well as speak.

The standard format is for lots to be drawn to decide in which order finalists should speak. They would then be invited to speak for ten minutes. A good general rule with these (and any other) speeches is not to be afraid to repeat yourself; repetition does have impact. So tell people what you are going to tell them, tell them, and then tell them what you have told them.

Generally finalists will talk for a short time about their own background, and why they think that they would be a suitable candidate to fight this particular seat. They would then spend a little time displaying their own knowledge of the seat, based on their local knowledge or research. This should lead on to a brief description of the campaign which the finalist would fight in order to win the seat (if in opposition) or to hold on to the seat (if it is currently held by your party but the sitting member is standing down or is up for reselection).

If your party does not hold the seat your research on the constituency should have included the sitting MP. It is very easy to check up on the Parliamentary activities of a sitting MP through the Parliament website. Constituency activity can be researched through the local newspapers.

Your speech should end with a rallying cry, re-iterating all the points you have made, and designed to convince the audience of your suitability and capability. Memorising your speech is also a good way to impress your audience. At the least you should only rely on prompt cards with a few bullet points. Reading out a prepared speech comes across as stilted and amateurish. If you want to impress your audience, research your speech well, and memorise it.

After each finalist has made his or her speech the selection meeting then moves on to the question and answer session. If all of the candidates have spoken well, it is often this part of the meeting which enables the party members to finally make up their minds. Questions can be on a panel basis, whereby each candidate is asked identical questions, an open basis, or a combination of the two.

Questions that are offensive or discriminatory should be ruled out of order by the Chair. However, as with the earlier rounds, there are often pointed questions about how much time the candidate will have to nurse the seat – often aimed at candidates with heavy family commitments or demanding jobs. A variation of this is to ask how the candidate (if not local) will cope with travelling to and from the constituency for evening and weekend engagements and whether, if selected, they will move to the constituency. Really detailed and parochial questions might be asked to try and trip up or stump non-local candidates. The golden rule in these situations is: be honest, do not bluff. If you do not know the answer say so, but add that if selected you would ensure that you quickly became completely up-to-speed on all local issues.

Another frequent line of questioning at selection meetings is designed to try and find out where candidates stand in the political spectrum. All political parties are broad churches with members stretching across a wide political spectrum. The Conservatives have Thatcherite and One Nation wings, Labour has old and new divisions, and the Lib Dems are drawn from two distinct liberal and social democratic traditions. Unless you have firm intelligence that the local party is distinctly inclined towards one wing or another, aim to plant yourself firmly in the centre – where most elections and most selections are won.

It is important to treat every question – and every questioner – seriously. Try and remember their name, and include it in your answer. If the question is a particularly good one, or a particularly hard one to answer, say so. If it is a particularly stupid question, resist the temptation to point this out. The questioner might just turn out to be a branch chair or the partner of the local party chair! In any event they will have a vote.

For a great many local party members periodic selection meetings are the one occasion where they get to exercise real power. They generally enjoy the occasion and take it seriously. Depending on who they had before, local parties may be looking for somebody who will make a good constituency MP. Alternatively they may be looking for somebody who will have a glittering career and go on to the front bench as quickly as possible and perhaps make it into the cabinet in time. Do not assume that the local party will always go for the local candidate. Over the years local candidates usually make many friends and allies: they also often acquire many enemies who will relish this opportunity to even the score.

Whether there have been two, three or four candidates in the final round the result has to be decided by a secret ballot. The methodology varies from party to party and from constituency to constituency. Sometimes it is simply the case that the candidate with the most number of votes wins. Other times there are a series of ballots, with the candidate with the least number of votes being eliminated each time, until one candidate ends up with more than fifty per cent of the vote.

The winning candidate is then expected to make an 'impromptu' valedictory speech. He or she should praise the other candidates, thank the party members for the confidence they have shown in them, and say how much they look forward to working with them in the months or years ahead. A ritualistic denunciation of the opposition usually goes down well at this point of the proceedings.

Council seat selections

The selection procedure for local councillors is much less onerous than that for a national seat. There is no central party selection procedure, although candidates can be vetoed by party headquarters in rare cases. There is also no final selection meeting where candidates have to address the entire local party membership.

The main requirements to become a candidate for council elections are that you have to:

- Be a member of the party.

- Live or work in the relevant local authority area, or own property there.

- Be eighteen or over.

- Be a UK or Commonwealth citizen, or a citizen of an EU member state.

Other than that, it is mainly a question of character and experience. Obviously your work for the local party will be a factor, but this can sometimes be considered less important than your work or life experience. It is also often the case that a local party will seek to have a good gender balance amongst its candidates, and they may also try to select candidates to reflect the ethnic make-up of the area.

The competition for selection at local council level varies enormously. One factor will obviously be winnability – both in terms of individual seats and the likely performance of your party within the local authority area. Another factor will be whether there are a large number of former councillors who have previously lost their seats and are looking to make a comeback. Finally of course, the standing and morale of your party nationally will have a big impact locally.

In the days when councillors were unpaid or only received expenses it was often difficult to get enough people to stand in every ward in a local authority. Today, with most councillors being paid upwards of £10,000 a year (and cabinet members a great deal more), it is rarely a problem finding candidates to fight winnable seats. There is also not usually a problem finding paper candidates to fight non-winnable seats – either these potential candidates just want to help the party out, or they want to gain experience to fight a better seat next time.

As with Westminster selections there will generally be a paper sift – to weed out the mad, bad and dangerous. After that, all candidates – sometimes including sitting councillors who have been told they need to re-apply for their seats – will be interviewed by a selection committee made up of constituency officers and branch officers. Depending on how they perform at these interviews, candidates will then be offered seats to fight. It is generally not a good idea to turn down an unwinnable seat: it may damage your chances of getting a better seat next time around.

 Warning: Electoral history is littered with examples of candidates who have been told that they are merely paper candidates for unwinnable seats. An unusually heavy swing on the night can lead to accidental councillors – and your spouse or partner might not share the delight of your new colleagues!

Council elections

Local authorities are divided into Principal Councils (which themselves are divided between County Boroughs and Non-County Borough Councils) and Non-Principal Councils (made up of Parish, Town and Community Councils). Principal Councils can be unitary authorities (such as London Boroughs) or non-unitaries (such as district and county councils). The Local Government Commission has a remit to conduct a rolling review of the structure of local government in England. In Scotland, Wales and Northern Ireland all local authorities are unitaries.

Local councillors are elected for a fixed four-year term. In some councils every seat is up for election simultaneously, whilst in others one third of all councillors are up for election in three out of every four years. There are also proposals to have councils elected by halves. There are usually two or three councillors per council ward.

More people are entitled to vote in local elections than in general elections. All UK, Commonwealth and EU citizens are entitled to vote – provided they are on the Electoral Roll and are not debarred for some other reason (such as age, mental incapacity or disqualifying criminal conviction). UK citizens living abroad are not entitled to vote in local elections.

The timetable for local elections is straightforward compared with that for general elections. Elections are always held on the first Thursday in May – unless directed otherwise by the Secretary of State in the event of an emergency (such as the Foot and Mouth crisis). The notice of the election must be published at least 25 days before the election, and nominations must be handed in by midday, 19 days prior to Polling Day.

Candidates for local elections must be nominated by a proposer and seconder, and eight other people entitled to vote in the relevant area. Unlike with Parliamentary elections, no deposit is required in order to stand in council elections.

As with elections for the Westminster Parliament, candidates are strictly limited as to the amount they can spend on their campaign. The current limit is £600 plus 5.0 pence per elector. This figure is reduced where there are joint candidates standing in the same ward, and it is varied from time to time – so always check with your agent or the local Returning Officer.

Getting Started

Adoption meeting

These days there is no legal necessity to have a formal adoption meeting – where the local party officially appoints you as their candidate. This is usually now accomplished by a motion at the end of the selection meeting.

There are, however, good reasons for holding such a meeting. After the tension of a selection meeting, it can be quite therapeutic to have a rally-style meeting where you can deliver a carefully prepared speech designed to reinforce your position and enthuse the local activists. You can also either invite the local press, or send them a short press release – with photograph – of the occasion.

The adoption meeting can also be used for fund-raising purposes. After your uplifting speech – and a supportive speech from your local party chair – it is perfectly acceptable to pass round a collection bucket or to leave envelopes on the chairs for members to put donations in. Just bear in mind that you have to cover the costs of setting up the meeting, and any donations of over £50 have to be recorded and reported to the Electoral Commission.

Building a team

If you have been selected as a local candidate your team may well already be in place. Assuming that they are largely happy with your selection, all that you have to do is to work with the existing personnel within the existing local party structure. However, you need to bear in mind that during a general election your local party is suspended for the entire duration of the campaign, which is why you will need to set up an alternative structure.

If you are a non-local candidate, or if there is no real structure in place, or if you are a local candidate but you do not have the full support of the local party, you may have to effectively start from scratch. This can be very difficult, and could take up a lot of your time and energy in the early days. However, without a team who you trust and can work effectively with, your campaign is pretty well doomed from the outset.

Below are some of the roles which you can assign if you are fortunate enough to have a large team at your disposal. Very often, however, it is simply a case of doing the best you can with the human resources at your disposal.

Agent

Many local parties cannot begin to consider employing a full-time qualified professional agent. If they are lucky, they might have a part-time agent or the equivalent, a constituency organiser, or an organising secretary. Some local parties have taken the bold and logical step of employing an agent between them. If you have none of the above options you will have to prevail upon a supporter to take up the role.

Having an election agent is a legal requirement, although you are permitted in law to be your own election agent. He or she will have to liaise with the local authority Electoral Registration Officer (the official charged with the responsibility for the preparation and maintenance of the register of electors), collect enough signatories (of persons on the electoral register) to get you nominated, and get you registered to contest the election. Your agent will have to advise you on what you can and cannot do, say or spend during your campaign. He or she will also have to set up and control your election bank account (known as the Agent's Account), and fill in the forms detailing every item of expenditure incurred during the course of the campaign.

All parties offer a crash course on the roles and responsibilities of being an election agent – I have been on one myself and it only lasted one day. They also provide supporting literature and timetables. But do not be under any misapprehension – being an election agent is a difficult and onerous task.

Chair

After your election agent your local party chair is the most important person to you. He or she will – hopefully – support you and your agent, and ensure that local party workers do just that; work in support of your campaign. Within reason it is worth doing almost anything to keep your local party chair onside. Either deliberately or through withholding full support your local party chair can doom your chances of victory from the outset.

This post is nearly always time limited. Sometimes a simple Buggins turn system operates, whereby one of the vice chairs simply takes over without a contest. However, sometimes there are elections – and they can be very hotly contested. My advice for any candidate (or sitting MP) is to not get drawn into these contests, or indeed any aspect of internal party politics.

Once the actual election campaign begins your local party goes into abeyance and your chair (and other officers) technically have no standing. However, they will still carry great weight with the local volunteer workers, and if you win you will have to work with them – so keep them involved and treat them with respect.

Fundraiser

When it comes to election campaigns, the normal scenario is that the national party pays for the central campaign but local parties are expected to raise the money to fight their own battles.

If you are extremely fortunate your local party may have sufficient reserves to fight a strong campaign without any additional fundraising. However, even if this is the case, they may not want to invest their reserves in your campaign, and most candidates are expected to fill their own war chest. You will need a fundraiser, and that person can often (but not necessarily) be your local party treasurer.

Some people are happier to contribute to something tangible like an election campaign, rather than just making a donation. You can either write to them requesting a contribution, or hold fundraising events. Your local party members can be expected to contribute some money, as can other supporters who (for various reasons) have never actually joined the party. As a general rule the Conservatives raise a lot of money from local businesses, and Labour from local trade unions. The Lib Dems are often forced to rely on members alone.

Quite often, however, the main burden of filling the war chest falls on the candidate themselves. Being a candidate can be a very expensive business, especially if you have to buy or rent a second home, or travel long distances. This strain can often be compounded by the need to find the money to fight the actual campaign – either from your own pockets, or from long-suffering family or friends. There must have been many millions of pounds wasted by unsuccessful candidates in nursing seats over the years. Sometimes the only consolation is the chance to fight a better seat, a second crack at the same seat or a nice profit on the second home you bought in order to give your candidature local credibility.

Press officer

If you are lucky enough to have a professional journalist or public relations professional as part of your volunteer team it would be a good idea to appoint them as your press officer. Although the local press will still want to meet you – and on occasion deal with you direct – having a communications professional on your staff able to deal with routine press releases and media handling can be a real asset.

IT manager

Again, if you are fortunate enough to have an information technology person on your team then you really should try and persuade them to take on responsibility for your IT during the campaign. They could help you to get the best out of your hardware and (more importantly) your software. Not all local parties have fully trained agents, and even if they do they may not be fully computer literate. The various software packages used by the main parties are very powerful but they are also fairly complex. The Lib Dems use Election Agents' Record System (EARS), the Conservatives use Bluechip, but are moving on to Merlin, and Labour used to use Labour Contact, but are moving onto Contact Creator. Training and support is available for all of these packages, but an IT professional will always be able to get more out of them than a gifted amateur.

Your IT manager will also probably co-ordinate the team who input data into your voter contact management system. Their job will be inputting canvass returns during the course of the campaign, and the data from telling slips on Polling Day. They will also have to be able to print out updated knocking up sheets once the telling information has been inputted.

Posters

Having a large number of posters up can be a great boost for party workers, and a strong indication to the electorate that your party is fighting hard and doing well. Window posters can largely be left to your street campaigners to distribute. However, if you can try and appoint somebody whose specific role it is to identify key large poster sites, secure the permission of the relevant person, and ensure they get erected (and replaced if knocked down or damaged).

Canvassers

Your canvassers are your shock troops. They are mobile, confident and committed. It may be that you or your agent (or chair) want to lead these elite troops yourself. Otherwise, choose one of their number who is widely respected and give them the role.

Telephone canvassers

Some local party members want to help with the campaign, but are unwilling or unable to knock on doors. They can often be persuaded to do some telephone canvassing, which initially will be to a script but over time they will become more confident and feel able to deviate from it. Having a person whose job it is to recruit, co-ordinate, train and motivate telephone canvassers can be worthwhile.

Leafleters

Again some party workers are mobile, but don't feel confident enough to talk to people on the doorstep. Organising them into delivery teams is time consuming, and if you have somebody with the organisational and motivational skills to take on this job then give them this assignment. If you can build up a decent delivery network it makes a huge difference to the amount of literature you can put out.

Postal votes co-ordinator

Many elections are swung on postal votes. They also have to be handled (pun intended) extremely carefully. If there is somebody who you can trust to drum up postal votes enthusiastically but scrupulously give them the job.

Committee room co-ordinators

Ideally you should have a committee room (usually in a member's house) in every ward. On the day, the efficiency or otherwise of these committee rooms could dictate the margin between victory and defeat. You need somebody who knows the local area – and the local members – to plan out well in advance where these tactical headquarters will be situated. Committee rooms may not be computerised, and they may therefore have to rely on old-fashioned hard copy systems; 'Reading Packs' in the case of Labour, 'NCRs' in the case of the Tories, and 'Shuttleworths' in the case of the Lib Dems.

Opposition researcher

This is in effect your intelligence officer. It is somebody whose job it is to find out as much as possible about the opposition's campaign and about their candidate. They should therefore be the co-ordinator and keeper of your newspaper cuttings file, and your collator of samples of the oppositions' leaflets.

It is also their job to highlight any contradictions in the enemy's campaign, and any dubious aspects of their candidate's past life. If you have a defector from the opposition's ranks, and you can trust them, give them this role. They will know more than most about the workings of the opposition's local party, and they will be better placed to second-guess their reaction to any political or policy initiative.

Your intelligence officer should attend any open meetings the opposition candidate might hold, and he or she should bring away any literature handed out and make mental notes (to be written up later) of what is said. They should also be charged with opposition SWOT analysis:

- Strengths
- Weaknesses
- Opportunities
- Threats

Tellers

Some members only want to help out on the actual polling day. For them, telling (i.e. checking which local electors have cast their votes by asking for their Electoral Roll Number and feeding this information back) is a relatively undemanding and usually quite sociable task. However, many tellers will only do an hour or two, so you will need somebody to organise your telling rota well in advance.

Make sure that your tellers are aware of the fact that they have no official standing in law, that the electorate does not have to provide them with any information and that their activities are totally governed by the polling station's Presiding Officer. The Presiding Officer will tell them where they can stand or sit, and their instructions must be obeyed in all respects. Tellers should never approach voters on their way into the polling station, and they should never ask them how they have voted.

Polling agents

You are permitted to appoint Polling Agents who (unlike tellers) are allowed into polling stations. You are allowed to appoint up to four for each polling station, although only one is allowed in at any one time. Their main job is to look out for 'personation', which is somebody masquerading as someone else in order to hijack their vote. This is extremely rare, and frankly there is not a great deal of point in appointing people specifically to this role; just appoint some of your telling slip collectors or members of your canvassing team who can make the odd visit to a polling station just to check that everything is in order.

Counting agents

Counting agents, on the other hand, do perform a valuable function. They can turn up at the count and sit opposite the official counters, making sure that they are putting votes in the correct pile. With many thousands of votes being counted there are inevitably some mistakes, and a sharp-eyed counting agent can find you a few votes or cause dubious votes to be examined. They are not allowed to touch any ballot papers, but counting assistants are obliged to react to any queries and (if necessary) take up any issues raised with the Returning Officer – the official charged with overseeing the conduct of the election and the count.

You can also send your counting agents along to the opening of the postal ballots, which are conducted periodically ahead of the actual count. Again, if they keep their eyes peeled they can get a good feel for how the postal ballot race is panning out as the envelopes are opened and the ballot papers are verified and put into piles for counting on Polling Day. However, they should be warned that broadcasting any intelligence they have gleaned whilst attending these openings is a criminal offence.

Appointing your active helpers as counting agents is a good way of extending the period of their active assistance into the night and the small hours of the following morning. It is a role seen as a reward and a perk. Having worked hard on a campaign most active politicos want to be in at the kill to share the elation – or join in the commiserations.

Get Out The Vote

Everything you do during your whole campaign builds up to the climax which is Polling Day. Unless your plans are in place for that day, all of your efforts could be wasted. If you have somebody with experience and a strategic brain who is not involved in the day-to-day slog then give them the crucial task of planning the final 24 hours and make them your GOTV co-ordinator.

The alternative is to rely on your agent or chair to see the campaign all the way through, including this last crucial 24 (or more often 36) hours. Given the amount of jealousy and internal warfare prevalent in so many local parties, this can often be the best option.

Local Communication

Having got yourself selected you need to inform the local electorate of the fact, and tell them about yourself and your priorities.

Rather than produce a smart (and expensive) leaflet the best way is often just to use your local party's (hopefully) regular newsletter – whether this is termed an In Touch, Focus or Rose. This piece of literature should include a picture of you, some details of your background, your personal priorities and your plans for making life better for local people.

One tip is to get supporters who are not able to campaign on the streets to write out the addresses on the envelopes for carefully targeted letters. This is very time consuming, but really personalises the exercise and consequently has much more impact. You can even scan in the candidate's hand-written letter, which often has more impact than a word-processed version.

At this stage, unless an election is imminent, it is probably better to keep literature low-key. Pictures of you shaking hands with the party leader could be counter-productive during the immediate post-selection phase. Pictures with local dignitaries, electors or activists are far more appropriate, especially if there are identifiable local landmarks in the background.

During the 2005 general election I used a picture of my agent's very attractive wife Jo and their baby daughter Hettie in my election literature. The picture was taken outside a local school, and I was roundly told off by the Chair of Governors at a hustings meeting for exploiting his school for political purposes!

Creating a newsletter announcing your selection is also a good way of testing and gauging the ability of your local party office and workers to produce a piece of literature, and distribute it.

When it comes to the actual general election campaign, all of the main parties offer literature packs based on a set template. They contain some national news and policies, but have plenty of space available for pictures and details of the local candidate and campaign. These packs are generally extremely good value, and do take away a lot of hassle in terms of design and print at a crucial time, so you would be well advised to take them. In the meantime, however, you should try to form a good working relationship with at least one local printer.

It is vital that any literature you put out – whether it be a leaflet, poster, knocking-up flyer, sorry you were out card, etc.– has an imprint. This is the final line on the bottom of any piece of literature which tells the voting public (and the authorities) who has produced and distributed it.

The standard form this takes would be along the lines of:

Promoted by Freda Bloggs on behalf of John Doe – both at 1 The High Street, London SE1 1AB

Printed by Acme Printing Ltd, 111 Commercial Street, London SE10 1YZ

 Warning: Failure to use an imprint can lead to an immediate legal challenge by your opponents. You could face a heavy fine and even the invalidation of your election.

E-bulletins

Sending out e-bulletins has several big advantages over traditional hard-copy leaflets:

- Firstly, they are free. Of course you have to invest time in designing and writing them, but there are no physical printing costs.

- The format makes it easier to target particular wards and you can adapt your bulletin according to local issues and priorities.

- Finally, no physical distribution is required so you can use your deliverers on other projects.

You will have to invest in gathering the email addresses in the first place, but once you have them you can send the recipients regular bulletins. There are a number of ways of doing this. You can actually buy them in bulk from mailing houses. More often though, you just build up your list through your members, via regular canvassing and through people signing petitions. These petitions can either be hard copy, gathered on the street as you circus or operate your street stall, or electronically on your website, encouraging people to submit their email address.

If you are going to send out e-bulletins there are two things which you need to be careful of:

1   You are still obliged to include an imprint showing who has produced the bulletin and on whose behalf you are sending it out.

2   Recipients must have the option of unsubscribing if they no longer want to receive your emails.

Local newspapers

Local papers tend to be widely read, and people generally have more faith in them than in national newspapers. A paid-for paper may only have an official circulation of (say) 3,000-5,000, but the number of people who actually read it is often double the number of those who buy it as it is passed round family and colleagues. Free newspapers – in theory at least – are often supposed to go to every household in a town or borough. Some people only read them for the advertisements, but others read the news and comments pages as well.

Local newspapers are usually either completely politically unbiased, or more subtle in the way in which they express their bias, than the national newspapers. They will often carry a weekly column from the local MP, but sometimes they will allow the main opposition party candidate in the area to also have a regular column. The great thing about local newspapers is that people not only read them, but on the whole believe the stories and take them at face value. It is much harder to mis-report or misrepresent a local story in a local newspaper than in a national newspaper.

As soon as you are selected you should send a press release – with an accompanying photograph – to all of the local newspapers (paid for and free). This should tell them a little bit about yourself (stressing your local connections) and your plans. You should also put down a marker stating which local issues you will be campaigning over.

Before you actually send the press release you should telephone the offices of the local papers and ask to speak to the editor. Tell him or her that there is a release on its way (preferably by email), and ask if you can meet them. A meeting can either be held at the paper's offices over a coffee, or over a beer or glass of wine at their local. Local journalists are not well paid and they have very small entertainment allowances, so some modest hospitality is often welcome.

It is vital to build a good working relationship with the local newspapers. You should aim to meet all of the editors and reporters. This is not as hard as it may seem as most local papers have only got two or three people on their editorial staff. Aim to meet them all within a month of your selection, and try to build up a relationship of trust with them. They need stories and pictures to fill their papers and you need the free publicity which they can give you. Exchange mobile phone numbers and promise to keep them up-to-date with what you are doing. If you are going to have any exclusives to dish out, share them equally around the local papers.

Most importantly, tell the local editors and reporters that you are available at any time of the day or night to comment on local or national stories. They will put you to the test, but if you can come out with an intelligent comment off the top of your head ten minutes before their deadline they will genuinely appreciate it. If you can make that comment amusing or controversial they may even learn to love you.

 Warning: Just don't become a 'media tart' – somebody who is so desperate to get coverage that they will say or do anything. The objective is to get yourself pictured or quoted in the local press, but only in a way which will impress the electorate.

Letters

The letters pages are the most well-read parts of any newspaper – local or national.

Whereas big national newspapers such as *The Times*, *The Daily Telegraph* or *Guardian* are not able to print all of the letters sent to them each day, local newspapers actually have trouble filling their letters pages. What is more, most of the letters which are sent in are, not to put too fine a point on it, very parochial and very boring. This means that a well written, reasonably short letter will have a very good chance of being published. If the letter is also amusing, all the better, and if it links a national issue to a local issue then better still.

If you are local and have not been selected but have ambitions to be so, then get in the habit of writing to your local papers every few weeks. Do not send the same letter to different newspapers, and do use a rota to make sure that you write to them each in turn. Obviously if one newspaper never prints your letters, then concentrate on the others. The purpose is to get name recognition – a vital asset in any election campaign.

Once you are selected as a local candidate you are much more likely to get your letters printed. On the other hand, you probably have to be more circumspect – and less amusing – in what you write. Ahead of the starting gun being fired for an actual election campaign, the normal convention is for candidates to style themselves as 'Prospective Parliamentary Candidate', or 'Parliamentary Spokesperson'. Technically you do not officially become a candidate (no matter when you were selected) until Parliament is dissolved, and this is when your election expenses are triggered

I have never believed in the maxim that 'there is no such thing as bad publicity'. There certainly is such a thing, and many a political career has been ruined by adverse publicity in local and national newspapers. However, given how expensive leaflets are to print and distribute, it is worth making every effort to get on with your local newspapers, and to persuade them to give you as much coverage as possible.

Warning: Some local parties and even candidates have been known to send in letters to local papers under either a false name and address, or under somebody else's name and address. Needless to say this practice, if not actually illegal, is certainly immoral and foolish. If the local newspaper decided to check out the letters (which they sometimes do) and caught you out, they would quite rightly heavily criticise you in their pages. If you want to vary the message – and the messengers – then set up a letter writing panel with a number of local people who are happy to write letters on a local theme which they not only agree with, but are happy to say so in print.

Local groups

As well as building up a relationship with the local papers, you should also aim (as soon after your selection as possible) to get around as many local groups as possible.

The groups you need to concentrate on are residents' groups, faith groups, voluntary groups, trade union branches, Chambers of Commerce and Rotary Clubs. Once news of your selection hits the local papers you will receive a number of invitations to visit and address groups, and you should accept them all if at all possible. Even if the group is likely to be naturally antipathetic to your party, you can at least convince them that you personally are a decent person and not worth actively campaigning against!

First-time voters

You can identify first-time voters from the Electoral Register. Every candidate is entitled to a free copy of the Electoral Register in either electronic or hard copy form. This will also show (in the case of first-time voters) their date of birth, so send them a birthday card; hopefully they will be impressed, and may even vote for you.

Although there is now much less voter loyalty than in times past, your first vote is like your first bank account; you will probably stick with it unless there is a good reason to switch. So getting those first-time voters on side could stand you in good stead not just for the election to come, but also for those to follow.

Election Timetable

The UK Prime Minister has a luxury which very few of his or her equivalents in other democracies possess; they can dictate the timing of the general election. As long as it is called no later than five years from the date Parliament was appointed under a Writ of Summons, the Prime Minister (technically subject to the consent of the Monarch) has the ability to call a general election at any time.

Traditionally, elections in this country have been held on a Thursday, but it was not always so, and it does not necessarily need to be so in the future (indeed Prime Minister Gordon Brown has said that he would like to experiment with weekend voting). The majority of general elections are held in the spring or early summer – April, May or June – but there have been October elections and any month could in theory be chosen (although there are obvious drawbacks to holding a general election in August or December). As local elections have (under current legislation) to be held on the first Thursday in May, this has become the favoured date for general elections as well.

When the time comes the Monarch will issue a Proclamation dissolving the existing Parliament and issue a Writ summoning a new one. Technically the Monarch does this on the advice of the Privy Council, although in fact it is on the advice of the Prime Minister. There is usually about a week between the Prime Minister announcing the election and the issue of the formal Writ dissolving Parliament – although this is not necessarily the case. This variable gap is one of the explanations as to why some general election campaigns seem to go on much longer than the 17 working days they technically consist of. The other explanation is the fact that weekends and Bank Holidays do not count towards the 17 days.

Here is the current timetable for general elections, as laid down by the Electoral Commission in their guidance for Returning Officers:

DAY 0	Proclamation summoning new Parliament, dissolution of old Parliament, issue of Writ
DAY 1	Receipt of Writ
DAY 3	Notice of election Deadline for registration of political parties intending to field candidates at the election
DAY 6	Last time for delivery of nomination papers Last time for notice of appointment of election agents Statement of person nominated Last time for changes to existing absent vote details, for example cancellation of existing arrangements, redirection of ballot papers etc
DAY 11	Last time for new applications to vote by post or proxy
DAY 12	Last day to make alterations to the register of electors to correct clerical errors or implement a court decision
DAY 15	Last day for notice of appointment of counting agents and polling agents
DAY 16	Last day to replace spoilt or lost postal ballot papers
DAY 17	Polling day
DAY 35	Last day for receipt of return of agents' election expenses
Day 42	Last day for receipt of return of candidates' election expenses

These days refer to working days, excluding weekends or Bank Holidays, which means that the actual campaign will be three and a half weeks long.

There is also a small gap (usually but not always a week) between the Prime Minister (with the approval of the Monarch) announcing the general election, and this formal timetable taking effect. Parliament uses this time to quickly pass any legislation which has got cross-party consent, and to wind up its formal proceedings.

 This is the formal timetable for an election. However, political parties are increasingly on an almost permanent war footing. It was Dick Morris, Bill Clinton's election guru, who invented the concept of the 'long campaign' (or the 'permanent campaign') whereby the next election campaign began immediately after the result of the previous one had been called. Tony Blair, a close friend and ally of Bill Clinton's, brought the concept of the permanent campaign to these shores.

Election Expenses

You can spend whatever you like ahead of the actual election campaign, giving richer parties – and richer candidates – an obvious advantage. However, once the campaign begins, there are very strict limits on what candidates can spend.

Currently the limits are £7,150 plus 7p per entry on the register of electors in a county constituency (generally rural areas), and £7,150 plus 5p per entry on the register of electors in a borough constituency (generally urban areas). As mentioned earlier, for a council election the current limit is £600 plus 5.0p per elector. Bear in mind, however, that these figures can be changed at any time, so double check them when your election is actually called.

All Parliamentary candidates must (at the time of submitting their nomination papers) also submit a £500 deposit, which will be returned, provided they manage to get at least 5% of the votes cast. They must also attract the support of at least ten people (including a proposer and seconder) who are on the electoral register and who are prepared to sign their nomination papers. These measures are in place to discourage frivolous candidates, although it has not altogether succeeded in this objective. There is no deposit required for candidates standing for election to local authorities.

What you actually spend your money on is largely up to you. However, you cannot pay for canvassers and you cannot treat (i.e. entertain) your helpers or bribe the electorate!

 Warning: You would be well advised to try and get enough nominations to fill two (or even three) nomination sheets. If one of the nominations is invalid, it can invalidate the whole sheet – so you will need a spare. It is also a good idea to submit your nomination form early, so that it can be checked – and if there is a problem you still have time to try and find other valid nominators.

Donations

There are very strict rules governing donations to national political parties at headquarters and local levels.

You can only accept donations (and that means money, goods or services in kind) from:

- An individual registered to vote in the UK
- A UK registered company or association
- A UK registered party

As mentioned earlier, any donation with a monetary equivalent value in excess of £50 has to be recorded and declared.

A full declaration of all donations – and all expenditure on your campaign – has to be delivered to the Returning Officer no later than 35 days after Polling Day for the Election Agent, and seven days after that for the candidate.

Eligibility

Not just anybody can stand for election.

You must be:

- At least 18 years old on the last day of nominations
- A UK citizen, or a citizen of a qualifying Commonwealth country, or a citizen of the Irish Republic.

Being an EU citizen does not qualify you to stand for the Westminster Parliament – although you can stand for European Parliament elections and local authority elections.

Equally, certain categories of people are explicitly prohibited from standing for election as an MP. They include prisoners serving sentences of more than 12 months, undischarged bankrupts, and people found guilty of electoral offences. They also include some categories of persons working for the Crown (including members of the armed forces), as well as Peers and Bishops who are entitled to sit and vote in the House of Lords, and Priests or Deacons of the Church of England.

Uniform – What To Wear

Like any army, if you are going to take part in an election campaign you will need a uniform. This is for the purposes of identification (whose army do you belong to) and protection (in this case from the elements).

Rosettes

Wearing a rosette, of whatever hue, serves a number of purposes.

Firstly, it makes it obvious to the public – the electorate – that you are out and about. You are active, you are taking this campaign seriously, and you have boots on the ground. In other words, there are troops who you can call upon to help you with your campaign. It is important to demonstrate this, not least because it is not always the case that a candidate does have helpers he or she can call upon. This is a show of force.

Secondly, wearing a rosette is part of the bonding process and helps to mark you out as a team. You may be from different areas, you may be wearing different uniforms, but you are all on the same side and you are all fighting for the same army. Wearing rosettes is good for morale.

Finally, wearing a rosette can save you an awful lot of time. As you gain experience as a canvasser you will come to learn that – for whatever reason – the electorate does not always respond honestly to questions from canvassers. They might want to send you packing in the shortest possible time by promising to vote for you. Alternatively, they could be supporters of another party who want to tie you up and waste your time. In this case, implying that they might vote for you if they can have an in-depth discussion about your full range of policies could tie you up for half an hour. If you are out and proud with a big rosette in the face of the resident, their immediate reaction might be to slam the door in your face, in which case you have all the information you need. Alternatively, if you look in their eyes the moment they alight on your rosette, that will give you a far more honest and trustworthy indication of their voting intention than any words they may utter.

So wearing rosettes shows the public you are serious, it helps your team to bond and it can save you time on the doorstep.

I was once canvassing in a European election in a run-down North London council estate. The door was flung open by a huge, heavily tattooed man who as soon as he spotted my rosette started to bellow at me and finger jabbed me backwards down his garden path until I reached the pavement and could turn and retreat. All the while he was giving me some detailed anatomical advice and an in-depth analysis of the make-up of my family tree.

I marked him down as 'Against' and thought no more about it. However, the following week a BBC camera crew asked if they could accompany me whilst canvassing and I agreed. After a couple of hours of knocking on doors and getting very little reaction they asked if it was always this dull. I replied that it could be quite interesting, and took them back and positioned them across the road from my tattooed friend. I knocked on his door, and sure enough he flung it open and raised his voice – and his finger – to give me a repeat of the previous week's performance. Unfortunately he then spotted the camera crew, smiled beatifically, shook my hand and invited me in for a beer. Needless to say the BBC crew were very disappointed!

Footwear

Napoleon said that an army marches on its stomach. This, of course, is nonsense. An army marches on its feet, and footwear is crucial. During my campaign in Edmonton in 2005 my agent, Francis Ingham, and I wore pedometers. On a full day's leafleting we would often cover 15 miles, and our record was 17 miles – the best part of three quarters of a marathon. Without the right footwear this would have been impossible.

The first rule – whether you are male or female – is no high heels. They get stuck, they slow you down, and eventually they cause problems for the Achilles tendon, which will rule you out for the rest of the campaign.

Secondly, bearing in mind our wonderful British weather, footwear has to be waterproof. That does not mean you have to wear Wellington boots, but you should avoid shoes with holes in the sole or those with leather soles which soon crack and let in water.

The ideal shoes are the kind of comfortable business shoes with cushioned soles made by some of the better shoe manufacturers. They are expensive, but they will last and they protect your feet whilst you are pounding the pavements. The alternatives are trainers or deck shoes, but they are neither as smart nor as comfortable.

Clothing

There is no golden rule for what you should wear whilst campaigning.

If you are leafleting, then you need to dress for comfort and speed. What you wear is less relevant, although if you are wearing a rosette (which you should be) you need to bear in mind the impression you will leave behind with the electorate. If you are canvassing, it is much more important to look smart. If you look scruffy or unkempt, it gives the electorate the impression that you don't care what they think about you.

Another important factor is whether you are the candidate or not. The electorate (and probably your own team) will expect you to be more smartly dressed than the other members of your campaign team. There is no rule about whether a male candidate should wear a suit and tie or a female candidate a business suit. You should dress in a way which feels comfortable to you, but which you also think will appear suitable to the electorate.

Of course you have no control over what the electorate is wearing when they open the door to you. I have had the door opened to me by members of the public in a huge variety of day and night attires – which they are just about wearing! On one occasion a very attractive young lady opened the door to me wearing a very small towel which barely covered her ample assets. Locking my gaze firmly on her eyes I explained that I was the local candidate and would be grateful for her vote. Smiling back at me she explained that she was just about to have her bath – and that I was welcome to join her. Stuttering about my party's stance on family values I beat a hasty retreat and abandoned the rest of that road for the day. I also marked her down as 'Against' in order to spare my colleagues from future temptation!

Rain protection

Given that most elections statistically speaking take place in the month of May it is inevitable that campaigners are going to encounter a fair number of rainy days and evenings.

Less enthusiastic campaigners sometimes use the rain as an excuse not to go out. Obviously it is less comfortable, and leaflets can indeed get soggy, but there are only so many days in a campaign, and it is going to rain for a fair proportion of them, so you really cannot afford to lose the opportunity to be out and about. What is more the general voting public might – just might – be impressed that you are campaigning in these conditions, and they might look a little more favourably on your cause.

That does not mean, however, that you should not take precautions to protect yourself from the rain. Waterproof shoes are an absolute must. An umbrella can be useful, but obviously takes up one hand, which can make it hard to post a leaflet through a door or to mark a canvass card. So sometimes an anorak or raincoat is preferable, as it will leave your hands free. Finally, of course, don't forget that you will need a pencil or biro capable of marking damp and soggy canvass cards.

Glasses

If you are canvassing, even on a sunny day, it really is not a good idea to wear sunglasses. The electorate want to look you in the eye, and that is a lot harder if you are wearing shades – trendy or otherwise. Wear glasses with clear lenses or, if you can wear them, contact lenses. Apart from any aesthetic improvement, they are much more effective in the rain!

Hats

One word – don't.

Equipment – What You Will Need

As with any army, you will need the right kit to go to war with. Some of the equipment you will need you will already own – it is just a case of remembering to take it with you, and of taking enough spares to help out less organised comrades.

Other equipment is more specialised, but either your local or your national party should be able to help you out – or at least point you in the right direction.

Vehicles

As the candidate you will need your own command vehicle. This should (if possible) be large enough to carry at least five people plus a substantial amount of literature. Ideally this vehicle should not be too flash or expensive. In days gone by it would have been advantageous to drive a British car, but nowadays that is less important and, frankly, well nigh impossible – unless you can afford an Aston Martin.

It really is vital that you are able to drive yourself. Non-driving candidates are very rare, and nearly always cause a lot of resentment as they have to be ferried everywhere. Assuming that you do have a driver's licence, make sure that you hang onto it. Watch the speeding points, and never, ever drink and drive. A candidate who gets done for drink driving can pretty well forget any chance of getting elected.

John Flack, who stood in Southgate in 2001, unwisely admitted in a newspaper interview that he owned four cars. The opposition gleefully seized on this, and promptly dubbed him 'Four Cars Flack'!

Speaker vans

There are two schools of thought on speaker vans (or speaker cars). It is now very easy and cheap to buy a public address system which clips magnetically to the roof. Some people regard them as being a very easy way of getting your message across to large numbers of people. Others regard them as a nuisance, more likely to put people off than to persuade them to turn out and vote for you. A good compromise is to only use them on Polling Day and only in your really solid areas.

In order to save your voice – and to allow somebody else to drive – it is a good idea to record a short message on a loop which can be played repeatedly.

In 1997, I was driving a speaker car for Michael Portillo at a time when our party was extremely unpopular. We started off parked outside railway stations with him outside the car talking into the microphone. Such was the level of abuse he received that at the next station he stayed inside the car and spoke from there. The reaction was scarcely any better, and after that we just kept constantly on the move!

Collecting voters

Despite the fact that postal votes are now readily available to anyone who wants them, many elderly and disabled people still prefer to vote in person. Therefore having a small pool of drivers and vehicles who have time to ferry them to and from the polling station is worthwhile. When they are not doing car calls, this fleet can be used at the polling stations picking up telling slips.

However, you have to bear in mind that this can be a very time-consuming exercise. There is also, of course, no guarantee that the people who you ferry to the polling station are going to vote for you.

I once arrived for a scheduled car pick-up to be met by an elderly man dressed in shirt, tie, cardigan – and nothing else. He explained that he had been having a bit of trouble in the 'downstairs department', but would be with me shortly. I explained to him that the election was not really that close, and that we would arrange for him to have a postal vote for future elections!

Mobile phones

Today virtually everybody has a mobile phone and everybody (including political campaigners) wonders how they ever got by without them.

What campaigners are apt to forget, however, is that on polling day they will be in action for at least 12 hours and talking on their mobiles for a fair proportion of that time. So what is absolutely essential is that you fully charge your phone the night before, and that (if possible) you take a spare battery with you. Failing that you must make sure that you have a mobile phone charger which fits into the cigarette lighter in your car. Without a spare battery or car charger you will almost inevitably find yourself out of contact in the final crucial hours of a campaign.

Again, most people now have hands-free kits (or Bluetooth) in their cars. If you do not, and you are the candidate, get one organised before the campaign, otherwise you will have the choice of being out of contact when you are driving, or having to constantly pull over to take calls or being spotted driving illegally talking on a non hands-free mobile phone – not an ideal scenario.

Make sure that all the key members of your team have each other's mobile numbers programmed in. Just as bad as running out of battery power is not being able to track somebody down because nobody has their number.

Pens

As mentioned above, you do need a writing implement which can function in the rain. It is also a good idea to have several biros or pencils, in case one runs out or is broken, or you decide to split your forces.

Torches

Most canvassing and leafleting is done during the spring and summer months and therefore during daylight. However, if you are out late in the evening, or during the autumn or winter months, a torch can be very useful for marking canvass cards – and seeing where you are going!

Clipboards

If you are out canvassing life really is a great deal easier if you have a clipboard. This not only anchors the canvass sheets (and prevents them being blown away), but also makes it far easier to mark them up. What is more, you can also clip postal vote application forms and a map of the area to the back, as well as a supply of small window posters.

Another advantage of a clipboard is that if there are just two of you out canvassing, instead of having one person on the board and one knocking on doors, you can use the 'board drop' technique. Each canvasser memorises the name and address of the residents in the next house to be canvassed, then leaves the clipboard on a convenient garden wall and goes up to ring the doorbell. The other canvasser can then come along, record the result of their previous effort, memorise the names of the people in the next house, and then leave the clipboard for their colleague. This technique effectively doubles the number of houses that two people can canvass in a given period.

Maps

Maps are essential whether you are canvassing or delivering. If you are canvassing a map will show you the most logical order in which to work the streets. If you are leafleting it will enable you to mark off the roads which have been done and you can then hand the marked map back to your agent or campaign manager at the end of the day.

You should be supplied with a map by your constituency or campaign office and would be well advised not to photocopy maps yourself in case you infringe copyright. However, having an A to Z or equivalent in your car is a good idea, especially if you are mutually aiding and campaigning in an area other than your own.

Having a constituency map should also help you to avoid embarrassing mistakes. During one campaign we strayed over the border into a neighbouring constituency, delivering leaflets as we went. I received an irate phone call from my colleague who was fighting that seat, wanting to know why we were 'bombing Cambodia' – a reference to the USAAF's habit of 'accidentally' ending their North Vietnamese bombing runs over that neighbouring (and theoretically neutral) country.

Food and drink

Having denied that an army marches on its stomach, you will need to refuel if you are out campaigning for any length of time.

If you are out for an entire day it can be a good idea to stop off for lunch. However, a heavy lunch can actually slow you down in the afternoon, and alcohol is best left to the end of the day – especially if you are driving!

Carrying sweets is a good idea. They may not be good for your waistline – but hey, think of all of the calories you have been burning off. Most people end up slimmer at the end of a campaign. My agent in Edmonton claimed to have lost a stone and a half – despite our having a few beers or glasses of wine at the end of each day's campaigning!

Leafleting

Next to canvassing, leafleting is the most important campaigning activity – and there is a great deal of technique involved. If you and your campaign team know the ropes and have refined your leafleting techniques you can cover a considerable number of roads during the course of a day's leafleting.

The purpose of leafleting

Unless you are a candidate in a local authority election, or a Westminster candidate selected but with a full four or five years to go before the next general election, then you have no chance on knocking on every door in your patch. If you are a regional or list candidate for the European or Scottish Parliament or Greater London or Welsh Assembly then obviously you have got no chance of covering all of the ground no matter how early you are selected.

That is where leafleting comes into its own. You can (along with your distribution network) deliver leaflets to every single letter box – hopefully several times during the course of a campaign. The purpose of these leaflets is to get name recognition as the candidate, and brand recognition for the party you are representing.

Leaflets can also explain to the electorate the policies of your national party and your own personal priorities as a local candidate. Bear in mind, however, that the vast majority of the general public does not share your fascination with politics – or with yourself. Whatever form your literature takes, you have got (it is reckoned) about six seconds to convey at least part of your message in a leaflet as it makes its inevitable passage between doormat and bin.

Flats

Whether you are canvassing or leafleting the techniques involved in dealing with flats are very different from ordinary street campaigning.

For a start, you have to gain access. Some flats are open access, but increasingly they are either entryphone or warden controlled.

On the other hand, once you are in it is relatively easy to either canvass or deliver – and generally speaking it is warm and dry.

Open access flats

The number of blocks of open access flats is declining as councils and residents try to make life more difficult for vandals – and (by proxy) canvassers. Many open access flats are deck access. The rule of thumb (as with all flats) is to start at the top, and at the farthest end of any corridor or deck. If you are confronted with an angry resident – or a fierce dog – it is easier to beat a hasty retreat if this simple rule is followed. Take the lift (if there is one, and it works) to the top floor, and work your way down using the stairs.

Warden controlled access

If flats are warden controlled it is usually for a good reason. The residents may be elderly, disabled or handicapped. Either way, it is unlikely that the management will allow you in – at least without an appointment. If you are the candidate, ask the management for a time when you can come along and address the residents and appeal for their votes. If you are leafleting, it is worth asking if the management will kindly distribute your leaflets or leave them out in a common area.

If residents are elderly, it might be worth suggesting that as many of them as possible are offered postal votes. Some elderly people relish the chance to go out and vote in a local or national election, but if they are frail or disabled it can take upwards of an hour to get them to the polling station and back. And there is no guarantee, of course, that they will be voting for the party which provides them with a lift.

Entryphone controlled flats

The purpose of installing entryphones in flats is to keep out undesirables. This does not, of course, include candidates or volunteers performing their democratic duty!

There are a number of ways of getting into controlled access flats. The most obvious is to arrive armed with the flat number or telephone number of a member or supporter. You can then ask them to buzz you in.

If you don't have this information (or you don't know of a supporter in the block) then ring the flats one by one, explain who you are, and ask to be buzzed in. Most of the time this technique will work, but it can be time consuming.

Most blocks of flats have a tradesmen's button. These sometimes only operate between certain hours, but it is always worth a try. On occasion there is a blank button next to the tradesmen's button, and you have to press the two simultaneously for it to function.

Finally, if you have the time and the patience you can simply wait outside until somebody arrives or leaves. Assuming you look reasonably respectable they will normally be quite happy for you to go in.

Outside letter boxes

For the deliverer, this is the ultimate bliss. You don't have to gain access to the flats, and a series of letter boxes all grouped together means that you can sometimes deliver a score of leaflets in a couple of minutes.

Make the most of these opportunities – they are few and far between!

Garden gates

The issue of garden gates is one which most campaigners have been confronted with at one stage or another. There is one golden rule: If the garden gate is open, leave it open. If it is closed, leave it closed.

Many campaigners have been confronted with an irritated resident who accuses them of not closing the gate on their way out. Having this resident upbraiding them as they work their way down the street is not good for morale – and could put other residents off.

Even worse is if you have damaged a gate by trying to close it when it is either too flimsy to bear being moved or it has become fixed in place by long-term lack of use. This can lead not just to loud complaints, but also to possible claims for damages from you or your campaign.

Fences

Almost as difficult as the issue of garden gates is that of garden fences.

As the starting gun of an election is fired time inevitably becomes more and more tight – and the temptation to cut corners increases. If you are particularly athletic the temptation is to step or leap over fences; partly to save time, and partly to show your colleagues how fit and youthful you are!

The general rule is: don't jump over fences. There are a number of reasons for this, any one of which should dissuade you from this activity:

- Firstly, you have no idea what is on the other side. If there is an obstacle then you could seriously injure yourself, and then 'for you, Tommy, the campaign will be over'. It is simply not worth the risk.

- You may damage a resident's property. This can be either the actual fence, a potted plant on the other side, or a child's bike or toy, etc. Either way, the chances of your gaining that person's vote are reduced to slim or non-existent.

- Many residents are either scared by somebody walking across the front of their window, or they are just plain irritated by it. If you are then knocking on their door – without having made use of their gate and pathway – there is a fair chance that they will send you packing.

The only possible exception to this no jumping rule is if you are leafleting (not canvassing) and there is an obvious well-worn trail along the front of houses where the postmen and milkmen have obviously been taking shortcuts for some time. Under those circumstances it might be worth the risk – it will depend on just how urgent your delivery is.

Letter boxes

If there is one issue which unites campaigners of all parties (as well as any other leaflet or paper deliverers) it is the sheer variety of letter boxes in use – and the patent unsuitability of so many of them.

The first variable is that of positioning. Letter boxes can be situated pretty well anywhere on a door, but the main locations are:

- Dead centre. The old-fashioned location for a letter box; half way up and half way across. This is the ideal location, and should be the industry standard. Hard to fit on glass doors, however.

- Right-hand side. These are generally used with glass doors where a central location is impractical. For some reason these always tend to be not only vertical but also very small. Additionally, they tend to have a strong spring, and a set of brushes designed to keep drafts out. Consequently pushing leaflets through is a major challenge, and they can often end up either stuck or a crumpled mess on the doormat.

- Bottom of door. These tend to be slightly larger than the right-hand side versions, and therefore easier to put leaflets through. However, they can take their toll on campaigners with back problems (and even those without!)

- Top of door. For some bizarre reason some householders choose to have their letter boxes located not in the centre of the door, not on the right-hand side, and not on the bottom edge. No, they have them located at the top. Fine for those with dodgy backs, but not so good for the vertically challenged.

- Continental style. Whether for security or other reasons, more and more residents are now choosing to seal off their standard letter box and instead have a continental-style detached one. These can be located either by the side of the door, or attached to the gate (where there is a long drive and locked gates).

Apart from location, other letter boxes issues include:

- Springs. Some have such strong springs that you need both hands – and considerable muscle-power – to prise them open.

- Draft excluders. Again, some letter boxes have such effective draft excluder brushes that it is almost impossible to force a leaflet through – especially if they happen to be damp.

- Nails. It is not unheard of for some letter boxes to have exposed nails or screws either through wear and tear or a clumsy effort at DIY. Very bad news for fingers.

- Dogs. Most dogs will start to bark as soon as you get near a front door. This is good news because it alerts you to the fact that you have to proceed with caution, and make sure that your fingers do not protrude through the letter box. Far more deadly is the silent dog who lies in wait for the unwary postman or campaigner. The first thing they will know about its presence is when a dog's teeth clamp firmly onto their fingers. This does not happen very often, but it does happen. If you try to protest to the dog's owner they will either just point at some 'beware of the dog' sign (which appears in every other household whether they own one or not), or fall back on the time honoured 'well he's never bitten anyone before'. For the sake of the party you have to grin and bear it – and go and get a Tetanus shot.

If you want to avoid the possibility of injury by nail, screw or dog you have a number of options:

- Just deliver very, very cautiously.

- Wear gloves. These will, however, only offer partial protection. They are also very uncomfortable in a hot spring or summer campaign.

- Take along a device (a stick or ruler) to push the (folded over) leaflet through. With practice this can be extremely effective. Make sure, however, that no policeman or Community Support Officer could mistake your device for an offensive weapon.

Speed of delivery

As a very rough rule of thumb it takes approximately one hour to deliver one hundred leaflets.

Of course this will vary enormously. Variables include: the fitness – and motivation – of your deliverers; whether you are delivering to flats or houses; and, if you are delivering to houses, whether they have drives or not. There is a huge difference between delivering in a road of terraced houses (where the letter boxes can be just three or four metres apart) and delivering in the countryside or outer suburbs where every drive takes a few minutes to walk down.

In any event, it all evens out. Most constituencies have a mix of houses and flats, and roads with no drives or long drives. And, of course, the opposition are having to deliver to exactly the same letter boxes.

One rule which really should always be obeyed is to never have deliverers leapfrogging each other down the same side of the street – they will have to walk twice as far to deliver one leaflet. Tell them to split up so that one is doing one side and one doing the other. If one finishes before the other they can loop round and finish off the last few houses.

Warning: No matter how pushed for time you are, or how inconvenient the letter boxes, make sure that your leaflets are pushed all the way through. If you don't you could well find that unscrupulous campaigners for another party simply come along behind you and remove all of your leaflets – replacing them with their own!

Other Methods Of Voting

Proxy

Proxy votes are generally used by people who, whilst entitled to vote in the UK, live or work overseas. They designate a friend or relative to vote on their behalf – to be their proxy – having firmly established which party they wish them to vote for. Such expatriates are registered to vote in the constituency in which they last lived in the UK.

Postal

The Blair government changed the rules relating to postal votes and made it far easier to apply for them.

In the past voters had to have a valid reason to apply for a postal vote, such as extreme old age, or infirmity. In order to help boost turnout these restrictions were scrapped, so that anybody who wants to can apply for and receive a postal vote – either for a specific election or for all future elections (unless notice is given to the contrary). People now apply if they travel a great deal, work long hours or simply can't be bothered to make the trip to the polling station.

The easing of these restrictions has had the hoped for increase in turnout but it has also caused a big increase in instances of electoral fraud. One problem is that a head of household can apply for postal votes for all of the members of the family. Another is that postal votes have been intercepted – especially in blocks of flats or houses in multiple occupation. A final problem – which has been proven in a series of court cases – is that over-zealous party workers have either been prevailing on electors to vote for their party or have even filled in the postal vote themselves.

Procedures have now been tightened up, with voters now having to give their date of birth, and sign the postal voting form, which can then be checked against the signature used when they originally applied for a postal vote. The Electoral Commission has now said that party workers should not handle postal votes unless they have already been completed and sealed. There will undoubtedly continue to be instances of the postal voting facility being abused. My advice to all candidates would be: do not offer to help any elector fill in their ballot, and do not handle any ballot papers. You may miss out on a handful of votes but you will avoid any possibility of a challenge should you be elected.

Due to the increasing popularity of postal votes, the Returning Officer will probably hold several 'openings' ahead of Polling Day. You will be notified of when these are to take place, and the candidate, election agent and counting agents are entitled to attend and observe. The idea of these sessions is not to count the postal votes, but to verify them by making sure that the declarations of identity and signatures are valid. This saves a great deal of time on polling day.

Although you are not allowed to handle the postal ballots, or to take notes, you can get a reasonable feel for how you are doing in this particular area of the battlefield just by observing closely.

The Electoral Registration Officer is obliged by law to keep two separate lists covering proxy votes and postal votes. Candidates and their agents are entitled to receive free copies of both lists, which they can put onto their systems and incorporate into their standard canvass returns. It is always worth canvassing people with proxy and postal votes, firstly to remind them to use their vote, and secondly to ascertain their voting preference and (possibly) to persuade them to vote for you.

 Warning: It is a criminal offence to broadcast any intelligence you have gleaned by attending the opening and verification of postal ballot forms.

Other

As well as proxy and postal voting there have also been experiments with voting by email or SMS text message, and in having mobile Polling Stations and even ones in local supermarkets. Depending on the advice of the Electoral Commission – and the decision of Parliament – these may be extended in elections to come.

Electoral Address

Your party will publish its national manifesto within about a week of the election campaign starting. However, you will also be expected to produce your own personal manifesto – or election address as it is usually known.

Your manifesto will not be expected to differ too markedly from your party's national one. If it does, you will get in trouble with the party national headquarters and the press may pick up on the fact and make great play of it. The electorate might also wonder why you are standing for that particular party when your election address differs so radically from the national party manifesto.

There are exceptions to this, usually relating to matters of principle. Many Conservative candidates have insisted on taking a tougher stance on the EU in their own election addresses than the party nationally. When I stood for Parliament in 2005, I 'came out' against the Iraq war – a stance which earned me a verbal rocket from the Area Campaign Director, but no actual sanctions.

The three main national parties all offer election packs which provide standard template versions of everything from posters and knocking-up leaflets to election addresses. These have general national party pictures and policies, but they also have plenty of space for the local candidate to have photos (often a studio picture, plus several location shots and local features) plus a description of who they are and what they stand for. They also often have space for a photograph of the candidate shaking hands with the party leader.

Crucially these centrally produced local manifestoes also have a blank area where the name and address of local voters can be overprinted. If you buy this central pack, a locally designated printer will overprint the name and address of every householder in your constituency, and deliver them to a mailing house for sorting. Once sorted by road, they are then delivered to the Royal Mail who are obliged by law to deliver them for free. You can even get a second bite of the cherry by having a second election address delivered to the second named person in the household.

This is one of the best deals you can avail yourself of as a candidate. You incur no hassle, and although the cost is quite high (usually about £3,000) the money really cannot be put to any better use.

Canvassing

The purpose of canvassing

Many activists – and agents and organising secretaries – do not seem to have a very clear idea as to what canvassing (or voter identification or voter ID as it is sometimes called) is actually for. There is an abiding myth that by sheer force of personality and the laser-like application of logic it is possible to convert the electorate on their doorstep. Sadly, this almost never happens. If somebody wants to engage you in lengthy discourse on the doorstep the odds are that they are a stalwart supporter of your opponent who simply want to waste your time.

Canvassing is the political equivalent of speed dating. The objective is to work out the voter's intentions in the shortest possible time. If you are standing for a Westminster constituency you will have approximately 60,000 voters in your patch and approximately 30,000 doors to knock on. The odds are that neither you nor your team will have a chance to knock on every door. So if you spend five, ten or (heaven forbid) fifteen minutes trying to talk one waverer round, you are probably denying yourself the chance to knock on another half a dozen doors.

You should not just be knocking on doors in a random fashion. You should be working from canvass sheets, run off by your campaign office, which are based on the Electoral Roll. This includes everybody who is entitled to vote and who has registered to vote – some people for religious or other reasons choose not to register. Previously the Electoral Roll was only updated once a year, but since the Representation of the People Act 2000 there is now a system of rolling registration whereby it is continuously updated throughout the year. The final date for updating the rolling register for any particular election is the same as the final date for the nomination of candidates.

If you are standing for council there is at least a chance that you can get round to knocking on every door – provided you have been selected in good time. Wards do vary in size (as do Westminster constituencies) and one major variable is whether your council has two or three member wards. However, as a very rough rule of thumb, you may (between you) have to try and contact 8,000 constituents in 4,000 households.

There are several reasons for putting your troops on the ground and going door to door. They do not include persuading opponents to turn their coats. The objective of canvassing is purely and simply to identify your firm supporters, wavering supporters, and opposition 'switchers'. One reason for this is so that you can target them with pledge letters (i.e. letters to those who have pledged to vote for you) during the course of the campaign. More vital than this, however, is the paramount and overriding necessity to get those supporters – firm and wavering – to turn out on Polling Day and actually vote. The last thing you want to be doing on Polling Day is knocking up the electorate and reminding them of the fact that it is Polling Day, particularly when some of the people may be supporters of your opponents. You have to know ahead of that day exactly who your supporters are – and it is them (and only them) you want to be alerting on the day. In close elections it is always the party that 'knocks up' most effectively which wins the day.

Time consuming as canvassing is, there are other reasons for going door-to-door. If you are the candidate it is essential that you knock on as many doors and meet as many people as humanly possible. Word will soon spread that you are (hopefully) personable, and fighting an energetic campaign. And even if you cannot convert the public, you might just persuade them that you are a decent enough person not to bother to turn out in order to cast a vote against.

Another good reason for canvassing is to gather essential intelligence. This can be hard intelligence, such as evidence of fly-tipping, or poorly maintained roads or pavements in an area, or it can be 'soft' intelligence, such as a general feeling that the incumbent is past their sell by date, or that the local authority is or is not doing a good job. These two forms of intelligence can help you to refine your campaign in terms of the local issues which you are highlighting.

It is an old military maxim that time spent on reconnaissance is never wasted: equally, in political campaigning, time spent on the doorstep is never wasted.

Pets

Pets can be an opportunity – or an outright menace.

Many pet owners are inordinately – even insanely – fond of their animals. It is electoral suicide to ignore a voter's pet. You have to notice them and compliment the owner on their beauty, cuteness, intelligence, etc. If you own a pet of the same species make that point, and say how much you miss the pet when the duties of electioneering keep you away from home.

Be very wary about stroking pets, however. The animal in question could take an obvious dislike to you, in which case you can pretty well wave goodbye to the vote in question. Even worse – from your point of view – the cat, dog or whatever in question could scratch or bite you. What are you going to do – sue?

Children

Similar rules apply to children. You certainly can't ignore them, but you should not under any circumstances attempt to touch them in any way. The days of politicians kissing babies are long gone; these days you are likely to be met with screams of protest or even accusations of abuse.

However, the presence of young children does give you your opening line. If they are pre-school age you can ask the parent which school they are hoping to attend. If they are in school uniform, you can sometimes get brownie points by working out which school they attend (the name might even be on their sweatshirt or jumper). If you are a school governor you should point this out to the parents, by way of demonstrating your local involvement, and parading your knowledge of education issues. It does not always work, of course. If you are the incumbent or the candidate from the governing party any dissatisfaction with local schooling is likely to be vented at you.

A very large percentage of the electorate have children, grandchildren, nephews, nieces and godchildren. They will want to be sure that you are aware of local schooling issues, and other factors which affect young people, such as street crime and local leisure facilities. Make sure that you are well prepared to answer any questions relating to these areas with your party's local and national policies.

Pit stops

Just like running a marathon, if you are going to be out canvassing for hours on end you will probably (unless you have a cast-iron bladder) need to relieve yourself (what the US military refer to as a pressure de-fuel).

You can't ask to use an elector's facilities, so you need to be aware of alternatives. Some local authorities still maintain public conveniences – either free or those tardis-like paid-for cubicles – and it is in your best interest to have a good working knowledge of where they are located. Otherwise, your best bet is usually local garages or cafés.

One very good tip is to avoid drinking more than one cup of tea or coffee before you set out. You may feel that it helps get you going first thing – but it will almost certainly make you feel that you have to go at some stage later in the day.

On the other side of the coin, you should make sure that you have access to something to drink while you are out and about – especially if the weather is hot. Ending up in hospital with dehydration is not going to be a great boost to your campaign – although you might pick up some good campaign intelligence!

Canvassing techniques and tips

Over time everyone develops their own canvassing techniques. However, there are certain do's and don'ts for making your canvassing more efficient and effective. Some of the tips (such as how to handle garden gates and gaining access to flats) have already been dealt with. This section deals with the far more difficult – and important – aspects of how to interact with the voting public.

Doorsteps

When you approach a door you will be faced with one immediate choice; doorbell or knocker? Unless it is taped over or there is a note to say that it is not working, always try the doorbell first – but listen to make sure that it is working and audible. If there is no response after about thirty seconds then try the doorbell again. If there is still no response then try knocking fairly loudly. However, do not knock too vigorously, as this can come across as aggressive.

Having done this, step back off the doorstep. There are two main reasons for this:

1 Many residents view visitors through a glass window or spy hole in the door. This is easier for them to do if you are standing about a metre away.

2 More importantly, you are standing on the threshold of somebody's home. If you are standing hard up against the door this can look intimidating. It can also look like you wish to enter the house, which is the last thing you want to do.

So just stand back, give the resident some space, and wait, making sure your demeanour is relaxed and not impatient.

Some novice canvassers have been known to ask why there are so many local residents who have the surname 'Friedland'. This is in fact the name of a major doorbell manufacturer, and they put the name in the small slot where the residents' names are supposed to go. Many residents simply never get round to replacing the manufacturer's name with their own!

Here's another golden rule: never enter a voter's house. Apart from anything else, it invariably takes a long time. You will be invited to sit down and possibly have a cup of tea. You may then be regaled with the voter's life story and that of their children and grandchildren. It is very hard to get way – without being rude – once you are in somebody's house.

You must also bear in mind that the terribly nice person inviting you in might simply be looking to waste your time. After all, if you are a supporter of the opposition, what greater service can you perform for your party than to tie them up for as long as possible?

There are also good security and legal reasons not to go in – especially on your own. The very hospitable voter you are talking to may in fact be dangerous. Alternatively, they could be demented, and you could end up accused of stealing something or molesting them.

So never go in anywhere on your own – and also remember that if there are two of you it is taking up twice as much time. If you are the sitting MP or a sitting councillor, there may be valid reasons why you may have to go inside to inspect a problem or a nuisance. But if so, go in with somebody else, and try to avoid sitting down and accepting any hospitality. Instead, try and get the voter to come along to the more formal setting of your regular surgery.

Body language

In any form of human interaction body language is extremely important. It conveys just as much information – if not more – than the spoken word. That goes for you – the canvasser – as much as for your target audience.

So having rung the bell (or knocked on the door) and stood back, you need to wait patiently for a response. Once the householder has opened the door they should then immediately be confronted with two things:

1 A smile. The universal symbol of friendliness and the strongest indication that you mean them no harm.

2 A rosette. The universally-recognised symbol of the party you are representing.

I like to think that nine times out of ten I can tell whether somebody is a supporter or not just by the look in their eyes when it first alights on my rosette. As well as that instant – and very hard to disguise – response, there will then be other 'tells' (indications of the householder's true feelings).

If the householder is antipathetic to your cause he or she may involuntarily close the door a fraction. Or they may just step back half a pace, to create a bit more space between you and then. Even worse – and this is pretty well fatal to your cause – they may fold their arms across their chest in a protective gesture. Whether you are speed dating, looking to make a sale, or soliciting for votes, these are all fair indications that you are wasting your time and highly unlikely to succeed with this person.

A councillor friend of mine was once canvassing when he knocked on an elaborate Victorian door replete with panels of stained glass. The gentlemen who opened the door spotted his rosette, gave him a volley of verbal abuse, and then slammed the door so vigorously that one of the stained glass panels fell out and shattered – leaving them staring eye to eye through the gap. The councillor grinned broadly, posted a leaflet through the gap, and walked smartly off down the path!

Script

It is always a good idea to have a basic script in your head. You don't always have to use it, and you will have to vary it, but some kind of a stump script is worth having.

A typical opening gambit might be:

> *Good morning/afternoon/evening Mr/Mrs/Ms X (you should have their name on your canvass sheet). I am Fred Bloggs, and I am standing for this seat on behalf of the Conservative/Labour/Lib Dem Party. As you may know there are elections on the xth of May, and I was wondering whether I could count on your vote?*

Some canvassers presage their remarks with an apology for disturbing the householder. I consider this to be unnecessarily defensive. You are standing for public office: you have a right – and a duty – to knock on as many doors as you can.

There can be a number of responses to this opener, from an emphatic yes to an emphatic no (sometimes accompanied by some advice as to how to perform an anatomically impossible feat of contortion).

If it is a straight yes – fantastic, mark them down as a firm pledge. If they are especially enthusiastic, you could push your luck and ask if they would like to join the local party, or even join your delivery network.

If the response is not a straight yes, but not hostile, it is worth asking if there are any issues which are of particular concern and trying to convince them that your personal priorities – and your party's policies – are in tune with those concerns. However, do not spend too much time on any single voter. Just thank them for their views, mark them down as a 'possible' and move on. A useful disengagement technique is to say something like "I can see you are busy so I won't take up any more of your time".

Train other members of your canvass team to rescue any canvasser who has been stuck on a doorstep for an inordinate amount of time. If it is the candidate who is stuck, just send somebody to tell them that another resident in the street would like to meet them.

If the response on the doorstep is a firm no, that is nearly as good as a firm yes because at least you have a definite answer. However, that is not quite the end of the transaction. Ask the householder who they will be voting for – that is still useful intelligence as it will help you to gauge how the split in the 'anti' vote is breaking down. You can win an election with just 35% of the vote provided the other 65% is split evenly between the other two main parties.

As well as finding out which way that person is voting, you also need to find out how other members of the household are going to vote. Never assume that all members of the same household vote the same way – they sometimes do not. You will know from your canvass sheet (or what the Americans call 'walking lists') how many people of voting age live in the house. Once you have found out the voting intention of the person who answered the door, the simplest thing to ask is "and do you all vote the same way?" Very often (but not always) the answer will be yes. If the person's partner votes for a different party, they will usually know that and tell you quite happily. If there are offspring in the household who are over eighteen the parents may know how they vote, but it's less likely. In any event, you can always ask to speak to other members of the household if they are available.

As well as finding out how people intend to vote at the next election, it is also useful to ask how they voted at previous elections. There are two reasons for this:

1 It will help you spot any trend or movement from one party to another.

2 Assuming you have this information on your canvass sheet, it will help you to judge whether the householder is giving you a bum steer or not.

Some people claim not to be able to remember how they voted last time, even if local elections were only a year ago. This is possible – but unlikely. What they mean (but are too polite to say) is that they did not vote for your party!

Lies, damned lies and the electorate

It is an undoubted, but very sad, fact that a large proportion of the electorate now feels that it is perfectly acceptable to lie to politicians. The rationale for this is that they feel that politicians constantly lie to them. It is because of this growing trend that assessing body language is just as important as listening to what people tell you.

Telling porkies can also serve a practical purpose: Most people want to clear you off in the shortest possible time and promising to vote for you normally does the trick.

There are increasing numbers of voters from ethnic minorities on the Electoral Roll, and their cultural, ingrained sense of politeness and what is the correct way to behave comes into play. For some communities – especially from the Indian subcontinent – saying no (especially to somebody who is in effect a guest at their door) would be considered very rude. The simplest solution is to pledge their vote to anybody who asks for it. There is no real answer to this unless you have a member of that community with you who can perhaps judge whether the pledge is real or simply politeness. Otherwise, you are again forced to rely on body language.

At the recent Ealing Southall by-election all three of the main parties were receiving very encouraging canvass returns. This was because the local electors – many of whom were Sikhs, Muslims or Hindus – were just nodding politely when asked if they would be voting for the canvasser's party.

Canvass teams

On any given day the number of volunteers you will have available to go out canvassing will vary considerably.

The ideal size of the team will vary, depending on the abilities of the person on the clipboard marking up the canvass returns. His or her job is to send canvassers to the correct door, armed with the names of the registered voters who live there and any information available as to their previous voting habits.

So the clipboard minder – who is in fact the canvass manager for that team – will stand by the relevant door or gate and say something along the lines of "Smiths, four of them, all previously Labour" or "Jones, three of them, nothing known". This gets a little more complicated where the household is split, or where there are a large number of surnames in a house or flat in multiple occupation. There the choice is either for the canvasser to jot down the names (unless they have a superb memory and can remember them all), or for the clipboard minder to stand there and record them one by one.

The job of clipboard minder should usually be given to the most experienced – or perhaps bossiest – member of your team, but it should never be the candidate. A good clipboard minder can run up to four canvassers. Any more than that, and canvassers will be queuing up to report their findings, and momentum will be lost. So if your team is bigger than five, split it and have two people on the clipboards.

If there are just two of you (and ideally teams should be bigger for morale and presentation reasons) there is a technique whereby you can both canvass. This is known as the 'board drop'. As you go to a door (having memorised the names of the residents) you place the board on the wall of the house you are going to. Your colleague then comes along, picks up the board, marks down the findings of their last knock, goes to the next door, memorises the name, and places the clipboard on the wall or pavement. You then overtake them and do the same thing. In effect, this doubles your canvassing capability.

Won't say and won't vote

There are always a fair number of people who will not discuss their voting intentions. There are also those who cannot vote, for personal, professional or religious reasons.

Some householders are just deeply private, and are reluctant to discuss anything as personal as their vote. I normally simply say that if they can just tell me their voting intention, we will not have to trouble them again. This sometimes works, but if not I never press them. In fact I usually mark them down as 'won't vote' so that they are not troubled again.

Other people who generally won't tell you how they will vote include those who work for the local authority. They might be involved in the electoral or counting process or they might simply not want the information to be known by local councillors.

There are several classes of people who are currently not allowed to vote: these include prisoners, in-house mental patients and Peers of the Realm entitled to sit and vote in the House of Lords. You are quite unlikely to encounter any of these classes of person on the doorstep – but you never know. Under the terms of Human Rights legislation the restrictions on prisoners and the mentally ill may be lifted. And if there is to be an elected House of Lords, the ban on their voting in elections will almost certainly go.

Some religions forbid their adherents to vote. The two best known are Jehovah's Witnesses and the Plymouth Brethren. If you are working from canvass sheets based on the electoral register you will probably not encounter them as they will almost certainly not be registered to vote. There is, however, a certain ironic pleasure in disturbing the domestic peace and tranquillity of a Jehovah's Witness!

Even with constantly updated rolling electoral registers you will from time to time find yourself looking for a voter who has recently passed away. When you do encounter this, all you can do is apologise to the relatives for disturbing them, express your condolences and mark this down clearly on your canvass sheet so that the family is not disturbed again during that election.

Sorry you were out

No matter what day of the week or time of the day you knock on doors there are always going to be a fair proportion of people who are out. Of course you may have the chance to canvass that road again at a later date, but in any event it is essential to always have a stock of cards with you saying 'sorry you were out when I called' and giving contact details so that the resident can let you know if there are any issues which concern them.

These cards also serve as evidence that you have been working the streets and have knocked on their door. It also reinforces name recognition; a crucial factor in any election at any level.

By the very nature of things most canvassing takes place during evenings and at weekends. Apart from anything else, most candidates (even if they are sitting MPs) have day jobs. Obviously there will always be a fair proportion of people who are out at any particular time, but what you will also find is that people can be in but extremely busy. This can range from cooking tea or bathing the kids to watching the football or their favourite soap. When told this on the doorstep my response is very simple: "Just tell me how you are going to vote and you can get on with what you are doing, and we won't trouble you again." This technique is remarkably successful in soliciting a fast – and honest – response.

Telephone canvassing

In an ideal world every voter would be canvassed in person – preferably by the candidate. We don't live in an ideal world. All parties and all candidates have limited time and limited resources. With telephone canvassing you can cover an awful lot of ground very quickly.

You are always going to have local supporters who for reasons of age or infirmity are not going to be very mobile. You might also have people who are too shy to knock on doors and discuss voting intentions. However, give them a script, a few minutes training, and some support and they can very quickly become effective telephone canvassers. Obviously they will still encounter people who are not home but at least they can leave an answerphone message (again according to a script). What is more, people are often more honest on the phone than they are face to face, so the quality of the information you are getting can be as good – or better – than door-to-door canvassing.

There are always going to be people who object to being canvassed by telephone. All you can do is apologise, and say that you simply do not have enough personnel to knock on every door. Some people have signed up to the Telephone Preference Service, which means that they do not want to receive cold-calls. However, all political parties run their lists through the TPS system, so you should not be placed in a situation where you are phoning a person who has opted out. There is sometimes a lag-time of a few weeks for the opt-out to be registered and passed on, but that is not your party's fault and you cannot be penalised for this.

Telephone canvassing can be difficult, and sometimes demoralising. The best thing to do is set up a small bank of telephones, and try and make sure that there is a team working them together. The camaraderie and mutual support will override a string of negative calls – or the odd abusive response!

Canvass returns

Apart from the psychological impact of having teams working the streets and knocking on doors the real objective of canvassing is to fill in those vital canvass return (voter ID) sheets.

Once these have been returned to your local party campaign headquarters somebody will key in the results, and over time a picture will start to emerge. You will start to build up a solid bank of pledges; those voters who have promised to vote for you. These will be supplemented by your 'possibles'; those people who (if they do vote) will most likely vote for you. Depending on how confident you are about your canvassers, I would count these 'possibles' at no more than 65/35 in your favour.

You will also start to build up a picture of the strength of your opponents. As I said earlier, you by no means have to have a majority of the votes to win a seat under the first-past-the-post system. If your opponents' votes are fairly evenly split, you can get away with a much lower percentage figure than if it was just a two-horse race.

If your current and previous canvassing has been efficiently done you can also begin to spot trends. The days when individuals – and whole families – used to automatically vote for one party or another are gone for good. Voters do float, and they do switch. By comparing your canvass returns with those from previous elections you should be able to spot any trends and track the migration of votes from one party to another – hopefully yours. This should help you to shape your message and amend your literature as you appeal to the disaffected voters of one party or another, giving you a better chance of luring them into your fold.

As you build up a good canvass – and anything over 50% is pretty good nowadays – you can also build up a good picture of your good wards and even your better roads. This will enable you to concentrate your limited resources in the right areas during the pre-campaign period, during the actual campaign, and (crucially) on Polling Day.

As your troops on the ground feed back more and more crucial intelligence to your headquarters, the picture of the battleground should become clearer, and you should be able to plan your way towards victory.

Campaigning

We have dealt at some length with leafleting and canvassing. These are the two main aspects of campaigning, but they are by no means the only methods. Here are a few other techniques which can be used during the course of an election campaign.

Circussing

As the name implies, circussing is about creating a bit of razzmatazz and making a splash.

The best time to go is Saturday morning, usually in shopping centres, or at other times over the weekend when large numbers of people are gathered (such as a local fete). The basic idea is to turn up mob-handed (you will need at least eight to ten people) with the candidate and work the crowds. You will need rosettes, and possibly poster boards, leaflets and something to hand out; balloons for children are always popular.

The idea is not to be static. You should work your way round the shopping centre, down the high street, or through the fete greeting people, introducing the candidate, and handing out leaflets and balloons. Once you have worked your way through do not retrace your steps – just load up and head off to a different venue.

If you are confident of the number of supporters you will have, and of the type of reception you will get, invite the local press along. If nothing else they will hopefully print a picture of you talking to local people.

Circussing should be fun and you should look like you are enjoying it. You will be seen by a large number of people in a short period of time, and if you look confident and appear to be having fun they will feed back positive reports to family and friends.

The idea of circussing is a bit like Blitzkrieg – you need to be constantly on the move. I once left my rather elderly deputy chair locked in the campaign bus. We had arrived at a car park round the back of our high street destination and as the younger circussing team piled out, I 'plipped' the lock prematurely – leaving her stuck in the back. We sprinted off and by the time we got back forty minutes later she was very hot – and very bothered. If Help the Aged had been around I could have been in big trouble!

Street stalls

Street stalls are a more passive and fixed form of circussing. You just pitch a table in a market or on a high street, and (as with circussing) have leaflets and balloons to hand out, plus perhaps a petition for people to sign. This gives a point to your being there, and also helps you collect names, addresses and email addresses.

Some local parties regularly pitch their street stall in the same place and at the same time each week. This is usually in one of their stronger areas, perhaps a high street, market or shopping mall where large numbers of people pass, a high proportion of whom they reckon are supporters of their party.

An alternative is to move your stall around. This means that you can take in your strong areas and also go into areas which traditionally support your opponents. This can unsettle the opposition, and let them and the public know that you are serious about making inroads into their vote. It is the political equivalent of parking your tanks on the opposition's lawn.

Posters

Having a good display of posters is beneficial to the morale of your workers and voters. It also sends out the message to wavering undecided voters that you are working a seat hard, and that you are getting results.

In rural, and some suburban, areas there is often a real battle to secure sites for huge display posters at busy junctions and along key routes. As local people travel around the constituency, a strong display of large posters can have a psychological effect.

In urban areas, window posters are much more common – although some residents are prepared to have large posters erected in their front gardens.

Here the battle is to get quantity, and to try and ensure some displays in every street. Party members should be asked to display a poster (or series of posters) for the duration of the campaign. Canvassers should always have a supply of posters with them, so that any strong supporters can be asked to put up a poster as soon as they have pledged you their support. Leaflets should also have at least one panel which will work as a poster with just your candidate name and party on it. One trick is to hand over a poster with the sellotape already on, so that the supporter feels more inclined to stick it up immediately. If you have interestingly shaped posters (such as the Lib Dem diamonds) another trick is to ask the householder to put them in the window straight away, so that you can indicate from the outside whether it is straight.

There are other variations on the poster theme. In 1997, Labour invested in posters on wooden staves, like mini versions of estate agents' boards. They were unlikely to survive much wind, or the attentions of local youths or political opponents, but what local candidates did was to secure permission to only erect them on the day of the election. They then erected them in front gardens the night before polling day. As polling day dawned, a forest of Labour posters were revealed, and this was the precursor of a Labour tidal wave which would sweep away many Conservative MPs.

Giant posters can be very expensive – and very time consuming. Our then agent in Enfield Southgate, Malcolm Tyndall, reckoned that he spent half of the 1992 general election campaign on the roof of the local party headquarters trying to secure a giant ten foot poster of Michael Portillo which was in constant danger of blowing away and winging its way across Enfield.

You also have to be careful about the wording on posters. A former CCO agent told me that he had to explain at great length to Sir Percy Grieve's agent why having 'Grieve for Solihull' was not such a good slogan to have plastered on posters throughout the constituency!

Loudspeaker vans or cars

We have already touched on the use of loudspeaker vans – or cars – in the section on vehicles.

If you need to make a noise, and a splash, and show that you are in the game then speaker vans are great. If you need to get out the vote on Polling Day in your safe areas, they are fantastic.

Other than that, however, speaker vans alert your opponents as well as your supporters to the fact that it is Polling Day and they can also really annoy the local residents. Just as they have succeeded in lulling little Johnny or little Jemima to sleep, some idiot comes down the street blaring away on a loudspeaker and undoing all their good work. There are certainly better ways of winning hearts and minds.

Hustings Meetings

There is a convention in most constituencies that there will be at least one hustings meeting to which all of the candidates – even the lunatic fringe ones – will be invited. This 'semi-official' hustings is often organised by the local churches, takes place in a church hall, and is chaired by a local faith leader. If they have any sense, the incumbent – who has the most to lose – will accept this invitation, but no others.

This is likely to be the best attended and best organised of the hustings. Questions are usually on a panel basis, which means that the same question is asked to each candidate. It is advisable to get as many of your supporters along as possible, to ask helpful questions, and to applaud your replies. The local press are likely to report events such as these.

Several other organisations may try and organise hustings meetings. These can be local residents' associations, local trade unions, or pressure groups. Again during the normal course of events the contenders will accept all invitations, and the incumbent will try and duck them. These events are unlikely to be as well attended as the semi-official hustings, frequently they are not well run and are often less disciplined. They can, in other words, turn into a bit of a slanging match or a bun fight. Not much fun if you are the incumbent with the most to lose and trying to hang onto your dignity.

During one campaign that I fought, the Lib Dem candidate (who lived five miles away) had not been seen campaigning and had not attended any hustings meetings. I sent him a map showing him the route from his home to the constituency, with the location of the next hustings meeting clearly marked. I then sent a picture of me posting the map to the local papers. My PR stunt backfired badly when he not only showed up at the next hustings, but he performed brilliantly – showing all the rest of us up!

Distraction Campaigns

So far we have assumed that every campaign is a real campaign aimed at winning a particular seat. This is not always the case. Some seats are, in practical terms, impossible to win. Others are so unlikely that it takes a once in a generation landslide to change their colour. However, it is possible to play on the paranoia of your opponents – particularly the sitting MP – to lure them into devoting resources to a seat which they are never going to lose.

The idea of a distraction campaign is as old as military history itself. All military commanders have sought to confuse their enemies by launching feints and trying to disguise the direction of their real assault.

The Soviets took this ancient technique and turned it into a military art form: they called it *maskirovka*. As the Nazi divisions rolled into the vast Russian steppes the Red Army deployed thousands of pre-fabricated fake tanks and artillery pieces. The idea – which worked spectacularly well – was to draw fire from German aircraft and artillery, and draw Panzer divisions away from Soviet armour and infantry. This worked extremely well in World War II, when aerial reconnaissance technology was quite basic. The Soviets, however, were still trying this trick during the cold war in the seventies and eighties, when US satellites could read number plates on cars and the health warning on a packet of cigarettes. What worked in the 1940s did not work so well in the 1980s.

The idea of a distraction campaign is still used by political parties. Because the intelligence (in both senses of the word) of political parties is not always that good, it is still possible to deliberately mislead your opponents as to your true objectives.

I ran such a campaign in Edmonton in 2005. The sitting MP had a majority of nearly 10,000, and was never really under threat. Our job was to convince local Labour activists – and most Enfield Labour councillors were from Edmonton – that we were serious about capturing the seat, or at least in slashing its majority to marginal levels. We spent large sums of money before the official campaign started, and the legal maximum once it had. We distributed over 250,000 leaflets (especially targeting roads where we knew Labour councillors and activists lived), and made extensive use of the local press and speaker vans. But we did no canvassing at all – everything went into leafleting, circussing, speaker vans and cultivating the press.

We had absolutely no delusions about winning Edmonton, but we believed that if we could distract the Enfield Constituency Labour Party enough, and keep the Edmonton councillors out of Enfield Southgate, we might just be able to win back that totemic seat. And we did – by 1,747 votes.

Target Wards

In the first section of the book I talked about how the strategic planner at party headquarters would identify target seats which they would need to capture (or hold) in the forthcoming campaign.

Equally, at local level you need to plan and target as well. If you are standing as a local councillor, there could be one swing polling district which will decide who wins in your ward. If you are standing for Parliament, then equally there could be one key ward which will decide the outcome of the whole campaign locally.

You should be able to identify the key battleground by studying the results of previous elections. If there is a ward which is split, you can target it and attempt to capture it outright. If there is a ward which has changed hands in the past, you might want to pay it particular attention. If your party has previously held it, you might have a good chance of recapturing it. If you only captured it last time out, you need to make sure that the opposition does not win it back.

As well as relying on previous electoral records, you should also rely on your own canvassing. If your canvass returns suggest that there is a swing in your favour in a particular area, you should target that area and try and accelerate the process. Equally, if your canvass returns suggest that there are potentially a large number of 'switchers' from another party to yours, you should fashion your literature in such a way that it actively encourages that trend.

Finally, as I have said previously, canvassing is all about gathering intelligence – and you need to act on that intelligence. If your conversations on the doorstep identify a particular issue which is concerning local residents, you should articulate their concerns and promise to try and do something about it. These issues can be as local as a bad road junction or the lack of a bus stop, or something more substantial like a hospital closure, a proposed by-pass or a new housing development. If you can shape your policies and your literature to help to give voice to the concerns of local residents in a particular area on a particular issue, and you can realistically promise to help solve that problem, that could provide the crucial breakthrough in a vital area.

Polling Day

Unless you have a plan in place for 'D Day', and have marshalled your forces effectively, all the preparation over the previous years, months or weeks will have been completely wasted. Most elections are won by the political party which gets its supporters to vote on the day. Whatever your own canvass returns have shown you, and whatever the opinion polls might be telling you, differential turnout can turn a campaign on its head. If you have been polling 35%, and your main opposition 40%, but you persuade 60% of your supporters to actually vote as compared with your opponent's 50%, then you will win. The final 24 hours of a campaign are worth at least 50% of the effort of the entire campaign. Unless you get it right on the day, all the effort which has gone in previously will be a complete waste of time.

The night before

Polling Day actually begins the night before. You and your most dedicated supporters must be out distributing last minute leaflets and pledge letters.

This literature can simply be a reminder that the following day is polling day. Alternatively, it can be a last minute shock or revelation which might sway any last minute waverers. In 1997 the Labour Party largely used '24 hours to save the NHS' leaflets, highlighting any real or imagined threat to local hospitals. Some Conservatives in 2005 (including myself) used last minute leaflets to emphasise their opposition to the Iraq War.

If you have any dramatic revelations about your opponent or his or her campaign this is the time to get it out. There is just time for it to make an impact on the electorate's consciousness, but not enough time for it to be effectively rebutted.

I would normally run this stage of the campaign from 6.30p.m. the evening before (when your helpers would generally return from their day jobs), to 10.30p.m. that night. You then just have time to go to the pub for a couple of drinks, and a final run-through of the plans for the big day itself.

Dawn raid

So having got to bed at (say) midnight, you now need to be up at 3.30a.m. for a 4.00a.m. start. This is (literally) the dawn raid.

The idea is to put out very last minute leaflets in just your good areas, identified in your weeks of canvassing. You can either put out final pledge letters to your core supporters, or general 'Today is Polling Day' leaflets through every door in your good wards or roads.

You have to be really careful on dawn raids. Kicking over milk bottles, tripping over cats or just making a noise when pushing your leaflet through the letter box can wake up the neighbourhood. Not every member of the general public shares your obsession with politics or your belief that polling day is so vital that sleep has to be forfeited in the pursuit of victory.

Wake somebody up in the small hours of the morning with your last minute leaflet and you can pretty well wave goodbye to their vote.

There are some rare exceptions to this rule. Whilst canvassing on one occasion a woman subjected me to such a tirade of foul and personal vitriol that I made a mental note of her address. On Polling Day I made a special detour to her home at 4.00a.m., pushed an opposition leaflet through her door, rang the doorbell for thirty seconds – and fled. Childish I know, but she deserved it!

Stations

At about 7.30a.m. there is a strong argument for breaking off from distributing your last minute leaflet door-to-door and moving on to your local railway or tube stations (assuming you have any).

Between 7.30 and 9.00a.m. you will catch commuters heading off to work. They may already have voted. They may or may not be pleased to see you. They may or may not take your leaflets – but they will note that you are out and about early and taking this election seriously.

Human beings have a strong herd instinct. If they see the people in front of them refusing your leaflets, there is a strong temptation to do likewise. If you can persuade just one person to take your leaflet, however, it is an almost invariable rule that the next half dozen will almost certainly take one as well.

The best technique is to smile and talk. Hold out the leaflet and just say 'good morning – can I give you a leaflet about the election'. You will be wearing a rosette so the commuters will know which party you are from, but this neutral phrase indicates that you are imparting some information as opposed to propaganda. It is also a good idea to run this phase of the operation in pairs. If you have a couple of dozen people declining your leaflet – or even having a go at you – this can be demoralising. There is safety – and comfort – in numbers.

Finally, assuming that the morning reaction has not been too bad, there is a good case for repeating the exercise during the evening rush hour – say between 6.00p.m. and 7.30p.m. Some people will tell you that they have already voted (in person or by post), but others will be heading to the polling station on the way home, or to collect their partner to go off to vote together. What is more, people are generally in a better mood heading home from work than vice versa!

Getting out the vote – Fighting a conventional battle

The traditional polling day operation demands a lot of planning and a great many troops. If you are fighting a by-election or you are a target seat, party headquarters will expect you to plan and implement a full, conventional Polling Day operation.

Most political parties are on the cusp now. Party membership levels have fallen so low, and active participation levels even lower, that it is now impossible to run a full polling day operation in anything like every seat. That is why the concept of having target seats was invented, and why it is so vital.

To run such an operation you will need:

- An agent – full or part-time, qualified or volunteer.
- The support of your Chair and officers.
- The active support of your local councillors.
- At least 150 foot soldiers – all assigned to specific teams and given specific objectives.

Mutual aid

Since so few local parties can muster that level of support, mutual aid is vital.

This can take the form of an informal local arrangement whereby a local party with no hope of winning sends support to a neighbouring constituency which could win. On other occasions your national party headquarters will instruct supporters in no-hope seats to go and help those in winnable seats.

Occasionally mutual aid can take the form of a national organisation which, whilst technically apolitical, has a strong quarrel with one party or another, sending volunteers to help in target seats. As an example, in 2005 many members of the Countryside Alliance targeted particular anti-hunting ministers, and helped Conservative candidates with leafleting.

Usually, however, mutual aid is organised by party national or regional headquarters. It involves bussing in volunteers (often students), sometimes from one end of the country to another. The Lib Dems and Labour have always been much better at this than the Conservatives. The Tories tend to be territorial and reluctant to travel and they value the autonomy of their local associations too much to willingly take orders from above.

The key with outside helpers is to make them feel welcome but then to get them out before they settle down and clutter up your headquarters. There is always a temptation to send them to your worst areas but this should be resisted, or else they won't come back. Make sure that they have a map marked up with their area of operations. And if at all possible send them out with a local guide who can prevent them getting lost and make sure that they have a number they can call if they get into difficulties.

Local party headquarters

Normally this will be your local party offices, although occasionally (especially in a by-election) other premises are hired for the duration.

This is where your agent and all of your IT equipment will be based. And this is where your ordnance will be stored; reserves of leaflets, rosettes, posters, pens, clipboards – all of the paraphernalia for an election campaign.

This is also where all of your volunteers will initially turn up, and where they will return in order to re-supply, return knocking up sheets and collect new ones. It is also, unless you are very careful, where they will hang around for a cup of tea or coffee, a chat and a rest. You will need somebody – a cross between a sergeant major and matron – to persuade them to collect what they need and then go. Otherwise not only will you be missing out on their services on the street, but they will also be distracting your headquarters staff from what they need to do.

The two main jobs of the local party headquarters on polling day are to gather and disseminate intelligence and co-ordinate the campaign on the ground. Incoming intelligence consists of telling slips from your tellers at polling stations, and knocking up sheets from your knocking up teams.

If you are running a full polling day operation, every polling station will be manned from when the polls open (7.00a.m.) until they close (10.00p.m.). Tellers feed back to local party headquarters the polling numbers of everyone who casts their vote. Once these numbers are entered into the computer system, they can be electronically crossed off so that the knocking up teams do not waste time on them.

The same is true in reverse. Knocking up teams go out with lists of supporters who (as far as is known) have not voted. If they identify those who have voted, they cross them off their lists and return the information to the local party headquarters. The idea is that between the tellers and the knockers up, every single supporter (who has previously been identified through canvassing) will have either voted (in person or by post), promised to vote or simply declined to vote (for whatever reason).

During the course of the day – usually by mid-afternoon – the agent will have some idea of what the general turnout is looking like and also the differential turnout between his or her party and the opposition. The agent should also be able to identify the wards or polling districts where supporters are not turning out and can draft in reinforcements to that area. They can also decide whether a dramatic *very* last minute leaflet should be designed, printed and distributed in those areas.

In order for all the data input, analysis and tactical decision making to run smoothly, it is essential that the local party headquarters remain as calm and controlled as possible and that the number of extraneous bodies is kept to a minimum.

Committee rooms

That is where tactical headquarters come into their own. These are known in Polling Day terms as committee rooms. They are often a local supporter's or councillor's front or back room. In days gone by there may have been committee rooms in every ward. Today the likelihood is that there are just a handful, probably in the good or target wards.

Their function is exactly the same as the local party headquarters – but on a local or tactical level. So they may control just one ward with up to three polling districts and polling stations. Their job is to get the information in from the tellers, and to send the knocking up teams out armed with the updated lists. Committee rooms may be computerised (as with the local party headquarters), or they may rely on old-fashioned carbon copy tear-off printed sheets (NCRs, Reading Packs or Shuttleworths).

As well as running their own small (but often vital) areas, committee rooms also have to feed their intelligence back to the local party headquarters. This can be done by messenger, phone or email but it is vital in building up an accurate picture as to how the battle is progressing.

As with the main party headquarters, it is essential that tellers and knockers uppers do not take root in committee rooms. Give them a tea or coffee and a biscuit, let them use the facilities and then get them straight back out there.

Telling teams

The job of a teller is to ask voters for their unique voter polling ID number. They are not allowed to ask which way they have voted, or to try and influence them one way or another. With this in mind tellers should approach voters on their way out of the polling station, rather than on the way in. Once secured, the ID number can be taken back to party HQ (or the local committee room), and when keyed into the system it will identify the voter by name and address. Many voters arrive armed with their polling card, and it is from this that you can get their polling number. If they do not have their card then you can just ask them for their name and address, which they do not have to give to you. If they have been canvassed, you can then work out (assuming that the canvassing has been done well) who they have voted for. You can also cross them off your list as a person who does not have to be knocked up and chased out to vote.

It is up to the discretion of the Presiding Officer at each individual polling station whether you are allowed inside the building. You may well find that tellers from the other parties are also in attendance. The normal convention is for hostilities to be suspended, and for tellers from all parties to share polling ID numbers and pass the time of day.

The problem with tellers is that you need an awful lot of them. Each polling station is open for fifteen hours. You can have three polling stations in a ward, and seven wards in a constituency. So if each teller only does two hours (although some can be prevailed upon to do more), you will need up to 150 volunteers just to do telling. You then need people to collect the telling slips, and deliver them to the local party HQ or committee room – and then others to key in the polling numbers and run off the revised knock up sheets. Finally, of course, you need those essential knocking up teams.

That is why, unless it is a by-election or a key marginal in a general election, most local parties will only run a partial telling operation. They will either just man their best wards, or will only man polling stations during peak voting times; generally 7.30a.m. to 9.30a.m. and 6.30p.m. to 9.30p.m.

Car lifts and slip collectors

As mentioned in an earlier section there are always people – despite the easy availability of postal votes – who will only vote in person. This can be the case even if they are especially elderly and frail. In fact, having read horror stories in the press a lot of older people do not trust postal votes.

It can take a good hour to transport an elderly or disabled person to the poll. However, it could be that one vote which wins it for you and to not offer a lift to an elderly or disabled supporter is not only harsh, it can be very bad PR.

The important thing is to try and stagger lifts throughout the day. In between taking voters to the polls, your drivers can be used to pick up telling pads from your tellers.

Knocking up teams

Your knock up teams are your shock troops, your Praetorian Guard. They need to be energetic, fit, dedicated and personable. As such, and because they know the local area and the local people, councillors often make the best knockers up.

Generally the key knocking up time is between 6.00p.m. and 9.45p.m. By then you should have been able to identify those people who have already voted, and run off knocking up sheets just showing those who are yet to vote.

Your knocking up teams need to work their way down the lists, crossing off those who tell you (and you have to take their word for it) that they have already voted. Once they have worked their way through all of their lists they just go back to the beginning and start again.

It is important for your knocking up teams to have good knocking up leaflets for occasions when nobody is at home. These should be bright and noticeable, they should remind voters what time the polls close, and they should encourage them to vote – for you.

Knocking up can also be done by telephone. Again, if the person is not in, an answerphone message can be left – and you will hopefully have the chance to try them again later.

The candidate

So what should your candidate – your most important person – be doing on this crucial day?

The answer is that they should be everywhere all of the time. The candidate should lead the leafleting raid the night before, and the dawn raid on polling morning. He or she should tour the committee rooms, and the polling stations (where they are allowed in, but are not allowed to talk to voters). They should be standing outside the railway or tube stations at peak times, and walking down the main shopping streets circussing at lunchtime.

With the exception of a couple of brief appearances to rally the troops and find out how the battle is going, the one place the candidate should not be is at the party headquarters. The job of the candidate is to lead his or her troops, in the trenches and on the battleground. Leave the headquarters to the agent.

Rolling Knock – Asymmetric Warfare

I have described above a conventional campaign based on a full polling day operation. I have also stated that (including tellers) you will need at least 150 people to conduct it. You might well find that you have nothing like enough bodies to conduct a full-blown campaign. You then have a choice of either conducting a limited campaign, concentrating on your key wards, or thinking outside of the box and deploying your troops in an unconventional way.

When I was election agent for David Burrowes at the general election in 2001, I developed a technique which became known as the 'rolling knock'. We did not have nearly enough activists to run a full conventional polling day operation with scores of tellers feeding information back to data collators who keyed it in, and then ran off constantly updated knocking up sheets to go out to the knocking up teams.

Instead we put together small teams of highly mobile, self-sufficient knocking up teams. These teams consisted of between two and four members, with one car per team, and they only went to our best wards and polling districts. They went out with just one list of supporters (firm pledges and possibles), and their job was to knock on doors from 9.30a.m. (once they had left the stations) until 9.45p.m. (just before polls closed).

In the morning many people were out, but those who were in and had voted were crossed off. Once they had reached the end of their allocated streets they simply started again, working their way through the addresses of all known supporters, excluding those who said that they had voted. By the time this process had been repeated three or four times a very high percentage of supporters had been knocked up and encouraged to vote. Where there was no answer a knocking up leaflet was left with polling details and a strong encouragement to vote. Where a voter was in and said that they had voted, we simply took their word for it, thanked them for their support, and apologised for bothering them.

You can still use tellers who are not able or willing to knock up to fly the flag (or display the rosette) at your key polling stations. This will persuade the electorate that you are making a fight of it, and is good for morale. You just do not bother to collect the telling slips, key in the polling numbers of those who have voted, or print out revised knocking up sheets. In other words your campaign has got a beginning (the tellers) and an end (the knocking up teams) but no middle – there is absolutely nothing in between.

This technique is far from scientific, and far from ideal, but the teams can operate totally self-sufficiently, without having to constantly return to local party headquarters to collect updated sheets. Depending on the number of troops you have available, you can operate a hybrid system: You can run a full polling day operation in your very best wards, and a 'rolling knock' operation in your marginal wards. It is simply a case of doing the maths, and deploying your troops in the most efficient manner possible – what the military call 'force extrapolation'.

In the 2006 London Borough elections I was asked to run the campaign in Palmers Green – a ward where the Conservatives had not been represented in a generation. With the agreement of the agent, Henry Lamprecht, we used the rolling knock campaign technique, and captured one of the three seats in the ward with a majority of 133. This was the only Conservative gain in the whole of Enfield.

The Count

So the weeks of campaigning are at an end, and the final 36 hours of frenetic activity have taken their toll. It is 9.45p.m. and the polls are closing in fifteen minutes. You have used the last few minutes to rally supporters in the roads where the polling stations are located, and everybody (not least the electorate) has had enough. What happens next?

If you are the candidate you go home, shower, change and grab a quick bite. You collect your spouse or partner (if you have one and if they are interested) and head off to the count, which is normally held in a local sports hall or civic centre. You should aim to arrive there by 11.00p.m. at the latest.

If you are the agent you will have headed straight off to the count. This is in order to supervise the arrival of the ballot boxes, which start to arrive very shortly after the polls have closed. You also need to marshal and supervise your counting agents, who will sit and watch as every vote is counted. These counting assistants are usually employees of the local council, keen to earn some overtime.

The count can be a real rollercoaster affair. Bundles of votes are stacked in a way which makes it easy for a seasoned observer to work out who is ahead at any time. However, the lead can change hands several times as ballot boxes from strong and then weak areas are counted in turn. A strong early lead can be overturned during the course of the evening. But as the count unfolds, veterans of previous elections get a strong feeling as to whether it is going to be their night or not.

The idea of the ballot being secret is actually a myth. Although nobody at the time you cast your vote, or at the actual count, can ascertain which party you have voted for, this can subsequently be traced. This is because each ballot paper has a serial number which is matched to the voter's electoral registration number. The purpose of this is actually to prevent electoral fraud. If the results of an election are challenged in the courts, the serial numbers of the ballot papers (which are stored for some time after the election) can all be cross checked against voters' polling numbers and the Electoral Register.

In the UK (unlike some other countries) there is no option to tick a box saying 'none of the above'. Voters sometimes use their ingenuity to spoil their ballot papers in a way which makes it plain that they do not approve of any of the candidates on offer. Sometimes they write individual – usually unflattering – comments against each name. Indeed I have even seen a ballot paper where the voter has taken the time and trouble to draw a very good (but not very flattering) cartoon caricature of each candidate in the box next to their name!

Any candidate can request a recount, and in theory there are no limits to the number of these which can be held. However, the Returning Officer (or often Acting Returning Officer as the Returning Officer is usually a symbolic post held by the local Mayor) has total discretion over this and has the power to refuse the request without explanation. If a candidate requests a recount where the winning majority is simply too large to be realistically overturned, many Returning Officers will allow one recount but no more. Sometimes recounts are requested by candidates who simply want to make the 5% threshold and secure the return of their deposit. If there are more than two recounts over the course of the night the Returning Officer will often call a halt to the proceedings, telling everyone to return at a specified time the following day. In the unlikely (but not unheard of) event of a tie, the winner is decided by the drawing of lots!

If you are the candidate you would be well advised to arrive with two speeches in your pocket or in your head; one for victory, and the other for defeat. In any event there are conventions to be observed. You will be expected to thank (in roughly this order):

1   Your spouse or partner.

2   Your opponents for making it a good clean fight (even if it has not been).

3   The police for keeping everything in order.

4   The returning office.

5   That proportion of the electorate who voted for you.

6   Your agent, chairman and campaigners.

If you have won, you should be magnanimous in victory. If you have lost, you should be dignified in defeat. This is not the time to deliver a partisan tirade.

Conclusion

If you have been through all of this and won it is (I am told) the most fantastic feeling. Any weariness is dissipated, any doubts dispelled, you can do anything, and will undoubtedly at some stage in the not too distant future become Prime Minister – or a cabinet minister at least.

If you have lost, you feel not just defeated but deflated and depressed as well. A bit like the immediate aftermath of running the marathon or giving birth, you will have firmly resolved never to do it again.

After a while, however, you will begin to miss the buzz and the excitement. As the opposition party stumbles and its poll ratings decline, you just start to get that feeling that next time, maybe next time, you might just do it...

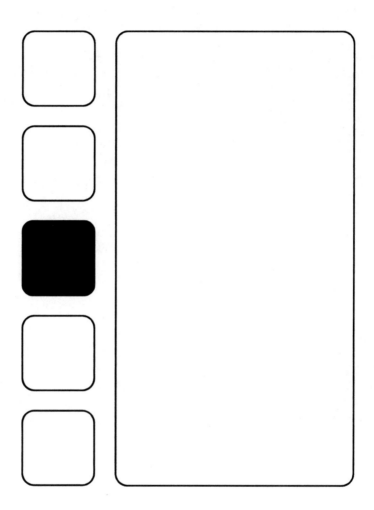

Appendices

The 50 most marginal seats

Constituency	MP	Party	Majority (July 2007)
Crawley	Laura Moffatt	Labour	37
Croydon Central	Andrew Pelling	Conservative	75
Sittingbourne and Sheppey	Derek Wyatt	Labour	79
Harlow	Bill Rammell	Labour	97
Romsey	Sandra Gidley	Liberal Democrat	125
Clwyd West	David Jones	Conservative	133
Battersea	Martin Linton	Labour	163
Medway	Robert Marshall-Andrews	Labour	213
Ceredigion	Mark Williams	Liberal Democrat	219
Gillingham	Paul Clark	Labour	254
Warwick and Leamington	James Plaskitt	Labour	266
Westmorland and Lonsdale	Tim Farron	Liberal Democrat	267
Solihull	Lorely Burt	Liberal Democrat	279
Guildford	Anne Milton	Conservative	347
Stroud	David Drew	Labour/Co-op	350
Dundee East	Stewart Hosie	Scottish National Party	383
Edinburgh South	Nigel Griffiths	Labour	405
Stourbridge	Lynda Waltho	Labour	407
Hove	Celia Barlow	Labour	420
Shipley	Philip Davies	Conservative	422
Rochdale	Paul Rowen	Liberal Democrat	442
Selby	John Grogan	Labour	467
Reading East	Robert Wilson	Conservative	475
Hornchurch	James Brokenshire	Conservative	480
Islington South and Finsbury	Emily Thornberry	Labour	484

Hemel Hempstead	Mike Penning	Conservative	499
Eastleigh	Chris Huhne	Liberal Democrat	568
Taunton	Jeremy Browne	Liberal Democrat	573
Preseli Pembrokeshire	Stephen Crabb	Conservative	607
Bromley and Chislehurst	Bob Neill	Conservative	633
Gravesham	Adam Holloway	Conservative	654
South Thanet	Stephen Ladyman	Labour	664
Manchester Withington	John Leech	Liberal Democrat	667
Wellingborough	Peter Bone	Conservative	687
Ochil and South Perthshire	Gordon Banks	Labour	688
Dartford	Howard Stoate	Labour	706
High Peak	Tom Levitt	Labour	735
Finchley and Golders Green	Rudi Vis	Labour	741
Somerton and Frome	David Heath	Liberal Democrat	812
Bethnal Green and Bow	George Galloway	Respect	823
City of Chester	Christine Russell	Labour	915
Harwich	Douglas Carswell	Conservative	920
The Wrekin	Mark Pritchard	Conservative	942
Hereford	Paul Keetch	Liberal Democrat	962
Oxford East	Andrew Smith	Labour	963
Carshalton and Wallington	Tom Brake	Liberal Democrat	1068
Wirral West	Stephen Hesford	Labour	1097
Eastbourne	Nigel Waterson	Conservative	1124
Portsmouth North	Sarah McCarthy-Fry	Labour/Co-op	1139
Cardiff North	Julie Morgan	Labour	1146

Data supplied by DodOnline, a division of Dods Parliamentary Communications Ltd

The 50 oldest MPs

MP	Date of Birth	Age in 2007
Ian Paisley	1926	81
Peter Tapsell	1930	77
Gerald Kaufman	1930	77
Robert Wareing	1930	77
Alan Williams	1930	77
Gwyneth Dunwoody	1930	77
Dennis Skinner	1932	75
David Winnick	1933	74
Joe Benton	1933	74
Michael Mates	1934	73
Richard Taylor	1934	73
Austin Mitchell	1934	73
Paul Flynn	1935	72
Eddie McGrady	1935	72
Frank Cook	1935	72
Glenda Jackson	1936	71
Ann Clwyd	1937	70
Alan Haselhurst	1937	70
Edward O'Hara	1937	70
Alan Keen	1937	70
Peter Viggers	1938	69
Nicholas Winterton	1938	69
Stuart Bell	1938	69
Geoffrey Robinson	1938	69
John Prescott	1938	69
Ian Gibson	1938	69
Michael Lord	1938	69
Ken Purchase	1939	68
John Horam	1939	68
Patrick Cormack	1939	68
Des Turner	1939	68
Anthony Steen	1939	68

Michael Meacher	1939	68
John Gummer	1939	68
Ann Cryer	1939	68
Frank Dobson	1940	67
William Cash	1940	67
Kenneth Clarke	1940	67
Brian Iddon	1940	67
Ben Chapman	1940	67
Barry Sheerman	1940	67
Tom Clarke	1941	66
James Cunningham	1941	66
John Butterfill	1941	66
Ann Winterton	1941	66
Doug Naysmith	1941	66
Rudi Vis	1941	66
David Marshall	1941	66
Rosemary McKenna	1941	66
Menzies Campbell	1941	66

Data supplied by DodOnline, a division of Dods Parliamentary Communications Ltd

Bibliography

Almanac of British Politics, The by Byron Criddle and Robert Waller, Routledge, ISBN 0415268338

Dods Constituency Guide, Vacher Dod Publishing, ISBN 090570259X

History of Britain's Parliamentary Constituencies, A, by Jacques Arnold & Patricia Arnold, Patricia Arnold Publishing, ISBN 0955509408

How to Win an Election by Paul Richards, Politico's, ISBN 184275100X

Media Guide to the New Parliamentary Constituencies by Colin Rallings & Michael Thrasher (eds.), The Local Government Chronicle Elections Centre, ISBN 9780948858451

Politico's Guide to Election Practice and Law by Susan Child, Politico's, ISBN 1902301811

Useful Websites

www.harriman-house.com/campaigning

www.electoralcommission.gov.uk

www.epolitix.com

www.parliament.uk

Relevant Legislation

House of Commons Disqualification Act 1975

Representation of the People Act 1983

Representation of the People Act 1985

Representation of the People Regulations 1986

Registration of Political Parties Act 1998

Representation of the People Act 2000

Political Parties, Elections and Referendums Act 2000

Representation of the People Regulations 2001

Electoral Administration Act 2006

Glossary

Acting Returning Officer

The official (often the Electoral Registration Officer) who actually oversees the conduct of the count.

Ad-van

A giant, mobile poster site.

Ballot Box

The sealed box in which votes are cast.

Blog

An online diary detailing an individual's thoughts, plans and activities.

Bluechip

Campaigning software used by the Conservative Party.

Board Drop

A canvassing technique which avoids the need for using a Clipboard Minder.

Boundary Commission

The body charged with ensuring that all constituencies have a roughly equal number of voters.

By-election

The procedure for filling an occasional vacancy between general elections.

Candidate

The person fighting the election (at whatever level) on behalf of their party.

Canvasser

A person who knocks on doors to ask electors about their voting intentions.

Circussing

A form of campaigning where a number of supporters accompany the candidate through a crowded area handing out literature.

Clipboard Minder

The person tasked with allocating doors to canvassers and recording their results.

Committee on Standards in Public Life

The body appointed to be the ethical watchdog overseeing all aspects of public life.

Committee Rooms

Tactical headquarters in charge of running Polling Day operations in a ward or polling district.

Constituency Agent

The trained and paid professional who runs a constituency alongside the elected volunteers.

Contact Creator

Campaigning software that will be used by the Labour Party in the future.

Counting Agent

A person authorised to supervise the counting of the ballot papers by the candidate and Election Agent.

Counting Assistant

The counters (often local authority employees) who count the votes at the end of Polling Day.

Deposit

Candidates in all elections (other than local and parish elections) have to deposit a sum of money (£500 for the Westminster Parliament), which is then forfeit if they do not gain a minimum proportion of the votes cast (5% in the case of the Westminster Parliament).

Differential Turnout

A situation where one party gets a higher proportion of its supporters to vote than the others.

Distribution Team

An organised group of leafleters.

Election Address

A local candidate's personal manifesto.

Election Agent

The person legally charged with the conduct of an election campaign on behalf of the Candidate.

Election Agents Records System (EARS)

Campaigning software used by the Liberal Democrats.

Election Expenses

The formal recording of all expenditure connected with an election campaign.

Electoral Commission

The body charged with overseeing the conduct of all elections.

Electoral Register

A list of all those in a constituency entitled to vote.

Electoral Registration Officer

The official charged with compiling and maintaining the Electoral Register.

Focus

The regular newsletter put out by the Liberal Democrats.

General Election

The time when Parliament is dissolved and all Westminster seats are contested.

Get Out The Vote (GOTV)

The Polling Day operation designed to ensure that as many of your supporters as possible actually vote.

Hung Parliament

A Parliament where no party has an overall majority.

Hustings

A meeting where candidates are questioned by the electorate.

Imprint

The words used to identify the printer and publisher of a piece of election literature.

In Touch

The regular newsletter put out by the Conservative Party.

Knocking up

The process of persuading your supporters to vote on Polling Day.

Labour Contact

Campaigning software used by the Labour Party.

Leafleter

A person delivering political literature on behalf of a candidate.

Lobby

Those journalists who are entitled to frequent the Members' Lobby and hold 'off the record' conversations with MPs and Ministers.

Local Government Commission

Body charged with conducting a rolling review of local government structure.

Manifesto

A detailed document outlining a political party's policies for an election.

Marginal

A seat which could go either way.

Maskirovka

A tactic used by the Red Army to distract and mislead enemy forces.

Media Tart

Somebody who is so desperate for publicity that they will say or do almost anything to get their name in print.

Merlin

Campaigning software that will be used by the Conservative Party in the future.

Mutual Aid

The process whereby one constituency helps another (usually a Marginal or Target Seat).

National Executive Committee

The Labour Party's governing body.

NCRs

A hard copy, print-out of party supporters used by the Conservatives.

Nomination

Names and details of at least ten local residents eligible to vote in that area are submitted in order for a candidate to stand.

Organising Secretary

Partially trained and sometimes unpaid person who runs a constituency which does not have a full-time professional Agent.

Paper Sift

The process of going through C.V.s and filtering out weaker candidates who have applied to stand for a position.

Party Election Broadcast (PEB)

A broadcast made during the course of an election campaign. The broadcast is free but the parties have to pay for production.

Party Political Broadcast (PPB)

A broadcast made following a major political event – such as the Budget or Queen's Speech. The broadcast is free but the parties have to pay for production

Phoney War

The period where war has been declared but serious hostilities have not started.

Pledge

When a voter promises to vote for you.

Pledge Letter

A letter reminding a voter that they have promised to vote for you.

Podcast

An aural message which is downloadable from a website.

Polling Agent

A person authorised to visit a Polling Station as the representative of the Agent and Candidate.

Polling Day

The day an election takes place.

Polling District

A sub-division of a ward.

Polling Number

A unique identifying number given to every voter.

Polling Station

The place (usually within a public building) where the electorate from a specific locality are directed to cast their votes.

Possibles

Voters who will probably (but not definitely) vote for you.

Postal Vote

The arrangement whereby anybody can apply to vote by post during an election campaign.

Presiding Officer

The person charged with running a Polling Station.

Press Gallery

Those journalists who sit in the House of Commons Press Gallery to report on proceedings.

Proxy Vote

The system whereby a UK citizen who lives abroad can designate a relative or friend to vote on their behalf. UK citizens living abroad are not entitled to vote in local elections.

Queen's Speech

The speech which the Queen makes in the House of Lords detailing the government's legislative programme.

Queensland Gambit

A ploy to lull supporters of the opposition into a false sense of security so that they do not bother to vote.

Reading Pack

Hard copy print-out of a party supporters used by the Labour Party.

Returning Officer

The person (often the Mayor) technically charged with overseeing an election campaign and securing and delivering a result – although the actual work is usually done by the Acting Returning Officer.

Rolling Knock

An unconventional way to run a Polling Day operation with minimal resources.

Rolling Registration

The system whereby the Electoral Roll is continuously updated – instead of being updated once a year as previously.

Rose

The regular newsletter put out by the Labour Party.

Rosette

A rose-shaped badge in the colours of a particular political party.

Shadow Communications Agency

Groups of communications professionals who provided their expertise free of charge whilst Labour were in opposition.

Short Money

The system whereby the taxpayer provides limited funding for opposition parties. So called because Ted Short, former Leader of the House, initiated this system.

Shuttleworths

A hard copy print-out of party supporters used by the Liberal Democrats.

Special Adviser

A party loyalist who has been appointed as a temporary civil servant in order to advise a Minister about party political matters.

Spin Doctor

A press officer whose job it is to present all news stories in the best possible light.

Street Stall

A table set up in the street to hand out literature and attract signatures for petitions.

Stump Script

A standard plea for voting support.

Stump Speech

A candidate's standard speech which they can adapt to any audience.

Switcher

A voter who is prepared to change their allegiance.

Target Seat (or Ward)

A constituency which has been identified as winnable by party HQ.

Telephone Preference Service (TPS)

A system whereby the public can forbid parties and salesmen from cold-calling them.

Teller

A person charged with the task of collecting the polling numbers of people who have voted.

Telling Slips

Pre-printed forms designed to record the polling numbers of people who have voted.

Turnout

The proportion of people entitled to vote who actually do so.

Voice Blasting

A technique for sending a pre-recorded message to thousands of voters by telephone.

War Book

Detailed plan covering every aspect of an election campaign.

War Room

The large open area at party headquarters where researchers, planners and press officers all work and interact.

Ward

A sub-division of a constituency.

Index

Also by Vincent H. O'Neil

Reduced Circumstances
Murder in Exile

EXILE TRUST

Vincent H. O'Neil

EXILE TRUST

THOMAS DUNNE BOOKS ❧ ST. MARTIN'S MINOTAUR
NEW YORK

SUFFOLK COUNTY LIBRARIES & HERITAGE	
07269884	
HJ	23/10/2008
F	£16.99

This is a work of fiction. All of the characters, organizations, and events portrayed in this novel are either products of the author's imagination or are used fictitiously.

THOMAS DUNNE BOOKS.
An imprint of St. Martin's Press.

EXILE TRUST. Copyright © 2008 by Vincent H. O'Neil. All rights reserved. Printed in the United States of America. For information, address St. Martin's Press, 175 Fifth Avenue, New York, N.Y. 10010.

www.thomasdunnebooks.com
www.minotaurbooks.com

Library of Congress Cataloging-in-Publication Data

O'Neil, Vincent H.
   Exile trust : a Frank Cole mystery / Vincent H. O'Neil.—1st ed.
       p.   cm.
   ISBN-13: 978-0-312-38064-9
   ISBN-10: 0-312-38064-X
   1. Private investigators—Fiction.   2. Fraud investigation—Fiction.   3. Identity theft—Fiction.   4. Florida—Fiction.   I. Title.
   PS3615.N48E95   2008
   813'.6—dc22   2008012500

First Edition: July 2008

10   9   8   7   6   5   4   3   2   1

For my nieces

ACKNOWLEDGMENTS

I would like to thank my editor, Ruth Cavin, her assistant, Toni Plummer, and everyone at St. Martin's Press who worked on this novel. I would also like to extend my appreciation to the many friends and relatives who read the earlier drafts of *Exile Trust* and provided their invaluable input. Many thanks.

EXILE TRUST

CHAPTER ONE

Frank, I need a favor."

Denny Dannon, the chief of police in my adopted home of Exile, Florida, spoke those words from an ocean-side dock. Tall and black, he was waiting when we pulled in after three hours of fishing in the Gulf of Mexico.

The boat was a small wooden number that I had first seen just a few days before. I had been looking for a missing cabdriver at the time, and had found him working as a deckhand on the charter fishing vessel *Miranda*. I had taken an instant liking to the little boat and its irascible skipper, and had hired them both when my old college roommate Mark came to visit.

I left Mark chatting with Captain Tom as I hopped onto the busy Davis pier that was the *Miranda*'s home. Davis is rich man's territory, with two yacht clubs in addition to the tourist docks, and Chief Dannon had driven a bit of a distance to meet me.

"How can I help, Chief?"

Dannon is one of the smartest guys I have ever met, as well as the patron saint and protector of the little town of Exile. I had solved the murder of a young Exile man a few months after coming to live there, and had gained a fair amount of Dannon's respect in the process.

"Frank, I've got a job for you. Someone complained to the State Attorney's office about the way the bank runs its safe-deposit area, and they're about to get a visit from some regulators." Exile has only one bank, so I didn't have to ask which one he was talking about.

Although I had solved two murders while living in Florida, my primary employment was as a fact-checker. I worked for insurance companies and local law offices on a freelance basis, and could see several possible tasks in Dannon's request.

"What do you want me to do?"

"Here's the situation: Some of the bank's safe-deposit records are badly out-of-date. They've discovered that the addresses and phone numbers on some of the older boxes are no longer current. They were hoping to contact the missing box-holders before the regulators get there, but they've reached a dead end on a few of them."

"Is that what the complaint was about?"

"From what Ollie told me, that seems to be the case." Ollie Morton was the bank's manager, and I had met him before. He was a thin, fiftyish man whose nerves didn't seem up to the job.

I digested Dannon's request while looking around the dock. Other charter boats were pulling in, and fishing parties or sightseeing groups were disembarking around us. It was late in the day, but the summer sun would not set for hours.

"I don't know much about banks, so humor me here. How could they lose track of someone who's renting a box in their own vault?"

"Ollie tells me the safe-deposit records have never been maintained on the bank's computers. They're kept on a card system filled out when the box is first assigned. So even if a box-holder submitted

2

a change of address to the main bank, that update usually didn't make it onto the ownership cards in the vault area."

"That sounds pretty easy to fix, then." I'd owned a computer business just a few years earlier, and for a moment thought I saw why Dannon had brought this to me. "They need to search the automated systems for the box-holder's name, and use that information to update the old address in the vault records."

"They've already done that, and it worked when the customer still had other business with the bank. But some of these box rentals go back a long time, and there are cases where the safe-deposit box is the only thing left over from an otherwise defunct account. Ollie's people have been calling around to confirm the addresses and numbers that they do have, but a lot of the time people have just hung up on them. So far they've got at least ten accounts where they're running into a brick wall."

It was starting to make sense to me, and sounded pretty simple at the time.

"So they want me to go knocking on a few doors to talk with the people who hung up on them, and then track down the customers who have actually moved away."

"Or died."

"Died?" Maybe it wasn't that simple. "How out-of-date *are* these records?"

"Ollie didn't go into that when we talked. He asked me to find someone to do the legwork, and of course they'll pay for it. It's right up your alley, so I came to you."

Considering the lack of details in this job offer, I decided to give myself an out.

"Of course I'll help, Chief, and glad to. But one thing: I'm not going to be able to resolve every one of these."

"Nobody expects that. Ollie said the complaint was pretty serious, but the regulators aren't going to come by for at least a week. He thinks they're giving him a chance to get a handle on things. It would help a lot if most of the names on the unconfirmed box-holder list had moved to the *previously* unconfirmed list when the inspectors get there."

"Sounds like they need me to come by right away."

"Tomorrow, if you can swing it. I know your friend is in town, but he was headed up to Tallahassee anyway, wasn't he?" I had introduced Mark to the chief the day before, and he had told Dannon he was mixing his visit with a little legal work involving a sister law firm in the state capital.

"Then tomorrow it is." I stuck my hand out, and we shook. I turned toward the boat, but Dannon spoke again, this time in almost a whisper.

"Frank, Ollie's not the most methodical fellow in the world. I don't want you to get involved with bank business, but don't be afraid to give him advice about keeping this organized. I'm talking basic project management, the stuff you did in your other life. The last thing we need is a hurry-up effort that leaves things worse off than before, where they can't tell what's been updated and what hasn't. Keep him straight, all right?"

Even less certain than before, I nodded and walked away.

Mark was standing at the end of the dock, looking out to sea, when I got back. I misspoke when I said I chartered Captain Tom and the *Miranda,* basically because I have almost no money and Mark had paid for our three hours on the ocean.

We had caught nothing, but Mark seemed to be having the time of his life. I stopped and watched him for a moment, standing there framed by the water and other sightseers, and was amazed by how much he fit in. Tall and dark-haired, Mark had played varsity tennis at our school and still managed to keep up his game despite the demands of his career. He was wearing a battered set of khaki shorts and an old sky-blue shirt with the sleeves rolled up to his elbows, and I had to work hard to remember the last time I had seen him dressed so casually.

Mark had gone into law school at about the same time that I started my computer business up north, and so of course we had spent a fair part of those years complaining to each other over the phone. The complaints had paid off, though, as my business found its legs right about the time that Mark landed a big job with a prestigious Manhattan law firm. He had disappeared into the firm's research stacks like any new corporate lawyer, and I had begun spending more and more hours at work while the economy softened and then swooned.

I barely came up for air to attend Mark's wedding to his longtime girlfriend Miriam, and by then my entire industry was in trouble. I kept hoping for the promised economic turnaround to occur, but it was always just around the corner. In a last-ditch effort to save my company, I brought in a pair of partners named Hammer and Lane who operated a venture capital outfit called Tammerlane Group.

The number crunchers at Tammerlane had changed their minds about my business shortly after coming on board, and then forced the place into bankruptcy with surprising speed. I had already plowed my entire savings into the company by then, and so I was left penniless when the gavel came down. My marriage—suffering under the weight of fourteen-hour workdays, little money, and blueblood in-laws who disapproved of failure—had collapsed at about the same time.

Just when things hadn't seemed likely to get worse, a dotty judge had decided I had wrecked my company on purpose. In a moment of pique, he had attached my future earnings as a means of paying off the same partners who had scuttled my business. Mark had come back into the picture then, proposing a stall tactic that only a lawyer could love.

It called for me to move somewhere warm, take odd jobs that would make almost no money at all, and convince Hammer and Lane that they'd already gotten their last penny out of me. Mark had taken over the role of negotiator, and intended to keep the ploy going until Hammer and Lane offered to settle. As for me, I moved to the Florida Panhandle because I had once enjoyed a happy spring break there, and began making just enough money to live on.

Mark had originally explained his visit to Florida as an update on the situation with my creditors, but he had brought little news. Hammer and Lane had recently divulged an interest in gaining control of some patents once held by my company, but that revelation did me no good. Those patents were currently the property of an angry insurance outfit in Hartford that had been forced to pay off a large chunk of my non-Tammerlane debt. Tammerlane's interest in them was doubly odd, in that the innovations supposedly protected by those patents were already obsolete.

I walked up behind my former roommate and tapped him lightly in the lower back. He turned away from the sea and smiled, and once again I wondered just why the high-powered city lawyer was so enamored of my little chunk of the world.

"What'd the chief want?"

"He's got a job for me. Somebody complained about the way the local bank runs its safe-deposit area, so right now they're scrambling to run down the current addresses of the box-holders."

Mark whistled. "Safe deposit. Walls full of locked containers rented by strangers. The banks don't want to know what's in them, and the box-holders load them up with things they don't want in their houses. Talk about a recipe for disaster."

"If you say so. I really don't know much about them."

"Try to stay away from the actual boxes if you can. Run down the customers, but let the bankers deal with the vault. If a complaint started this ball rolling, the regulators can't be far behind."

That sounded logical, but it was important to read between the lines when Mark doled out advice. In this case he was actually warning me to stay in the shadows when the regulators arrived. If his strategy with Hammer and Lane failed, he hoped to someday get my situation resolved through an appeal. To that end, he was constantly reminding me to keep my nose clean. As you might guess, that litany got a little tiresome sometimes.

"Will do. It sounds fairly simple, but they're in a bit of a hurry so I'm going to have to swing by there tomorrow morning."

"That's fine. I'll just head up to Tallahassee a little ahead of schedule." Mark had not elaborated on his legal duties in the state capital, although he had joked that it was a means of writing his visit off as a business expense. I doubted that, because Mark was an ethical guy and also quite wealthy.

I secretly believed he was trying to get some lawyer friends in Tallahassee to recommend me as the in-house investigator for their firm. He had mentioned the idea once before as a way of getting me a steady income, but I was not sure I wanted to go that particular route. Although I had knocked on plenty of doors as a background checker, and had helped solve those two murders in the bargain, I was a little leery of anything that might have me helping lawyers with a bankruptcy case. Or a divorce.

"But I'll be back in Exile in a couple of days, so we should plan to do something then." Mark had already been in town the entire weekend, and had so far shown no hurry to get back to New York.

"Sure the little lady won't mind?" I asked. Miriam Ruben was well along in her first pregnancy, and I was a bit surprised at how much time he was planning to spend in the Panhandle.

"Not so little right now." He laughed. "Nah, she was happy to get me out of her hair. She's scouting out a new place for us, a real house outside the city for when the baby gets here, only she doesn't think I know it."

"How *do* you know it?"

He smiled again, and changed the subject by pointing at my waistline. I had lost a lot of weight in the past few weeks, and it was about the only thing he hadn't liked down here.

"Come on, scarecrow. I'll buy you something to eat."

CHAPTER TWO

The bank was one of the town's oldest buildings, two stories of solid gray rock with wrought-iron bars on the windows. It faced the tree-lined park that was the main square in Exile, almost directly across from the police station. I called Ollie on Monday morning and asked when he wanted to see me, and he suggested that I wait until just after lunch. Mark adjusted his departure accordingly, and I donned a light suit after waving good-bye to his rental car. I crossed the bank's small lobby a little past one, looking for Ollie.

He was nowhere to be seen, so I approached one of the tellers and said I was there to meet the manager. The teller station resembled an airport ticket counter, and cameras watched me from at least three places. Regardless of what the bank looked like from the street, inside it seemed technologically up-to-date.

The software designer in me was wondering how a modern bank could have such a major records problem when Ollie emerged from a side door. I knew him pretty well, from banking at his establishment and seeing him around town over the months I had lived there. He always put me in mind of a small dog in a big dog neighborhood;

even when he isn't looking over his shoulder, you know that he wants to. I guess that's not such a bad quality in the man handling your money, but I had often wondered how he ever managed to drift off to sleep at night.

"Frank, good to see you, good to see you," he said, extending his hand while walking toward me. No sooner had our palms touched than he was steering me toward the door through which he had entered the lobby. We were both on the other side before it had a chance to swing shut.

Ollie was a tall man in his fifties, thin and slightly balding. He was a genuinely friendly guy, which is also a good quality in a local banker, but just then he was genuinely relieved to see me.

"Thank you so much for coming over right away, Frank. We have a lot to do and I have no idea when they're going to come down on us. Every one of these box records that we can update is one less indication that we're completely lost."

We went down a short hallway past a small office where people were banging away on computers, and I was shown into the safe-deposit area.

Or, more exactly, the main vault of the Exile bank. The circular door was enormous, taller than a man and at least three feet deep. It was a gunmetal gray, with a mechanism like a ship's wheel on one side at chest height. The wheel obviously locked the door when it was swung shut, but just then it stood open.

Inside, I could see row after row of locked silver doors set into the cream-colored walls. The vault was much larger than I had expected, with a big metal table bolted to the floor in the very center. Two men were standing inside, one old and one young and both wearing gray coveralls. Canvas tool bags lay at their feet, and they were fiddling with the open door of one of the safe-deposit boxes.

Off to my right, a woman was starting to remove items from a black metal box. The top of the container was flipped all the way back on a long hinge, and the shallow case looked like it would just fit inside the slot being worked on by the men in the vault. The woman wore a pair of plastic reading glasses on a neck chain, although I would later learn that she never took them off.

She was seated behind a large folding table set up perpendicular to the vault entrance. It interrupted the room's traffic pattern so completely that it had to be a recent addition. Two more folding tables were set up against the wall behind her, and several neat stacks of index cards sat on one of them. Seeing numbers printed across the tops of the cards, I assumed these were the much-maligned records of the safe-deposit area.

Farther away from the vault, two young women were loudly working the phones. One hung up right at that moment with a gesture of exasperation, huffing such a blast of air from an outthrust lower lip that it tossed her bangs. The other one was speaking rapidly, trying to explain the call before the individual on the other end could break the connection. The whole scene reeked of desperation, and I was reminded of Dannon's final request, the one where he asked me to keep Ollie organized, the day before.

"Lord, what a mess," Ollie intoned behind me in a voice that was close to cracking.

I would later come to agree with Ollie's gloomy assessment, but at that exact moment I was propelled to a place in my past that I did not care to revisit. It was the lady inventorying the safe-deposit box who did it. Not her personally, mind you; she was a thin, severe-looking black woman who could have been anywhere between forty and sixty, but it was what she was doing.

She removed a small, clear plastic disk from the box and examined it closely. It held some kind of coin, and when she had gleaned enough information she placed it in a cardboard carton next to the safe-deposit container. She then began writing on a clipboard, recording the item for the inventory.

That did it. I was suddenly transported to Connecticut, roughly two years in the past, to the building that had held my computer business. A team of movers was methodically boxing up the machines that my employees had once used to create software for our clients. Overseers from the creditors, the courts, and my own legal team hovered over each machine as it was packed, and it seemed that every other inspector wielded some kind of camcorder.

I had not wanted to be present when they picked over my bones, but my attendance had been almost mandatory. My lawyers had insisted that I get some people to videotape the contents of the business the day before, and the recording had not ended there.

"It's all a question of being able to show that the items were there, that they worked, and that you didn't damage them before they were taken away," one of the legal beagles had explained at the time, but I had only come to understand his wisdom much later. Hammer and Lane, never ones to miss an opportunity to kick me, had questioned how much of the company's equipment had actually been sold. They had even accused me of switching old machines for new ones, and only the videotapes had kept that from becoming yet another of their many victories.

Coming back to the here and now, I walked toward the woman conducting the inventory. By then she had picked up a small unmarked tin with a screw top, and was just about to open it when I stopped her.

"Don't do that." I could have said that more politely, and got the opportunity to do so when the woman looked up at me over the rims of her glasses. She didn't say a word, but the reprimand was obvious.

"Please don't do that."

That didn't exactly win her over, but she did put the tin back inside the box. She then shifted the same mute stare away from me and over to Ollie, clearly asking who I was.

"Susan, this is Frank Cole, he's going to be helping us. Frank, this is Susan Wilmington, she's in charge of our safe-deposit area."

"*Newly* in charge," Susan stated aggressively, still looking at Ollie. From the timber of her voice I decided she was closer to sixty than forty, and that I did not want to lock horns with her.

"I'm sorry, I just walked in and saw you were going to open that container—"

"Yes, so I could describe it for the inventory. That's what we're doing here, you know."

"I understand." I was getting nowhere with Susan, so I turned to Ollie. "Ollie, you need to get a video camera in here before you open any more of these boxes."

The two men in overalls overheard that part and began drifting toward the vault door. I had assumed they were locksmiths, and a quick reading of the patches sewn on their chests proved it was true. The older one's badge identified him as Al of Al's Hardware, and the younger one, a tall rangy guy with close-cut blond hair and a thin mustache, was labeled as Stan.

"A video camera?" Susan Wilmington stood up and inclined her head in a menacing way. "Mr. Cole, we've been drilling abandoned boxes for years in this bank, and I have never done anything more in the way of inventory than what I am doing right now."

I had not meant to break open this particular hornet's nest, and had not even known it existed prior to stepping into the vault area.

Even so, Chief Dannon had suggested that Ollie's approach to the current problem might be a tad disorganized, and he had asked me to watch out for that. Denny Dannon's wishes carry much more than the force of mere law in Exile, so I came back swinging.

"Maybe so. But right now you're responding to a complaint about the way this part of the bank is being run. Regulators are about to come in and tear this area apart, and you have nothing more than a written description of what's in the boxes you're opening. Without video proof, you haven't got any way to show that what's on the list represents what was actually in the box."

"Ollie, I'm not going to stand here and get accused of stealing." Even the girls working the phones had stopped to watch the fight that had magically sprung up in front of them, and I thought I saw the younger locksmith wink playfully at the older one.

"I'm not accusing anyone of anything. In fact, I'm trying to prevent an accusation from ever being made. You get a camcorder in here, one with a microphone on it, and you'll have some pretty good protection." I pointed toward the vault. "Tape the whole process from beginning to end. You start by announcing the date and time, whose box it is if you know, and then you get a close-up shot of the box number."

In case you're wondering how I suddenly became an expert on safe-deposit inventories, I'm not. I've spent a lot of time around private investigators while working as a fact-checker, and one of their favorite tools is a video camera. The work product from those film sessions is sometimes used in court, and so those PIs frequently provide a verbal commentary of what is transpiring on the tape. Some of their tips seemed to have rubbed off on me, magnifying what I had learned while cataloging my dead business years before.

I was walking toward the vault by then, largely to get away from the baleful glare of Susan Wilmington, but also to illustrate my point. I passed the two locksmiths and turned to find both Ollie and Susan standing close behind me. Ollie looked like a lost child who has just seen his parents approaching, and Susan looked ready to bash my head in.

"You get a nice tight shot of the box number, and then you step back and film these two gentlemen while they work their magic." I did not know what they did to get a box open, so I left it vague. "You take the box out, walk it over to this table here, filming the whole time, and open it up. You come in close again, pan it around, and that way nobody can say you took something out."

I looked at Susan.

"I know you wouldn't take anything. No one here would. But that's not enough." I pointed in the air, as if the walls of the building did not exist. "There are people out there who will claim something valuable was stored in their box, even though it's a lie, and so you need a video record of what was in the container when it was first removed from its slot. That way, you're covered."

I turned back to the empty table, pantomiming someone lifting the cover of the invisible box and removing its contents.

"Do the inventory right here, with the camera running the entire time. Hold up each item and turn it around so you film every side. If it's something that might be valuable, like that old coin in that other box"—Susan glared at me again, so I turned back to the container that wasn't there—"get a close-up shot and then read whatever identifying marks are on it. If there isn't anything, just describe it to the best of your abilities and move on."

Each point made me think of another, and I now turned to Ollie.

"Ollie, you're gonna want to have someone writing down the inventory while the film is rolling. That way you've got a backup list in case something happens to the tape, and you can include a copy of the list inside the storage box. Where are you putting the items once they're removed from the safe-deposit area?"

Ollie looked at Susan, who responded with lessening heat.

"We've got a locked cabinet in the supply area that we're using. There is nothing else in the cabinet, and I have the only key." Either some of what I was saying was rubbing off, or Susan was closer to my way of thinking than I had at first believed.

"Super. Film each item going into the new container, and you'll have a photographic record from the moment you opened the box to the moment you emptied it."

I looked around me and saw that the two girls who had been working the phones had joined the locksmiths near the vault doorway. They seemed downright impressed, as did the older of the locksmiths. The younger man was wearing a scowl, however, and spoke up as soon as the chance presented itself.

"Mister, I don't think we've got the time to do that for every one of these boxes."

The older one chimed in. "He's right, Ollie. I'm gonna have to charge you by the hour if you make us wait around for all this cinematography."

He might just as well have said that to the richest man on earth. The clouds were parting for Ollie Morton just then, and money was not an object.

"Well, we'll just have to make sure we've got our ducks in a row before you come back, then. It may take a little extra time, but the bank will pay for that, if that's what you want."

The younger locksmith clearly did not like this idea, but he expressed his disagreement as a question. More than one, in fact.

"Come back? What do you mean come back? And are we gonna

have people breathing down our necks the whole time we're working in here?"

Ollie was looking at the wall, deep in thought, so he probably only heard the first part of that. I believed he was deciding where to get a recording device, and he proved it with his answer.

"Come back is right. We need time to get a camera." He looked at me with outright pleasure. "And for me and Susan to sit down and talk a little more with Mr. Cole."

I got my first long look at the work area as I stepped out of the vault. Al and Stan were collecting their tools behind me, and the girls were headed back to the phones.

A quick survey of the office outside the vault spoke volumes about the safe-deposit area's neglect. The walls were a dull mustard color, and the paint was peeling in the corners near the ceiling. The rug was dull gray and water-stained, and there were no windows. A bright overhead light hummed loudly and bounced its beams off of the walls. It was not surprising that nobody wanted to spend their entire day there.

I glanced at the desks where the girls had gone back to the phones, and decided that no one actually did spend the day there. With the exception of a printed phone log and some scratch paper, the desktops were empty. With no photos or other personalizing items in sight, this was obviously a temporary work area for them. There was a third desk behind them, but it appeared long abandoned. A stapler lying on its side, a blotter with a thumbtack stuck in it dead center, and an empty pencil cup suggested that no one had occupied that desk for some time.

Ollie took my arm and walked me back through the door into the hallway. Susan went with us, after closing the lid on the safe-deposit container with a thud. Ollie led the way to a small conference room, and we sat down at a circular table that put me well within fist range of Susan.

As if that weren't bad enough, a teller poked his head in just after we sat down and called Ollie away. I had been hoping he would calm the waters, but it was not to be. Susan wasted no time once he was gone.

"Troubleshooter."

"Excuse me?"

"Troubleshooter. That's what know-it-alls like you call themselves. You come in where everyone is trying to work, you look around for a few minutes, and then point out everything that's wrong. As if the people who spend every day here haven't got eyes. Or brains."

I started to speak, but she wasn't having it.

"Listen, sweet pea." I'd heard that phrase a few times since moving to Florida, and in each of those instances it had been a put-down. "With the exception of the camcorder idea, you haven't said anything to Ollie that I haven't. Many times. I've been working here fifteen years, Mr. Cole. I've been in charge of the mortgage records, the car loan records, and every teller in this bank. I've been warning Ollie for at least a year that the safe-deposit area was going to jump up and bite us, but when that complaint came down the line you'd think I'd never opened my mouth.

"Well, enough's enough. You're not even an employee of this bank, and I'll be hanged if I'm going to work for you. So what's it going to be, Mr. Cole? You gonna stick with finding us the right addresses for these boxes, or am I gonna walk out of here and let you run this inventory?"

"I'm perfectly happy—"

"And another thing. Ollie's a good manager, but he's afraid of his own shadow, and he doesn't know everything that goes on in here. I'm the one who called in Al and Stan. Al had to close up shop to come out here, so now I'm going to have to call him back and smooth things over. Thanks to you."

"It takes two of them to open the boxes?"

"Drill the boxes."

I held up my hands in a gesture of defeat.

"They drill the entire lock mechanism out and replace it with a new one. And no, it doesn't take two of them to do it. Stan's new, Al's teaching him, and the plan was to have Stan take over so Al could go back to the store. Until you came along."

I had tried to surrender earlier, but I now saw that she wanted to continue fighting.

"I couldn't help noticing that they were working in there by themselves. Without a single bank employee able to see what they were doing."

I honestly thought she was going to hit me. She had been glaring over the rims of her glasses the whole time, and now her face screwed up into an expression of outrage.

"That's the second time you've accused total strangers of stealing."

"No it's not." I let my voice rise, resentful at the lack of appreciation. For an instant back in the vault, while explaining the proper way to run an inventory, I'd experienced a bit of a happy glow. It had been a long time since I had taken charge of a business situation, and I had enjoyed it. Now the glow was gone, and it had been taken from me just because I'd invaded some petty despot's turf. "I bet there's a manual somewhere around here that says who can go into that vault, and I'd bet big money that people who don't work here aren't supposed to be in there alone."

That had a strange effect on her. Susan had been leaning forward with her palms on the table, but now she settled back in her chair. She didn't say anything at first, instead looking at me with her head cocked slightly to the side, as if thinking something over.

"You might actually be worth having around after all, Mr. Cole. You're right about who's allowed to enter the vault unsupervised, so maybe we do need an outsider to remind us to slow down." She rolled her lips out of sight for a moment and then opened them with a slight smack, as if she had come to a decision. "You keep showing this kind of concern for the bank and its depositors, you and I might just get along."

CHAPTER THREE

We didn't wait for Ollie to come back, largely because I had reached a cease-fire with the individual in charge of straightening out the safe-deposit records. Susan offered to show me the office I would use to track down the unknown box-holders, and we headed back into the hallway.

"I've got a college degree, you know," she said softly as we walked.

"Florida State?"

"Farragut Community."

"I know one of the instructors there." I was actually dating the instructor in question, but things had recently cooled. Her name was Beth Ann Thibedault, and she was growing tired of waiting for my life to get started again. She had pointedly refused to meet Mark, the author of the plan to wait out my creditors, and I took that as a bad sign.

"Accounting? Business?"

"Photography."

We had just crossed back into the vault area, and Susan gave me a knowing smirk.

"So you didn't come up with that camcorder idea on your own."

"That's true, but I didn't get it from her either. She's not a big fan of video."

"I want you to meet my two assistants, Vicki and Anna." These were the two girls placing the phone calls. Vicki was a petite blonde, probably twenty, and Anna was a slightly older brunette. They were both working the phones again, so all I got was a wave.

"I'd like you to give them any information you come across, and limit your contact with the box-holders that you do find. We know what to say to them, so once you locate the owners, or their next of kin, get a good contact number and take it to the girls."

"How many of these unknowns are there?"

"Right now, ten. Three of them are far enough overdue in their rent for us to declare their boxes abandoned and drill them. The other seven boxes are a mix of slightly overdue payments and out-dated contact information."

We moved down a connecting hallway to a small side office. There were two more desks inside, each equipped with a phone and a computer. A large whiteboard hung on one wall, and there were no windows.

"A mix?"

She looked back toward the girls before answering.

"As you might already know, the safe-deposit records were not maintained properly. We did have someone working down here just a while back, but Ollie never gave her instructions to clean things up. Personally, I think the job would have been beyond her anyway."

"Why is that?"

"She didn't like being alone down here, and when she heard about the complaint she just up and quit." She read my mind before continuing. "And no, I'm not giving you her name. I imagine the inspectors might want to talk to her, but this mess really isn't her fault.

"Anyway, she wasn't down here all the time, and the tellers shared the duty when we issued a box to a new customer. Whoever was free at the moment would come down here, consult the register, find an unassigned box of the proper dimensions—"

"Proper dimensions?"

"Yes. We have several different sizes, with the rent going up for the larger boxes. Most people don't need the big ones, but it all depends on what they want to secure.

"Whoever was issuing the box would take down the customer's personal information, have them sign an access card, and issue a key."

"What kind of information went on the access card? It might be helpful."

Susan crossed to one of the computers and called up a spreadsheet. She had obviously prepared the room and its computers for my use ahead of time.

"Every scrap of information we have on the unknown boxes is in this spreadsheet. You'll notice I created extra columns where you can add any updated information and new points-of-contact if the person you've found is not the box-holder.

"To answer your question, the access card is just a signature card. If we don't know the customer personally, we do a signature check before we let them into the safe deposit."

"I assume they would already have the key."

"Can't open the box without it. But keys can get stolen."

"Signatures can be forged, too."

She gave me a strange look then, and I think she believed I was criticizing the bank again.

"Yes they can. Honestly, Mr. Cole, this is a simple bank with simple customers. The key, some form of identification, and the signature are all we ever ask for.

"To get back to the records, sometimes the teller issuing the key didn't completely fill out the form. They knew the contact data was entered into the bank's computers when the new account was opened, so they didn't see the need. Unfortunately, some of these relationships go back decades. In some cases a customer would close all their other accounts, but keep the box. In time their data dropped off the computers, and that half-completed card became the only record if we needed to contact the people who were renting the boxes."

"How is the rent paid?"

"Good questions, Mr. Cole."

"Call me Frank."

"Good questions, Frank. Most of the box-holders pay the rent as an automatic withdrawal from their other accounts, and so we've had a lot of success confirming box ownership from those records. But not everyone trusts the automatic withdrawal, and some box-holders don't have any other business with us. Some of those pay by check, and some of them are old-fashioned. They pay in cash, and it's easy to lose track of them if they don't have any other business with us."

"You can have a box if you're not one of the bank's customers?" My ignorance was starting to show.

"Box-holders are customers the same as any others, even if that's the limit of our relationship." She stopped for a second, and actually smiled. "Listen to me. I've been rereading our policies to get ready for the audit. That's why I sound like a talking ATM."

We shared a smile, and she went on.

"You can have a box without having an account, but the requirements are the same. You have to prove you're who you say you are, prove you live where you say you do, the same as if you were opening, say, a checking account." She looked troubled for an instant.

"And believe me, with the way the government has tightened up the money-laundering laws, this is serious stuff."

I didn't want to ask, but I had to.

"Susan, if that's the case, why are the records—" I stopped short of saying the documentation was messed up. Instead, I looked down at the computer screen and read one of the descriptions. "Say this one, the box you drilled two days ago, where there's a name and address but they're both listed as 'Unable to Contact'?"

"I know the case you're looking at. It was one of the rent-free boxes. Some of our bigger customers get the smallest-sized containers for free, and that account was closed years ago. So we've got a name, address, and phone number, but they're all way out-of-date. When we called the people who currently live in that house, they said the name sounded like an old man who owned the place before them. They think he died.

"That box should have been emptied when the other account was closed, or switched to a rent-paying status, but somebody goofed. We don't know if that account was closed when the old man passed away, or even if he's actually deceased. We're hoping you can help us with that."

I had a quick look at the list of what they had found inside the abandoned box. One item jumped at me.

"It says there was a service medal in there. A Navy Cross."

"Think you can do something with that? Trace the relatives, I mean?"

"Not me. But I know a guy who would be perfect for this."

"I'd love to help!" My friend Gray Toliver exclaimed from his living-room couch. His hair was almost white, but he had the energy of men half his age.

Gray was a retired navy man, and when it came to organization he was the opposite of Ollie Morton. Although he had left the service as a chief petty officer, he had more education than most admirals and had spent his final uniformed years playing with aircraft design at Pensacola.

I sat across from him, a soda in my hand, while the smells of a dinner cooking floated in from the kitchen. Gray turned his head and spoke in that general direction.

"Honey! Can I help Frank with a project for a few days?" I was relieved to see him overcome his initial excitement long enough to remember he was married.

"Of course you can, if it gets you out of the house," a pleasant Southern female voice called back. Gray was the first friend I had made in Exile, and he and I played chess together at the town beach on most Wednesday mornings. The seed of that acquaintance had blossomed when Gray had helped me sort the wheat from the chaff in my two murder cases, and I suspected that Gray secretly wanted to participate in what I do.

Emily Toliver walked into the room, wiping her hands with a yellow dish towel. I had been over to the Tolivers' house for dinner many times, increasingly so when I began to lose weight, and I had come to like Emily very much. She was originally from Georgia, but had moved to the Panhandle when Gray had been assigned to Pensacola. She was a large woman, tall and broad, with blond hair that was now almost completely gray. She always spoke with a soft, refined accent, and handled Gray with ease.

"So who do you think complained?" she asked, sitting next to Gray on the sofa. She'd been back and forth between the living room and the kitchen, and had heard the entire discussion.

I was surprised that I had not asked that question myself, and was

26

initially lost for an answer. While I was pondering this, Gray replied for me.

"Could have been anybody. A customer who didn't like having to wait to get to his box, a disgruntled employee, anybody."

"I really hadn't given this any thought until now, but if I had to guess I'd put Susan on the list," I offered.

"Sue Wilmington? I doubt that." Gray almost laughed at me.

"You know her?"

"We've been in Exile a long time, Frank. I think Gray and I know just about everyone by now." Emily answered that one, but Gray kept the thread going.

"Sue's got a hard head, but it's worth your life to say something bad about the bank when she's around. She's got too much loyalty to drop a dime on them, and besides, you said she wasn't too happy to be handed the job of cleaning the place up."

I imagined I had stepped on someone's reputation, and backed away quickly.

"Hey, I said I was guessing. Besides, the complaint isn't our concern. We're supposed to track down the former owners of ten safe-deposit boxes, or their next of kin if that's the case."

"Have you done anything like this before?" Emily asked.

"Nothing quite like this, but the tools are the same. I'm subscribed to some of the locator databases on the Web, and it's amazing how much you can find out if you start with a name and a recent address."

"I don't think I like that."

"You shouldn't. The amount of personal information that's out there is scary. But that's the starting point. Then there's a lot of phone calling or legwork to see if any of the leads you find in the databases turn into something real. It took me a while to get good at this, but a little deduction will take you a long way."

"Tell her about that bail jumper you tracked down, just by finding out his hobbies." Gray followed my more interesting assignments with enthusiasm, frequently grilling me as we played chess. At first I had believed he was simply trying to throw off my game, but time and many defeats had shown that he didn't need to.

"I can't take credit for that approach. One of the investigators I know mentioned it. He was chasing this bail jumper, and he started at the guy's last known address. The landlord had a box of the skip's possessions, and when my buddy looked through it he found a hot rod magazine with the skip's name on the address label. So he called the magazine's subscription department and tricked them into giving him the bail jumper's new address. He pretended to be the guy he was tracking, though, and I'm afraid I'm just not up to doing that."

"So how *did* you do it? If you didn't pretend to be the man you were looking for?" From the tone of her voice, I wondered if Emily believed that part of the story.

"The guy I was tracing liked to fly model planes, so I combed the Internet for model plane conventions. He'd used his own name to register at one, so I passed that on to the bail bondsman who was looking for him. Somebody else, on the other side of the country, caught him at the sign-in table."

"The other side of the country?" Emily was laughing now. "That sounds a little vague."

"I wasn't trying to be mysterious. It was in Idaho. I was trying to say that there are a *lot* of model airplane conventions, and I had to access a whole slew of 'Registered Attendees' lists because we had no idea where the guy had run off to. My fingers were bleeding by the time I found him."

We all had a good laugh at that, and Gray found a chance to mention Mark.

"So where's that city lawyer friend of yours?" Gray and Emily had gone out to dinner with us when Mark first got to town, but Gray had not warmed to him. Emily had been her charming Southern self, but Gray hadn't tried very hard to hide his disapproval. He felt I was wasting my life in the vain hope of wearing down my creditors, and that Mark was to blame.

"Up in Tallahassee. He says he's coordinating some work between his firm and a group up there."

"But you don't think that's it."

"Gray!" Emily sounded as if she were telling the family dog to be still.

"No I don't. I think he's trying to get me a job as the in-house investigator for one of the law firms up there. When you have one of those gigs, you don't have to get a PI license." I wasn't even sure I wanted one. Private investigations is hard work, and I was still content to do background checks and track down court documents.

"Would you want to do something like that?" Emily was reading my mind, and not for the first time.

"Not really. I still haven't gotten used to knocking on strangers' doors, and there's a lot of that in PI work." I was getting better at it, largely from practice, but there was another reason to shy away. The in-house law firm guys often end up working divorce cases, and that was just too darn close to home.

Gray knew this, and moved the conversation along.

"So. When do we start in the morning?"

CHAPTER FOUR

Gray jumped the gun just a little the next day. We had agreed to wait until the bank was fully open before showing up, largely to give Susan and her helpers a chance to get their work started before they had to deal with us. I walked in holding a cup of coffee in one hand and a briefcase in the other, and was buzzed into the back without so much as a word.

Walking into the vault area, I found Vicki and Anna busily working the phones again. Susan was not to be seen, so I juggled my load sufficiently to give the girls a wave as I went past. I was headed for the office Susan had designated for our use, and expected it to be empty.

I really should not have been surprised by what greeted me. Gray is a take-charge kind of guy, and he approaches new challenges with great enthusiasm. I doubt he slept much the previous evening, and Emily was probably pretty happy when he departed for the bank ahead of schedule. I imagine he talked her ear off with the ideas, which now covered the office walls.

Susan must have shown him the database, as he had already

drawn a chart on the whiteboard depicting the status of each of our ten mystery boxes. As if that weren't enough, he had also covered much of the remaining wall space with large sheets of paper. Each of these bore a box number at the top, and he had already outlined a strategy for finding the owners on three of them. He was writing on the fourth when he noticed me.

"Frank! Glad you're here." Gray turned around, marker in hand. "I think we should split up the boxes between us, five each. I'll obviously take the one with the Navy Cross in it, so I thought I'd give you first dibs on the next one. We can keep score on the whiteboard, make this a little competitive—"

"Gray." I said this in the same tone that I would use while trying to talk someone off the ledge of a high building.

He looked at me expectantly, the marker held poised as if he couldn't wait to write down whatever I said.

"I've never seen you in a tie before."

Gray stared at me a full beat longer, and then looked down. He was wearing dark trousers with black suspenders, a white dress shirt, and a gray tie. The suit's jacket was draped over one of the desk chairs, and he looked like the oldest banker in the building. I had dropped the formal attire after the first visit, knowing I would want to be comfortable. I was wearing a loose collared shirt and tan pants, and had even considered wearing shorts.

"Yes, well, I wasn't sure what the dress code was, so I decided to err on the side of caution. Too much?"

"Much." I placed the briefcase on the desk he was not using, and looked around appreciatively. "But you clearly hit the ground running this morning."

"Oh, I was running long before then." Poor Emily. I made a mental note to send her flowers. "It occurred to me, after you went home, that the navy man we're looking for might have belonged to the VFW or some other veterans' group. You'd told me his name, so I made a few phone calls, and bingo! He was a member of the VFW in Bending Palms, and they think he moved to Miami a while back. They had a full house there when I called, and their commander said he'd try and find out if anybody knew where he went. I'm supposed to call him this afternoon."

I sat down, chiding myself for being amazed. Gray had organized my last murder case after hearing a brief description of the facts, so I should have expected this.

"You've got a nice head start here. I imagine you've even got a plan."

He slowly put the cap back on the marker before looking at me with a hopeful grin.

"Okay, Chief Toliver, I surrender the captain's chair. Frank Cole reporting for duty. What's the plan?"

As things turned out, Gray's ascendance turned out to be a lucky development. I did not know it at the time, but I was going to be separated from the safe-deposit box investigation very soon. We did get to spend two days locating former owners before I was called away, and in that time Gray demonstrated a gift for this kind of work.

That's not surprising, given his personality and his background. In the navy, Gray had started out as a basic seaman just like anybody else. He had served on the decks of two aircraft carriers, and often said he had enjoyed the duty.

One day decades earlier, in the middle of a storm, an incoming plane had declared an emergency. Gray had been on deck with the other responders when the aircraft sliced through the black clouds and then basically disintegrated in the air. One of its detached wings had passed only a few yards over Gray's head and then buried itself in the superstructure behind him. While everyone else was sensibly running away, he had stood there, transfixed by a single question: How did *that* happen? The pilot had safely ejected and no one was injured, but that giant spinning blade had decided the course of Gray's life in the same moment of almost ending it.

Gray had transferred to an accident investigation unit shortly after that, and had dedicated the rest of his career to understanding what caused planes to crash. He specialized in wing performance, and frequently corresponded with the engineers who designed them. He had become a bit of an expert in airfoils, to the extent that some of the wings currently flying had been modified due to his suggestions. He had racked up two engineering degrees, and loved nothing in the world so much as a puzzle.

We made good time on the first day, closing out two of the ten unknown boxes. The ones that Al and Stan had already opened were the easiest, because they contained clues, and so we started with those.

One of our best clues was a woman's college ring that seemed out of place with the other items found in the same container. The lady's name was inscribed inside the band, and her alumni association put us in touch with her. That particular box had belonged to a man who turned out to be the ring-owner's ex-husband, and she was both elated and enraged that her missing ring had been found in his possession. She gave us his current Midwestern phone number, and we used this to confirm that the box was his. He told us he was preparing to do a stretch in prison at the moment, and asked us to forward his items.

Gray and I agreed that we had met the obligations of our job at that point, and handed the murky situation over to Susan. (When I later mentioned the gentleman's name to Chief Dannon, he laughed and told me that the convict-in-waiting held a high position on the town's list of underachievers. He had stolen something from everyone who had ever trusted him, so this was one of the few graduates of Exile High whose departure from the region was not considered a loss.)

We also closed out the box that held the Navy Cross medal, but that had proven tougher than I expected. Gray's lead at the Bending Palms VFW had only served to confirm what we already knew, which was that the box-holder had once lived in the area. We went out there Tuesday evening to talk to his VFW buddies, but they couldn't agree on where he had gone. They also contradicted each other on important elements of the man's history, which did not help. They did narrow his age down for us, though, insisting that he had won the medal in World War Two.

That wasn't much to go on, but in a moment of inspiration I asked them if he had ever mentioned children. That jogged their memories, as the medal winner was intensely proud of his son the doctor. They did not know what kind of doctor he was, or where he had gone to medical school, but they were reasonably sure that father and son shared the same name.

Armed with the son's name, profession, and estimated age, I had gone into the databases. I had found three possible names, and two phone calls later I was talking to the man's son. The father had passed away while vacationing out of state years before, and the son had closed out his affairs in Florida without ever learning about the safe-deposit box. He was quite pleased to hear from us, and we turned that one over to Susan as well.

Gray was pacing back and forth in front of the whiteboard on Wednesday morning, just before Susan told me about her visitor.

"Okay, let's review the bidding." I had learned that this was one of Gray's favorite phrases, a signal that he wanted to revisit the facts that we already knew. Large check marks now stood out on the whiteboard next to the two boxes we had cleared, and we were starting on the last of the three containers that the bank had opened.

"The contents are not much help this time." I sounded like a court stenographer. "There is a coin in a plastic case, but the dealer I called said it was not valuable and may have been kept for sentimental reasons. There is a union card in the name of the box-holder. There is a small tin with a screw top—"

I was interrupted by a rapid pair of knocks on the door, immediately followed by the door's opening. Susan poked her head inside.

Gray's inclusion on this assignment had yielded another unexpected bonus, in that Susan honestly liked him. Some of that amity now extended to me, and I could not decide if it was because I was Gray's friend, or because I had managed to stay out of her hair.

The reason did not matter at this point, as Susan's face bore an unusual expression. She had proven quite helpful in the last two days, and our progress was clearly lifting some weight from her shoulders. I had discovered that she never actually dangled her glasses on the chain around her neck, but now she was looking through the lenses at me instead of over them. When she spoke, her voice was almost deferential.

"Frank, may I speak to you?"

Gray went back to the inventory on box number three, and I stepped out into the hall. Susan was wearing a dress with a floral pattern so tiny that I could not actually assign the garment a color. She pulled the door shut behind me.

"Frank, I may have made a mistake on something, and I would like your help."

"Sure. What is it?"

"Don't say that until you know what it is. Didn't your mother teach you anything?"

I smiled at her, before seeing that she was truly agitated.

"Go ahead."

"This doesn't involve any of the boxes on your list. This one's paid up, and we've got a good phone number for the owner. At least I think we do.

"The problem is, a man walked in here Monday morning saying he was the box-holder's husband. He had the key, and he was on the access card. I didn't know him personally, so I asked to see his ID and he showed me his passport."

"Passport? Is that unusual?"

"It's an acceptable form of identification under bank policy. But you're right; most people show a driver's license. When I asked him about that, he said he'd lost his wallet the day before. He was wearing sunglasses and a baseball hat the whole time, a lot of the old-timers do things like that, but I swear he looked like the face on the passport . . . anyway, his signature checked out, and I let him access the box."

"He was an older gentleman?" I was guessing that the man with the passport might not have been willing to admit he wasn't allowed to drive anymore.

"His hair was mostly gray, but no, he wasn't that old. I was in a rush, so I didn't check his date of birth. I should have."

"You're not a bartender, Susan." I said this because she was so clearly embarrassed at the incident's retelling, and she smiled gratefully.

"I'd say he was sixty-five, seventy at most. He asked for one of the privacy rooms after we opened the box, and I walked him back there. He was carrying a briefcase, one of those big rigid things with two flaps for a top, like the lawyers carry into court—"

"I know what you're talking about."

Her voice had been slowly getting more strained, and she took a deep breath before continuing.

"I have no idea if he took anything from the box, or if anything was in it in the first place. We never do. He left, and things were so hectic that I didn't really give it much thought until later."

"Thought to what?"

"It was nothing more than a feeling, but that passport story bothered me. And he kept his hat and sunglasses on. I don't know the box owner, she's a woman named Dorothea Freehoffer, lives over in Preston, but I just couldn't let it go. I looked at her records, she's got a checking account and a savings account here, but neither one had the husband's name on it.

"So I called her. Twice. Yesterday, and now today. The phone machine at that number answers as Dorothea, and I've left messages, but so far nothing."

She was really starting to work herself up by then, and I had to wonder if the stress of the audit was the cause. What she was telling me didn't sound like much, so I tried to go with that.

"You say he had the key?"

"That's right."

"Sounds okay to me." I let out a small laugh, knowing what she really wanted me to do. "Whaddya say I take a drive out there, see if I can't find Dorothea, and make sure she sent her husband to the bank the other day?"

"That would take a big load off my mind, Frank."

"Sure thing. At the very least I can check with the neighbors and confirm that she lives where you think she does. If I don't meet up with her, I'll leave a note on the door asking her to call you at her convenience."

Susan handed me two of her business cards, along with the address. She'd had them ready when she knocked on the office door. I had just turned to go back inside when I thought of something else.

"Sue?"

"Yes, Frank."

"Just for fun, go ahead and describe Mr. Freehoffer to me."

Most of the private investigators I know would have loved the Freehoffers' neighborhood. It was suburban, on the low side of middle class, and packed with small houses on tiny lots. Many cars sat in their driveways in the middle of the day, and there were few high fences. This was a place where people knew a lot about their neighbors.

It was hot outside, but I was happy to get away from the office. I was not exactly chafing under Gray's harness, but prolonged exposure to his unrelenting inquisitiveness had worn me down. Besides, I wasn't really sure that he needed me there.

Not that I needed to be in the Freehoffers' neighborhood, either. Judging from Susan's behavior when she described her predicament, I was pretty sure that this was all a figment of her imagination. She'd been working on the safe-deposit area for so long, with the constant menace of the approaching inspection, that she was looking at a lost wallet and seeing a crime.

I came up with several explanations for the unreturned phone calls while I drove. For one, Susan had only just started making those calls, and a day's worth of unanswered messages does not add up to much. Additionally, it was possible that Dorothea was simply out of town. Discovering that she needed something from the safe deposit, she could have called her hapless husband and assigned him the chore just before he learned he had misplaced his wallet.

I was considering that explanation as I rolled up outside the address Susan had given me. It made sense, because it meant that the guy picking up Susan's phone messages was the same guy sent on the errand in the first place. Dorothea's wallet-less husband probably thought Susan was out of her mind, and had decided to let his wife return the calls when she came home.

That was all working for me when I climbed out of my car and rang the doorbell of the Freehoffers' yellow two-story house. It was making so much sense that I wasn't a bit surprised when no one answered. It might even have gotten me all the way back to Exile, except I was in no hurry and decided to go knocking on a few more doors.

That's when I found out Dorothea was dead, having taken a bad fall inside her house a few days earlier, and that her husband had predeceased her by at least a year.

I quickly learned that Dorothea's neighborhood was indeed the kind of place where everybody has something to say about everybody else, and also that speaking ill of the dead was practically a local hobby. My first interview was with a young mother who lived in the house off to the left of Dorothea's, and she seemed to find my questions therapeutic.

The strangest part of my job is the reaction I get when I tell people why I am on their doorstep. From time to time I have had to stretch the truth a little, as telling most people that you work for an insurance company usually gets you nowhere. In this case, however, I had every reason to play it straight. I had begun the interview by giving my name, saying I worked with the bank in Exile, and that we were trying to get in touch with Dorothea.

"Doesn't take you vultures long, does it?" the homemaker asked abruptly. "First the lawyers come by, now the bank, and that mean old woman hasn't been gone even three days. You guys are something."

"Gone? You mean she's—"

"That's right. Ding dong, the witch is dead." She said this without heat while balancing a toddler on one hip and looking back from the half-open door at another child seated in front of the television. "And I can't think of anyone on this block who's unhappy about it. She was an awful person. Do you know she once called the police and told them my kids were spray-painting graffiti on the walls of people's houses?"

She swept her free hand toward the boy watching the television. I'm no judge of these things, but I would guess he was not yet four.

"Do these kids look like they'd be able to spray paint anything?" She didn't wait for my answer, which was good, because I was still stuck on the news that Dorothea was not among the living. "Finger paint, maybe. She was mean, I tell you, mean! Ask Mr. Norbert on the other side. She ran over his flower bed so many times that he finally had to transplant it all to his backyard."

"Um, may I get your name?" I always carry a pen and notebook as part of my work, and began taking both of them out. "I'm going to have to report back to my boss at the bank about this."

"Paula Linden. And feel free to tell anybody you like that I wasn't the least bit sorry that battle-ax broke her neck."

"Do you know how that happened?" I asked, wondering at the same time just how she'd come into all this knowledge.

"Sure do. We practically had a block party last night. Everybody was talking about it. That lawyer showed up early yesterday morning with a couple of police officers, they went inside, and the next thing you know they were rolling her out. Wrapped in a sheet, and good riddance."

I was scribbling furiously, but I still had to know where she'd gotten the details.

"So one of your neighbors told you what happened?" I offered lamely.

"What have I been saying? There was a lawyer. He went door to door yesterday afternoon, telling people that Dorothea fell down the stairs and broke her silly neck, and asking people how well we all knew her."

None of this was making any sense, so I grabbed onto the part that was most outrageous.

"Ma'am, please forgive me, I'm playing catch-up here. Did the lawyer say why he was going door to door? I mean, that's a little unusual."

"Unusual? That's not the word, Mr. Cole. It's *creepy* is what it is, so you can bet he explained himself. He said he was trying to find out if any of us had been friendly enough with that old bag of bones to be holding on to something for her." She gave out a short laugh. "He must have been crazy, asking a question like that in this neighborhood."

"Holding on to something? Was he specific about what he was looking for?"

"Not at all. And I didn't ask. I laughed him right out the door, once he'd told me what happened over there. Sounds like that horrible witch got good and liquored up, tripped coming down the stairs, and woke up in the next life."

She sounded a bit disappointed that Dorothea's passing had been so quick and unexpected, but there was yet another question I had to ask.

"You said the lawyer brought the police, and that they found the body. Do you know where Dorothea's husband is? Why didn't he find her?"

She gave me a perplexed shake of the head, her lips parted to show that my stupidity had rendered her momentarily speechless.

"Her husband? That bum's been dead almost two years."

CHAPTER FIVE

Having stood in the sun for a long while, I felt entitled to a few minutes sitting in my car with the air-conditioning on. I had asked Mrs. Linden to describe the departed Andy Freehoffer, and her description matched the one Susan had given me of the impostor at the bank. Both men had been tall, somewhere north of sixty with dark graying hair, and not badly out of shape. They could have been the same man, except one of them was supposed to be dead.

Mrs. Linden had also described the lawyer, and that allowed me to scratch him off the enormous list of people who could be the impostor. He was mid-sixties like the other two, but of medium height and quite overweight. Mrs. Linden might still have been in the grip of post-Dorothea euphoria when she met him, but she had described him as friendly and polite. His name was Gary Patterson, and she let me have the card he'd given her.

I had asked her to describe Patterson's visit, particularly his questions regarding Dorothea, and her responses had clarified the picture somewhat. It still didn't make much sense to me that the family lawyer would be canvassing the neighborhood like that, but Patterson had provided a reasonable explanation straight off.

"He said that he was actually Andy's lawyer, and that they had been in business together. Dorothea had contacted him about making a will, and I guess he really wasn't ready for her to suddenly die." Paula Linden had elaborated on his visit, still standing in the doorway. "He said he was kind of scrambling, trying to figure out where all her stuff was."

"Her stuff?" I'd asked, still writing. "You mean, her assets?"

"Yes, that's the word he used. Her assets. He said he had a good idea of what was in the house, but he was checking around to find out if Dorothea had asked anybody to hold something for her. He was really nice about it, so I don't think he was suggesting that anyone took anything." From the way she said those last words, I could tell that the idea was so ludicrous to her that she wouldn't even consider it.

I was considering it plenty, sitting there in the car. I've known a lot of lawyers, and they come in all sizes. Some of them are jerks, some of them are not, and some of them are jerks who try to hide it. This Patterson might belong to the third category, pretending he was just getting a handle on Dorothea's affairs when he was really trying to determine if the unfriendly natives had helped themselves to Dorothea's property.

Patterson seemed to have been thinking along those lines, because he had grilled Paula Linden closely about the other neighbors and their relationship to his client. Sitting there pondering what I had learned so far, I started wondering about the lawyer's timing. From what Paula had told me, no one had known Dorothea was dead before that morning. Patterson and the Preston police had found the body, so there really wouldn't have been any time for the neighbors to loot the house. Unless he had some specific item in mind, something that should have been there that was not, his little fishing expedition didn't really make much sense.

That is, until I remembered Susan's visitor at the bank. I would have to confirm that Dorothea's husband was indeed dead and gone, but it seemed likely that the man holding his passport had been an impostor. Considering how closely his trip to the safe deposit had followed Dorothea's accidental death, I recognized that the impostor may have actually been something much worse. Although I had worked two murder cases since moving to Exile, I had not reached that level of paranoia where every household accident looks sinister. With that said, the impostor's appearance at the bank, holding Dorothea's safe-deposit key and her dead husband's passport, cast her sudden demise in a very different light.

This thinking brought the safe-deposit key back into my mind. Was that what the lawyer was looking for? Perhaps he didn't suspect the neighbors of petty theft after all. Maybe he was just trying to determine if any of them had been friendly enough with Dorothea to be holding her safe-deposit key in trust.

I'd had enough air-conditioning, and had scratched down some new questions for the other neighbors. It was time to knock on a few more doors.

Mr. Norbert was not at home, but I did get to inspect the deep rut that someone's tires had dug into his lawn where it bordered Dorothea's driveway. Paula Linden's house was to the left of Dorothea's if you stood in the street, and Mr. Norbert's was on the right. Like most of the homes on the block, his was a modest two-story dwelling with a small front lawn. It was hard to see if he had actually transplanted flowers from the danger area next to Dorothea's driveway to the backyard, but just thinking about Paula's horticultural observation reminded me of something else.

A PI once told me that investigators sometimes comb the entire street on which a subject lives, and forget to consult the back-door neighbor. Some canvassers end up knocking on doors five houses away from the target dwelling, finding out nothing, when the subject's closest confidant lives ten feet out the back entrance.

Other PIs lose the potential trust of people they hope to interview by walking through their yards, so I got in the car and drove around the block to the house that stood back-to-back with Dorothea's property. Keep in mind that most PIs knock on a lot of doors that yield them no information at all, so I did not approach this particular abode with any kind of special hope.

The lady who answered my knock was quite elderly. She stood a little over five feet tall, her hair was almost completely white, and she was wearing a light dress that may have been a nightgown. Although it took her a while to get to the door, she did seem happy to see me. I told her who I was and why I was there, bracing to hear the life story of a shut-in. I could not have been more wrong.

"Oh, I was wondering when someone other than that awful lawyer would come by! I was Dorothea's only friend in the world! Come in, Mr. Cole, come in! It must be terribly hot out there, would you like some water?" Her voice was soft but still strong, and got strained only when she uttered Dorothea's name. Following her inside, I decided that she wasn't spinning me a yarn just for the sake of some company. We walked down a short hallway adorned with family photos, and into a spotless kitchen.

"I'm Wilma Gibson. I've been living in this house for the last forty years. Worked at the electronics company until it closed, then I told my husband Harold, 'It's your turn,' and I quit working. Old Harold got on at the shipyard, worked there thirty years." She stopped walking, turned, and put a gentle hand on my forearm as she looked up into my eyes. "Dropped dead not two months into his retirement. What a gentleman."

I was not sure if she was pleased that he had lived long enough to guarantee her financial security, or that he had showed the good grace not to be underfoot once he no longer worked. I found out, almost immediately, that it was the latter.

Wilma began running the tap with her fingers in the stream, waiting for it to run cold.

"Gave me five children, and I just can't convince them that we have nothing to talk about anymore. Honestly, Mr. Cole, the only person I've been able to have a decent conversation with all these years was poor Dorothea. We'd both buried husbands, both been down the road and back again, and now look what happened. Fell down a flight of stairs, busted her neck, and the police and that lawyer wouldn't even let me see her."

She filled a glass with the now-cold water from the tap, and motioned with one hand toward a side doorway that led into a parlor of sorts. I could see Dorothea's back door from the window once we sat down.

"You spoke with the police?" I glanced at my notebook. "Yesterday morning?"

"Yes I did." She spoke grimly, as if experiencing physical pain. "I hadn't seen Dorothea in a day. I was getting worried, but she gave me her spare keys in confidence so I didn't just go in there. I was going to call the police myself if I didn't see her by last night, but they appeared on their own."

She waved an airy hand at the window, and I could almost see one of the Preston police walking around the back of Dorothea's house the previous morning, trying to see inside.

"One of the officers was standing on her back stoop, peering in like some Peeping Tom, and I rushed out there." She gave a small laugh when she considered this. "Well, I don't exactly rush anywhere anymore, but the officer was still out there when I got the door open and called out to him."

She'd mentioned having keys to Dorothea's place, but I didn't want to interrupt her. It was the easiest interview I'd ever done, and asking questions could only ruin it.

"I told them I hadn't seen her in a day, and that I was worried, but they just took those keys from me and opened her front door like I wasn't even standing there." Her face took on a harsher cast. "That's when that Patterson, that fat shyster, pulled one of them aside and whispered in his ear. Like I'm senile or something. Like I'm so old that I couldn't see he was talking about *me*!

"And then they were thanking me for helping them, and telling me to go home! I gave them the keys they needed, and they wouldn't even let me in there! I told them I wasn't *giving* them those keys, that I wanted them back, and do you know what they said?

"They said, 'We can see Mrs. Frechoffer's keys on the kitchen counter, ma'am, so we won't be needing these.' And handed them back like that was the end of it. As if I'd help them get inside a friend's house and then let them do whatever they darn well pleased."

The retelling didn't seem to be taking much out of her, but she stopped all the same, as if stewing away on the very memory.

"Did you come back here?" I asked gently.

"Come back here? Of course not! One of those young men had to stand outside with me because I told them I was coming in whether they liked it or not. So we stood out there, staring at each other.

"I knew something was wrong, Mr. Cole, and seeing her purse and keys right there in plain sight proved it. The other neighbors hated Dorothea, so she never left her money or her keys out in the open. First thing she did every time she walked in was put them away in a cupboard.

"And then that radio rig that the police all wear now, the one on the shoulder of the officer standing with me, starts just hollering. 'Get an ambulance.' 'Call the coroner.' And I knew they'd found my friend."

Needless to say, Wilma had not spent much time speaking to Dorothea's lawyer when he came to visit later that same day. He got around to every single house on both streets in a surprisingly brief period of time, but then again he knew what he was looking for. Unlike me.

I canvassed the area long enough to confirm what Paula and Wilma had told me. I met two more of Dorothea's neighbors, both of whom hated her passionately, and the only new thing I learned from them was that they believed Andy Freehoffer had run through a considerable fortune in his brief retirement.

I swung back by Wilma Gibson's house right after that, figuring she would be able to shed some light on what the other neighbors had said. She invited me inside again, but I had to keep it quick and so we spoke on the porch.

"Wilma, some of the other neighbors think Mr. Freehoffer was in money trouble. Did Dorothea ever mention anything like that?"

"Did she!" Wilma gave me a mischievous grin. "That was about all she ever talked about. She thought Andy had a lot of money socked away when he retired. She was absolutely mortified when it started to run out, and them living the good life in Miami at the time. Her husband might have been a big wheel real estate agent, but he couldn't manage money at all."

"Did Dorothea work? After her husband died?"

"That girl never worked a day in her life, Mr. Cole, and she was proud of it."

"So do you have any idea what she did to make ends meet?"

She regarded me strangely just then, as if looking into the sun.

"Mr. Cole, I'm telling you these things because you're trying to find out who went into my friend's safe-deposit box. I'd better not find out you were lying to me."

That kind of statement is usually followed by some choice piece of information, so I gave her my most earnest look and said, "No, ma'am, I'm not lying to you."

"All right then. I suppose it doesn't make much difference now anyway. Dorothea was a drinker, and one time when she was tipsy she told me that one of Andy's old business associates was helping her out. Financially."

"Did she tell you his name? Describe him, maybe?"

"No name, but you could say she described him all right. Dorothea got a little profane once she'd had a few, and she called him every four-letter word you can think of. Said he was a mean old skinflint, the money was barely enough to keep a roof over her head, that sort of thing. And you know what else? Whoever he was, he was too proud to hand her a check. Paid her in cash, like she was a street-walker or something. Some friend."

The afternoon was wearing on, so I thanked Wilma and left. I still had not broken the news to Susan back at the bank, and I needed to let her know that the man she had met was an impostor. I was not sure how to handle this, so I called Gray.

"Gee, Frank, and I thought I was having all the fun," he joked when I had finished bringing him up to speed. He did not sound sarcastic, and I got the impression he was still enjoying the safe-deposit work. "Seriously, I think you should get back here right away. Ollie and Sue are going to need to know what you've learned as soon as possible."

"That makes sense. Listen, I've been trying to figure this out on my own, but I'm not sure what the answer is. You have any idea if a law has actually been broken here?"

"I can't tell you exactly what the impostor would be charged with, but it's probably going to come under the general heading of bank fraud." Gray was one of those guys who knows a little bit about everything. "And that's plenty serious, even if that box was empty. You've basically got three sacred cows in this country, and if you mess with them in any way you're in big trouble. Mess with the mail, the stock market, or a bank and you're looking at big jail time.

"But the bigger issue here is who has jurisdiction. Ollie probably has to report this to about a half-dozen different agencies. I can't even begin to guess what those are, so we need to give him as much lead time as we can. Do you want me to pass on what I know, and you can fill him in when you get here?"

I had already considered that, and had decided against it.

"No, I want to get into the database first, and make absolutely sure that Andy Freehoffer is dead. Everybody here says he is, but what if he just ran off a couple years back?"

"That's good thinking, Frank." Gray sounded genuinely impressed. "Dead or not, the timing here is suspicious as all get-out."

"I hear you. What are the odds of someone taking a spill, and her dead husband cleaning out the safe deposit the next day? I'll tell you one thing: I'm glad I don't have to try and figure this one out."

How wrong I was.

I didn't get to stay at the bank long. The tellers knew who I was by then, and one of them buzzed me into the back area without missing a beat with the customers. I did not see Ollie or Susan as I passed through the vault area, although I did wave at Vicki and Anna before stepping into the office.

Gray was not alone. A young woman with Latin features was seated in my chair, and she broke off what she had been saying when I came through the door.

"Is this him?" she asked, tossing a careless finger in my direction while looking at Gray. I would have placed her age at close to my own, which would make her about thirty. She had cream-colored skin, curly chestnut-brown hair that came almost to her shoulders, and dark eyes. She was quite pretty, and had what looked like a nice figure inside the gray business suit she was wearing.

"Frank, this is Vera Cienfuegos. She's an assistant state attorney. Where you're from, she'd be an assistant DA—"

Vera wasn't going to let Gray control the conversation. When she turned and spoke to me, it was in the way you would send an errant student to the principal's office.

"Mr. Cole, I am going to have to ask you to leave the premises. My office received a complaint about your involvement in the safe-deposit situation here, and I've already spoken to Mr. Morton. I'll give you a few minutes to collect your things."

I'd had a tough day out there in the heat, and had come back with some very important information, so I was not pleased by this unexpected development. Even worse, I had run into far too many bossy lawyers during my bankruptcy, and I now discovered that Mark's visit had rekindled some of those memories.

"A complaint? From whom?"

"I'm not at liberty to say, Mr. Cole. What I can tell you is that I agree with the substance of that complaint entirely. I'm frankly shocked that Ollie let someone with your background anywhere near the safe deposit, much less gave you free run of the bank's administrative areas."

"My *background*? Where'd you get your law degree, Counselor? Bankruptcy isn't a crime."

Gray made a sound as if to intervene, but Vera was a professional who argued for a living, and she jumped right back at me.

"Your judge seemed to think it was. I read his decision, and as far as I'm concerned you got off easy. You mismanaged that business in ways that could only have been intentional, and cost a lot of innocent people their jobs. Not to mention losing your partners a great deal of money."

She stood up, revealing that she was a little under the average height for a woman.

"So you can see that the source of my Juris Doctor is not the issue here. This bank is about to be audited, its safe-deposit records are a shambles, and that is no place for a refugee from a Northern court."

"Vera, I already told you that Chief Dannon asked Frank to do this. Personally." Gray sounded both surprised and hurt, but that didn't hold any water with the legal rottweiler he'd let in the office. She answered him without taking her eyes off of me.

"Denny knows better than that, and I'm going over to see him next. Now I'm done explaining myself, Mr. Cole. I'd like to keep this low-key, but I need an answer from you: Are you going to leave now or not?"

My face was burning. Hearing a total stranger rattle off my bank-ruptcy judge's crazy suspicions as if they were facts was bad enough, but the whole scene before me made no sense. The pugnacious civil servant telling me to leave had been amiably chatting with Gray when I entered, and they obviously knew each other. Additionally, it sounded like she knew both Ollie and Chief Dannon quite well. It was more than I could take in, so I turned to Gray just in time to see him shake his head slightly.

Having lost this battle, I resorted to an old ruse that had stymied several Northern attorneys. Planting a sunny smile on my face, I nodded at Vera Cienfuegos while answering as if I was on the verge of laughing out loud.

"Whatever you say. Counselor."

Gray stood outside with me once I had packed my briefcase and thrown it in my car. The sun was still high in the sky, but the work-day was ending all around us. Exile's main square is surrounded by shops and small offices, as well as the police station and the bank, and people could be seen heading for their vehicles.

"Honestly, Frank, I did not know she was going to go off like that." Gray was clearly upset by the incident in the office. "I've known Vera for quite some time, and I've never seen her behave that way. If I knew she was going to start by taking a bite out of you, I would have given you some kind of warning."

I was leaning against my car, my arms clutched across my chest, and I pumped a thumb at the bank across the way.

"Who is she, Gray? I know she's with the DA's office, but she talks about Ollie and the chief as if she knows them quite well." I frowned before going on. "I don't think I've ever heard anyone un-der the age of sixty refer to the chief as 'Denny.' Who is she?"

"Vera's one of the sharpest kids to ever come out of this burg. I'm surprised you haven't heard of her. She went off to college after graduating first in her class at Exile High, and people pretty much figured that'd be the last we saw of her."

"That seems to be the pattern around here." I made this remark softly. The brain drain does not sit well with Exile natives.

"It really doesn't apply to Vera, though. She never moved back, but she landed this state attorney job straight out of law school, and she's been a bit of a long-distance protector ever since. What Dannon does locally, she does at a higher level.

"That's why she's here. She'd already heard the bank was in hot water, and then somebody complained to them about you. She didn't come right out and say this, but I'd guess she's not here officially."

"How could someone have complained about me already? We haven't been on the job but two days."

"I was thinking the same thing while I was talking to her. She insists the call was anonymous, but it had to be somebody familiar with your history." He stopped, getting his thoughts in order. "So who would complain? That's my question. And is it the same individual who ratted out the safe deposit in the first place?"

"If it's the same person, why would they be surprised that their first complaint brought in an outsider to help fix this thing? And if it isn't, who outside the bank knows I'm here? You and I have been a powerful amount of help so far, so I don't expect it's someone who works inside."

"Careful, Frank." Gray fixed me with a stern look. "You almost started talking Southern there. 'A powerful amount of help.' Just think what Mark would say."

We both laughed, and he continued.

"Maybe it is the same individual, and they don't want the safe deposit fixed before the regulators get here. Disgruntled employee, maybe."

"Or maybe a disgruntled *ex*-employee. Susan mentioned someone who worked down in the safe-deposit area, someone who quit when the audit was announced." I took a couple of steps up and down the sidewalk. "But that doesn't fit either. Why complain about your own area, and then quit when someone finally investigates?"

"Did Susan tell you anything more about this person?"

"No, and I doubt she would. Besides, why would a former employee care about who got hired to run down a few addresses for the bank?"

"I'll see what I can dig up when I get here tomorrow."

I looked at him for a few seconds. I had not realized he was still on the job. Gray finally raised his hands, palms up, as if showing that he'd washed for supper.

"What can I say? Vera thought we were doing a great job, and she wants the rest of these unknown boxes cleared." I was still staring, so he dropped his hands to his side in exasperation. "Besides, she likes *me* just fine. You're the one who had to go calling her names. 'Where'd you go to law school?' What did you think she was gonna do after you said that?"

We laughed some more, and then I heard a car horn behind me. It was Mark, back from Tallahassee, circumnavigating the town square. Gray looked over my shoulder and grimaced slightly.

"I keep forgetting to keep you away from lawyers. You're a completely different guy when one of these legal beagles comes into view," Gray stated flatly. "Listen, I told Sue and Ollie about the impostor, and they told Vera, so she's going to kick that one over to whatever jurisdiction wants it. It seems to me that you could finish that one up, maybe make sure this Freehoffer is actually dead. You might even talk with that lawyer guy who was asking around the dead woman's neighborhood. Just keep a civil tongue in your head when you do it."

He made a move toward the bank, and I knew he was going to take his leave before Mark walked up.

"You're still going to need my help with the online databases. You think they'd mind if I did that part as long as I didn't set foot in the bank?"

"Let's just decide that for them. I'd be dead in the water without that, and you're going to be doing that anyway with this Freehoffer thing. Call me tonight." He was already five feet away.

"All right. And Gray?" He stopped moving. "One thing's for certain. Somebody is watching this bank, from inside or outside. You be careful in there."

CHAPTER SIX

Mark walked up just after that, so I told him about the happenings in the safe-deposit area and the death of the widow Freehoffer. He'd returned in a buoyant mood, but that quickly evaporated when I told him about my meeting with Vera Cienfuegos.

"Where is she? Did she leave already?" he demanded, his lower jaw sticking out and his eyes sweeping the main street like a hawk's. He was still wearing a suit from his business in Tallahassee, and unconsciously began straightening his tie as if gearing up for battle. "The last thing we need is some Podunk civil servant calling Judge Carter and making it sound like you're causing trouble down here."

Carter was my bankruptcy judge, a mean-spirited old man who seemed lost in a fog when he wasn't yelling at someone. Privately, Mark and I referred to him as Judge Crater, hoping that he might disappear like the famous missing judge of the 1930s.

"Mark, it's not going to do any good to lock horns with her. I tried it, and she's one of those types that won't hear a word you say."

"You think I can't handle this?"

"I think you're a corporate lawyer here on business, and that she's a big fish in the little Exile pond. Didn't you tell me that you're always careful around local lawyers when your case is in their jurisdiction?"

"No." Mark's face became slightly strained, and he raised an index finger for effect. "I said we *hire* a local lawyer whenever the case is in a small town. You never know who plays golf with the judge in those places."

"Do you do that in court?"

"What?"

"Put on that face that says no matter how much it hurts you personally, you have to make everybody see the truth? It's really effective." Actually, it was a little annoying.

"How would you know? You've never been in court with me."

"I mean right here, right on the sidewalk in Exile. I'm buying it completely."

He put a hand on my shoulder and pushed me so that I had to take a step or two back to keep my balance.

"Don't mock my profession," he advised quietly, breaking into a smile.

"Oh, I plan to take advantage of it. You're going to work now, Counselor. I know the reference lady at the library, and they've got access to all those fancy legal databases there."

"And what am I going to look up?"

"I'm going to determine if Andy Freehoffer is actually dead, and you're going to find out just what business he was in."

Mary Beth Marquadt was the reference librarian I mentioned, and I had gotten to know her quite well over the previous months. Though extremely old, she was sharp as a tack and had steered me to the right source of local news more than once. She was quite pleased to meet my friend Mark, and sat us in front of two computers in the reference section. Mark was unfamiliar with the setup, so she hovered over us like a substitute teacher supervising two delinquents.

Mark went into the legal databases, looking for mention of an Andrew Freehoffer in the area, while I confirmed that Mr. Freehoffer had indeed expired in the town of Preston two years earlier. It quickly took on the trappings of a contest.

"Got him," I announced.

"Me, too." I looked over at Mark's screen, and seeing that he had only reached a listing of legal cases involving the name Freehoffer, dismissed his claim.

"No you don't. Not until you've got a real article or case in front of you. Look here, I've got his obituary."

"You gonna trust the news? I've got a record of lawsuits here. It seems Mr. Freehoffer was in real estate."

" 'Real estate magnate Andrew Freehoffer was laid to rest in Sunny View Cemetery after a sudden heart attack.' "

"Magnate? The guy was a swindler. Look right here, he got sued more times than your average used-car dealer. False claims. False representation. Falsification of documents. What a guy."

Mark's rising voice earned him a shush from another patron, and Mary Beth cautioned him to keep his voice down. I kept reading from the obituary, but in an obedient whisper.

" 'Mr. Freehoffer's longtime business associate, Brian Temple, was in attendance.' You got any mention of a Brian Temple?"

"Do I? I wondered who he was. A longtime business associate, huh? He's named in half of these suits, but there doesn't seem to be a direct business link." Mark went silent for a moment, and then found what he was looking for. "Oh, here it is. Looks like Brian Temple was Andy Freehoffer's secret partner back in the eighties.

They each managed various real estate funds, seemed to change the names a lot, but whenever somebody was mad at one of them he seems to have been mad at the other one, too."

I stopped reading the obituary, and looked at the list of legal claims and accusations scrolling across Mark's computer. Mary Beth leaned in as well.

"Oh, I remember some of these." She breathed with satisfaction and pointed at the screen. I think our game had annoyed her, but she had kept up enough to recognize the cases. "Not these in particular, mind you, but there was a lot of land speculation around here back in the eighties. People were telling all sorts of outrageous stories about offshore oil, and of course half of it wasn't there at all. There were a lot of lawsuits, as I recall."

I went back to the databases and began searching for Mr. Temple. I found him in no time, largely because he was still a real estate developer with his own Web site. A good-looking man in his sixties looked back at me from the home page.

"His old partner's still operating." I turned my monitor so that Brian Temple could smile at Mark, as if assuring him the old roof had at least ten more years in it.

"I'd describe him as in his sixties, looks in shape, with graying hair."

"Yep. Maybe he'd be able to pass as Freehoffer, if he had his passport, a ball cap, and some sunglasses."

Mary Beth didn't understand that last bit, and watched as I printed out a color copy of Mr. Temple's photo. Apart from his resemblance to Andy Freehoffer's impersonator, Temple could also fit the mold of the former business associate who Wilma Gibson believed had been helping Dorothea Freehoffer pay her bills.

In case that sounds like I was moving a little fast, I assure you I was not. I did not automatically suspect Andy Freehoffer's old partner of being the safe-deposit impostor, or of being the business associate who had helped Freehoffer's widow. I had only a photo and a prior relationship to connect him to either of those activities, and many of the PIs I know have gotten themselves in trouble by jumping the gun in this fashion. He was worth talking to, though.

"One more thing." Mark had become somber. "Temple and Freehoffer won most of these cases. Looks like they had the right legal representation."

"I could introduce them to a good lawyer. Just met her, very cute, loves to fight, name's Vera Cienfuegos."

"Oh, don't you just adore her?" Mary Beth knew every graduate of the Exile school system. "And she's just your type, Frank!"

Mark and I went into a laughing fit so loud and long that for the first time since our college days, we got kicked out of the library.

We were still laughing when we got to the car. It seemed like a good opportunity to ask Mark just what he had been doing up in Tallahassee, but he beat me to the punch.

"Roomie," he began, still chuckling, "has it occurred to you that this widow Freehoffer might not have fallen down those stairs?"

He didn't sound like he really believed that was the case, but I had to tell him I'd already considered it.

"The timing is a bit much, isn't it?"

"That's what I was thinking. If you hadn't found proof that Mr. Freehoffer was actually deceased, I might be tempted to believe he swung by the safe deposit to get something. From what I read online, this guy was not above playing dead. I was thinking that he and the widow could have been working an insurance scam of some kind, and he decided to clean out the safe deposit when she tripped on the stairs.

"But now that we know he's in the ground, that means a total impostor, carrying the guy's passport and the safe-deposit key, went into the family box just after Mrs. Freehoffer took the plunge. I think that's a little suspicious."

"I thought the same thing about the passport. If the impostor helped Dorothea down those stairs, he might have gone looking for some kind of old ID in the house. He'd need it to go along with the key, and maybe a passport was the best he could do.

"But you know what bothers me about that? He knew the passport would work as identification, that Andy Freehoffer's name was still on an access card in there, and that he looked enough like him to pull this off. That's not something that just anybody would know."

"He also forged Freehoffer's signature. Whoever this is, he knew a lot about that family." Mark seemed to give this some more thought before continuing. "So what's next?"

"Well, tomorrow I'm going back to Preston. I'm going to check with the police to see what they think of this accident, particularly now that an assistant DA has let them know about the impostor."

"She might not be the one who tells them. We're in a nice hairball of jurisdictions, between the bank, the safe deposit, and this possible murder. Somebody will get around to talking to the local police, but it might not be Ms. Cienfuegos."

"She called the Preston police, all right," Susan Wilmington announced quietly. She had been walking toward us for some time, but we had been so lost in discussion that she seemed to have materialized straight out of the sidewalk. She was shaking her head in mild disgust. "I could hear you two halfway down the block. Would you please keep your voices down when talking about the bank?"

We both adopted the stances of misbehaving schoolboys, having practiced them a few minutes earlier in the library.

"Okay, cut it out. I'm not here to give you a hard time." She placed a hand on my forearm. "I was going to call you later to say I was sorry about what happened, Frank. Vera was a little agitated when she showed up, and when she gets going it's best not to get in her way. Both Ollie and I tried to tell her that we know all about your difficulties up north, but she wouldn't listen."

Mark raised a hand as if to ask a question.

"Before I introduce myself, just how do you and Ollie know about Frank's 'difficulties'?"

"This is a small town, Mr.—"

"Mark Ruben. I'm Frank's old college roommate."

"Mr. Ruben, Frank solved the murder of one of the townsfolk a while back, so everybody knows who he is and why he's here. In fact, about the only person connected to this town who didn't know was Vera."

She turned back to me.

"Vera said she would tell the Preston police about our visitor, what with the news you brought us about both the Freehoffers being deceased."

I held up the printed photo of Freehoffer's old partner Temple.

"This guy look familiar?"

She scrutinized it for several seconds before giving me a shrug.

"Maybe. The man the other day wore sunglasses and a baseball hat, like I told you."

"Do you think you'd recognize him if you saw him again?" I sounded like an old detective movie, but I had a point to make.

"I'm not sure."

"Keep your eyes open anyway. As far as the fake Freehoffer is concerned, you're the only one who can identify him. And with the police asking questions, who knows what he might do."

Susan shook her head tolerantly.

"Frank, I've got much bigger concerns than that right now. I really need you to find out who that man was. With the regulators coming down on us, that phony could cost me my job."

"Cost you your job? How would that happen?"

"Because I lied to you this morning. I never checked that man's signature against Mr. Freehoffer's."

A phone message from Chief Dannon was waiting for me when we got back to my place, echoing Susan's apology over the way Vera Cienfuegos had manhandled me. According to Dannon, he had come in for some of the same treatment when the assistant state attorney had stormed over to his office. She had meant to upbraid him for allowing me anywhere near the bank, but the chief felt he had settled her down a bit. He mentioned that Gray was welcome to continue the work we had started, and said he would be home all evening if I wanted to talk.

I was picking up the phone to do just that when Mark took the receiver from me.

"Frank, maybe you better let the chief of police quietly step off to the sidelines here." He set the phone on its cradle. "Honestly, I'm surprised he got involved in that safe-deposit situation in the first place. Banks come under a lot of different regulatory agencies, and if it turns out a crime was committed in that safe deposit, Chief Dannon could be in some pretty hot water for recruiting you."

"A crime? Nobody knew about the impostor or Dorothea until days after the chief asked me to get involved."

"That's not what I'm talking about. I'm talking about the initial complaint about the safe deposit being poorly managed. If it turns out that bad people were using the bank for bad things, Chief Dannon's involvement might start looking like a cover-up."

I had such a high opinion of Dannon that such a thought had never entered my mind. It should have.

"And now somebody has complained about you to the DA. Chief Dannon basically hired you for this job, so that second complaint has put him on the hot seat just a bit. Now that I've learned a little more about Vera's relationship to this town, I'm not certain she was overreacting by pushing you out the door. If I were you, I'd give the chief a little room for a while."

I wasn't sure what he was suggesting, so I asked.

"You think I should drop the whole thing?"

"Oh, not at all. Somebody needs to figure out who that impostor was if your friend Susan is going to keep her job. We can do that, and steer clear of the bank, by continuing to ask questions about this thing out in Preston. We're just going to have to be careful about who we talk to, that's all."

"I noticed you included yourself in this little project."

"That's right. The firm up in Tallahassee is tying up some loose ends from the thing I was working on. They asked me to stick around for a few more days. Besides, how am I going to keep you from antagonizing every lawyer in the state if I'm not standing right next to you?"

CHAPTER SEVEN

Despite Mark's concern about my unsupervised behavior, we made a plan that evening and split up the following morning. Mark's firm in New York had arranged for him to use the offices of an associated law firm in Davis if necessary. This allowed him to keep up with ongoing projects in New York while also helping the firm in Tallahassee, and I finally accepted that he had legitimate business down here.

In addition to that work, Mark was planning to review the various legal actions lodged against Andrew Freehoffer and his partner Brian Temple over the years. He had only been able to scan these items the night before, and wanted to gain a clear idea of what we might be getting into.

As for me, I was headed back to Preston. I wanted to speak with Wilma Gibson on the topic of Dorothea Freehoffer's visitors. Specifically, I wanted to know if Wilma had seen Dorothea in the company of any man who might be able to pass himself off as Andy Freehoffer in a pinch.

I also wanted to know if Wilma had noticed any strange activity in Dorothea's house in the evenings surrounding her neighbor's death. I believed that the safe-deposit impostor might have had to spend considerable time looking through the woman's house for the box key and some form of her departed husband's identification, and hoped Wilma might have seen something.

I called Gray from the road. His enthusiasm for the safe-deposit job was unabated, and the most recent complaint had only intrigued him more.

"We were only on the job two days when Vera came by, so that means somebody complained about you almost right off the bat. And I'm beginning to suspect that the same individual who called the state attorney's office about you is the same person who complained about the safe deposit in the first place."

We had discussed this, but it still seemed far-fetched to me.

"Gray, I think your initial impression is more likely to be right: Some troublemaker ratted them out about the safe deposit. Then we showed up to help, and we didn't exactly hide ourselves. You know what a small town Exile is. The bank's a big business, and just about everybody knows my story. I think the second complaint is nothing more than some gossip that got out of hand."

He seemed to consider that, but not accept it entirely.

"Maybe. But I keep coming back to what you said the other night about the bank being watched. A single complaint is somebody with a chip on his shoulder, but two complaints, right after each other, means somebody is paying an awful lot of attention to what we're doing. It makes me wonder about the first complaint."

"How so?"

"Like maybe it's more than we thought it was. What if somebody wanted to get at the contents of one of these boxes, but couldn't? Maybe they knew one of the boxes had something good in it, but didn't have the nerve to try and pass themselves off as the owner the way that other guy did, the one pretending to be Freehoffer.

"I asked Ollie what happens to the contents of an abandoned box, and he said it eventually gets turned over to the state and auctioned off. I think somebody got tired of waiting for the bank to recognize that a certain box was abandoned, and accelerated things with a phone call to get the contents of that box on the auction block."

Gray was doing a super job tracking down the owners of the abandoned boxes, but he was starting to suffer from one of the investigation business's occupational hazards: He was seeing things that weren't there. PIs had warned me about that, saying that if you spend enough time trying to figure out why sneaky people are lying to you, you'll end up seeing a conspiracy around every corner.

"Well, who knows?" I didn't want to take the wind out of his sails, and I certainly didn't want him to quit. "I think that's too involved a process for anything of value to actually end up on the auction table—"

"I wondered about that, and I looked it up online. Some pretty pricey stuff gets sold for pennies on the dollar at these things. And what if its value isn't monetary? If the guy simply wants the thing, why wouldn't he rat out the bank in the hope that the box would be opened and the item would get auctioned off?"

"That might fit, but it doesn't explain why the same guy would want me out of there. And if he's hoping to scoop something up on the sly, he's sure going about it a funny way, bringing in the DA's office alongside the regulators."

He went quiet again for a moment.

"I didn't think of that. I'm going to have to look at this some more."

"Okay, but I wouldn't waste a lot of time on it. Remember, the more of those boxes you check off, the better Ollie and Sue are gonna look." Susan's plea from the prior evening still rang in my ears.

"Got it. Hey, keep me in the loop on this Freehoffer thing. If the police aren't trying very hard, you're the only chance we have of figuring this out."

As things turned out, the police were trying pretty hard. When I turned onto the street where Dorothea Freehoffer used to live, it was a very different scene from the day before. A Preston police car was parked directly in front of the house, and a police warning sign was now posted on the front door. Two uniformed officers were standing on the lawn talking to two men I did not recognize. One was tall and thin, and judging from the convenience-store coffee cup and newspaper he was holding I'd guess he lived in the neighborhood. The other one wore a suit and tie and looked like he could use a diet.

I figured that Vera had informed the Preston law enforcement community of the impostor's visit to Dorothea's safe-deposit box, and that they were taking a closer look at the accident site. I wanted to make sure that was the case, but without having my name repeated to the assistant DA.

I have a hard time walking up to strangers and getting them to talk to me, and don't know too many ways of doing that without identifying myself. I sometimes soft-sell my relationship to the insurance companies and law firms who employ me, but that can go wrong if the interviewee starts asking questions right back at you. I doubted it would work with two police officers, so I chose the safest course of action and just kept my mouth shut.

I was dressed in shorts and a collared shirt, and had parked two houses up the street in the hope that I would be taken for a local.

Adopting an expression of dull curiosity, I walked up to the group and stopped.

The two police officers scrutinized me when I got there, but the tall thin man was talking and they continued to listen to him.

"I live next door, and I have to tell you I was surprised to see the police here the other day." The tall thin man was probably forty, dressed in casual brown slacks and a short-sleeved white shirt. I decided that this was Dorothea's other neighbor, the absent Mr. Norbert. "And then when they wheeled poor Dorothea out, well, it was quite a shock."

Paula Linden had put Mr. Norbert solidly in the anti-Dorothea camp for me, and the tire marks were still there on his lawn. I figured he'd either had a change of heart or was playing up the grieving neighbor angle to score some gossip.

Norbert stopped talking and turned to the overweight man, who was staring at me with an odd mix of interest and hostility. This made me guess that he was Dorothea's infamous lawyer, unable to choose between getting my name for further questioning and shooing me away from the police who were complicating his scavenger hunt.

"Mr. Patterson, you didn't think anything was wrong when you brought the police here the other day, did you?" Mr. Norbert was a gift from above, and very obviously digging for dirt.

"Actually, I did. I was very concerned that something had happened to Dorothea, as I've been telling most of your neighbors. But up until now I didn't suspect there had been . . . foul play."

"We don't know that for sure, Mr. Patterson," one of the policemen said. He was the older of the two, dressed in the dark blue uniform of Preston law enforcement, and sounded like he was in charge. "There was some strange activity with one of Mrs. Freehoffer's bank accounts, and we're just covering all the bases."

That sounded like a classic half explanation designed for public consumption. The police would need a story for the neighbors, now that they had returned to the scene of the accident, but they would not want to give away a lot of details. That was why they weren't saying which bank was involved, or that the specific account had been a safe-deposit box.

From the tone of the older officer's voice I guessed he still considered Dorothea's death to be an accident. That was probably why he had accepted my presence without challenge. I was prepared to identify myself if asked, but Mr. Norbert kept the attention off me.

"Well, that certainly sounds suspicious to me. Did she have any enemies, Mr. Patterson?" My PI friends salivate over nosy neighbors like Mr. Norbert.

"Not a one," Patterson replied, smiling pointedly at Norbert. Patterson had canvassed the entire area the previous day, and he was letting Dorothea's flower-loving neighbor know that he was aware of the friction between them.

Norbert took a step back, suddenly seeing that his dissembling curiosity might earn him a spot on the suspect list if Dorothea's death was ruled to be suspicious. Particularly if the police remembered that he had pretended to have been her friend when everyone else in the area said he was not.

I knew he was going to make his escape right after that, and figured it was a good moment for my departure as well. I wanted Patterson to follow me, though, so I continued the guise of the local homeowner.

"So you don't think there's anything to worry about?" I asked the officer who was doing the talking.

"No, sir, I really don't. The poor lady fell down the stairs, and I think the activity on her bank account is just a mix-up." He smiled at me reassuringly, but I had already pushed my luck too far and decided to get out of there before he had a chance to ask where I lived.

I heard Patterson excusing himself as well, and smiled inwardly when he came hustling down the sidewalk after me.

"Excuse me, do you live in the neighborhood?" he called, just loud enough for me to hear, once we were far enough away from the police. I turned around with a sunny smile on my face.

"No, I was just driving by when I saw the squad car and decided to stop. Bit of a police buff."

His interest vanished the instant he saw I could not help him with his search, and that was when I popped the question.

"What are you looking for?" I asked, enunciating each syllable while watching closely for his reaction.

I had to give him credit. He didn't crack even a little bit. Years spent defending Freehoffer and Temple had probably given him total control of his features, and my little private investigator's trick never stood a chance of tripping him up.

"Excuse me?" He said this with interested eyes, and took an extra step closer. He was on to me, and he wasn't backing down.

I met his gaze with a bemused expression of my own. I was not about to admit that I was partially amputated from the investigation at the bank, at least not to the guy who I believed was continuing the impostor's work.

"I asked what you're looking for. I was in the area yesterday, asking a few questions of my own, and the neighbors all said you were looking for something."

His face darkened just a bit, but he didn't budge.

"And who, exactly, are you?"

"Frank Cole. The folks at the bank asked me to look into the 'unusual activity' on Dorothea's account. Did the police tell you what that activity was?"

He kept the cloudy face for a long moment, gathering his thoughts. He leaned in even closer after a while, speaking in a whisper.

"Are you some kind of bank security?"

"No, I'm more of an investigator."

That did it. He decided I had no official standing here, and started moving away.

"I'm sorry, Mr. Cole, but as an investigator I'm sure you understand privileged information. Have a nice day."

He turned and started walking back toward the police, who had been ignoring us the entire time. I watched him go, and realized he had cracked just a bit after all. His excuse for questioning the entire neighborhood was his lawyerly duty to determine just what Dorothea owned. If that was true, he probably should have asked me to share any information I discovered.

"Walked away a little too fast there, Gary," I said under my breath, and then saw Wilma Gibson waving at me from behind Dorothea Freehoffer's backyard fence.

Whoever said we catch more flies with honey than with vinegar was absolutely right, and doubly so when it comes to the investigations business. There is certainly a dark side to this industry, where coercion sometimes crosses the line into outright violence, but as a fact-checker I have not encountered anything beyond rudeness and threats. I have had doors slammed in my face, been called some very uncomplimentary names, and once even had a woman older than Wilma threaten to beat me with a mop handle. In spite of all that, every now and then a little politeness pays off handsomely. Wilma was about to prove that.

She ushered me into her parlor for the second time in as many days, this time wearing a housecoat over her nightgown. I guessed she had thrown this on before running out into her backyard, but she clearly had something to say.

"Do you *believe* those policemen?" she asked, and I could tell she was not questioning their integrity. "They did it again! I walked up and asked what was going on, and they told me to go back inside! They were both there the day I let them into Dorothea's, and they acted as if we'd never met! It's ageism, I tell you."

She settled into her chair, shaking her head at the injustice of the world. I took her silence as my cue.

"They think someone might have been in Dorothea's house when she went down the stairs, Wilma. Did you notice anyone around her place during the weekend?"

"Oh, stop it!" Perhaps I had not curried as much favor as I had thought. "I don't watch the woman's house all day and night! I haven't seen anyone or anything. Even those two uniformed nitwits asked me that one."

She turned to the small table next to the chair. A tall reading lamp, several books, and the remote control for the television sat on its aged wooden top. The table had a drawer, and she opened it to retrieve a manila envelope a little larger than a sheet of copy paper. A business envelope.

She handed it across to me with an impish smile.

"I was going to call you. I thought about it all night, and I think you're the one I should give this to." Hearing that, I started to fear that Wilma was offering me some piece of personal memorabilia not remotely connected with the case. "I would have given it to those policemen if they'd shown me even one ounce of courtesy, but they didn't, so it goes to you."

The envelope was sealed, and I looked at her as if asking permission.

"Go ahead and open it!" she blurted out. "Dorothea asked me to hold that for her, and I've been *dying* to know what's in it."

Wilma was not quite as let down by the envelope's contents as I was, but that's only because I was as disappointed as you can get. She said she had been holding the packet since just after Andy Freehoffer died, so she probably deserved a better outcome after waiting two entire years. As for me, having much more knowledge of the case, I was hoping for a nice double-spaced "If I Die Suddenly" letter, preferably with photos.

The item inside was a large piece of heavy paper folded in half and then folded in half again. Fully opened, I recognized it as a nautical map of the coastline and waters around Exile. Closer examination revealed that it was some kind of planning document, with large pieces of seafront property identified as the intended sites for wharfs, warehouses, and offices.

A legend in the corner identified it as the confidential work product of an entity calling itself the Oswego Oil Company of West Texas, and placed the map's date of origin in the mid-1980s.

It might not be surprising to find such a document in the private papers of a real estate developer's widow, but as the contents of a secret envelope it was a letdown. After all, Dorothea had given this to her only friend in the world to hold for her, which suggested it was important enough for someone to steal. An impostor had gone to a lot of trouble to get into Dorothea's safe-deposit box, possibly looking for this very item. A secretive lawyer was canvassing the area, looking for something that Dorothea might have given to a neighbor. I felt this all added up to the reasonable expectation that the envelope would contain something a bit more substantial.

The map seemed quite old, and had no explanatory notes written on its front or back. If that wasn't quite bad enough, I am personally familiar with that segment of Florida coastline, and can attest that nothing represented on that document ever came into existence.

I walked around the block and back to my car with the envelope in my hand. Although I could not make heads or tails of its contents, I felt it was a major development. Dorothea had given the map to Wilma for safekeeping, which is the usual function of a safe-deposit box. An impostor pretending to be her long-dead husband had raided her safe deposit shortly after she had taken her fatal fall, and a lawyer had gained access to her house the very next day. He had brought the police with him on what I considered a flimsy excuse, and had then gone hunting for Dorothea's neighborhood friends, friends who might be trusted to hold something for her.

When Dorothea gave the map to Wilma, it showed she did not feel it was secure in her house. Although there are reasons for not putting certain things in a bank vault, such as not being able to get at them after business hours, the map's presence in Wilma's house suggested Dorothea did not trust the safe deposit either. Regardless of her reasons, Dorothea believed there were people who would steal that map if given the chance.

Though focused on the map, I had remembered to show Wilma the printed picture of Freehoffer's former partner, Temple. She recognized the name from Dorothea's drunken ramblings about her husband's real estate days, but did not recognize the man in the picture.

The Preston police were still outside Dorothea's house when I turned the corner, so I decided to speak with them. A brown four-door sedan had joined their cruiser in my absence, but its occupants were not in sight. I imagined they were detectives looking the place over, and reminded myself to keep the interview brief.

The older cop sat in the cruiser's passenger seat, so I walked up on his side. Both windows were down, and the two patrolmen looked bored.

"Hello again," I said, holding the envelope by my leg when I realized I was still carrying it. I hoped I would still be remembered as a local, and at first this seemed to be the case.

"Hello. What can I do for you?"

"Yes, Officer, the chubby gentleman you were talking to a little while ago asked me a couple of questions about poor Dorothea."

"I saw him."

"He said he was her lawyer, and I wasn't sure if that was true, so I didn't want to talk to him. *Is* he her lawyer?"

"Yes he is." He nodded amiably enough, continuing his assignment of rumor control.

I nodded back, keeping my eyes wide as if the sight of the radio and the uniforms was a new and exciting experience.

"How would I know something like that, Officer? In the future, I mean."

"You wouldn't. Don't talk to strange lawyers."

"Don't talk to *any* lawyers," the younger one chimed in, and they both laughed in a subdued way.

"But he was with you when you had to break in the other day. At least that's what people on the block are saying."

The older one motioned me away from the door, opened it, and stepped out. I thought I had pushed him too far, but he only wanted to stretch. He raised two muscular arms over his head, and his lower back popped before he answered me.

"We didn't have to break in. One of your neighbors had the keys. And we've known Gary for years. He lives just a few blocks from here."

"So what happened? I thought someone had to be missing for at least a day before the police would get involved."

I was really getting close to the line, and for the first time he started to look suspicious.

"That's normally the case, but like I said, we know him well, he was concerned for his client, so we took a ride out here with him. What did you say your name was?"

That last line was a surprise, but I understood what prompted it when I heard the new voice behind me.

"His name is Frank Cole, and why are you talking to him, Officer?" I turned to look into the calmly critical eyes of Vera Cienfuegos, assistant state attorney. She had been inside the house, and I had not heard her come out.

The younger patrolman climbed out of the car with deliberate slowness, and the older one answered Vera in a dull, detached voice.

"Do you want me to make him move along, ma'am?"

"That's all right." Vera was in a tan skirt-and-jacket outfit, and her hair was bunched up on top of her head. She wore a set of red plastic glasses, but the lenses were so slim that she hardly needed them. "Frank, let's take a walk."

It was not a request, and I became acutely aware that I was still holding Dorothea's secret envelope as we moved off.

"Frank, what are you doing here?" Vera's tone had softened, but it still made me uncomfortable.

"I'm still working on who impersonated Andy Freehoffer at the bank."

"You're not going to find the answer to that here. The coroner couldn't find anything inconsistent with an accidental fall."

"Seems like an odd coincidence, her falling like that and a total fake showing up at the bank with her key and Freehoffer's passport."

We had been walking this whole time, and I stopped at my car. Vera continued in the same reasonable voice.

"Yes it does, and that's why the detectives are going over the house. And so far they've found what the first officers on the scene found: nothing. No sign of forced entry, no sign of a struggle, and nothing of value is missing."

I wanted to ask about the safe-deposit key that had somehow found its way into the fake Freehoffer's possession, but I skipped it and went straight to the biggest arrow in my quiver.

"I'm told that Dorothea's purse and keys were in plain sight when the police got here with Patterson. And I'm also told that she never left them out in the open like that. She was a little leery of her neighbors."

Vera turned and looked back at the cruiser as if to melt it with her eyeballs, but the cops back there weren't looking in our direction. I didn't want them to take the blame for something I had learned from the neighbors, and I also wanted to know more about Patterson.

"The police didn't tell me any of that. I got it from walking around the neighborhood like Patterson did. You do know he went knocking on doors, asking if anyone was holding anything for Dorothea?"

The Vera I had met in the bank resurfaced at that point.

"Frank, you're about a second away from the back of that cruiser." She let that out in rapid fire, her eyes starting to squinch up with annoyance. "You come near this house again, and I'll charge you with interfering in a police investigation."

"So there is an investigation after all?"

"Investigate what? The coroner says she died of a fall, and that she was intoxicated when it happened. Drunk people fall and hurt themselves all the time. They also leave their belongings in strange places, so if you think there is any significance to her forgetting to hide her purse, you're even dumber than I first thought."

"So that guy who showed up at the bank, the one with her key and her husband's passport, he was just . . . what? Lucky?"

"Stay away from here, Frank. Denny might have a high opinion of you, but I don't. And stop stirring up the neighbors with your crazy stories."

She turned and walked off as if I were no longer there.

CHAPTER EIGHT

Take a look at the printouts. Anything match?" Mark was driving, and I was sorting through a large pile of paper he had brought with him from Davis. He had spent the morning at a law office there, digging into the various grievances lodged against Andrew Freehoffer and Brian Temple, and had not stopped at that. He had printed out maps of the various properties involved in the pair's court battles, and there were quite a few of them.

I was trying to see if any of them rested within the boundaries of the planned-but-never-completed oil company development on Dorothea's map, but the printouts were all different scales and it was not easy.

"I don't think so. A lot of these properties aren't even on the coast," I offered, still trying to find common landmarks on the various sheets.

"I don't doubt it. These guys had business all over northern Florida. I spoke with some of the paralegals once I finished reading the outright lawsuits, and I should take back some of what I said about Temple and Freehoffer." In addition to their other assistance, the paralegals had turned out to be quite knowledgeable about land deals in the area. Mark was driving me to the offices of one of the real estate men they had recommended as a source.

"First, these two weren't any more crooked than the average land speculator. When you compare the number of complaints to the stack of deals where they didn't get sued, suddenly it's not such a big pile. Second, the majority of these suits took place in the early nineties, so either they got smarter or their sales technique got better. Oh, and their lawyer was none other than the Gary Patterson you met this morning."

"Really? I thought he was some kind of estate lawyer."

"He is, now. He sounds semiretired, works out of his home, but back then he represented Temple and Freehoffer whenever they got pulled into court. Pretty able attorney, too. He got most of these suits thrown out just by showing that the buyers didn't run proper due diligence checks."

"Due diligence?" I remembered the term from my bankruptcy, but had been in too much of a funk to explore it at the time.

"Right. That's where a buyer takes a look at the thing he's thinking of purchasing. In a merger it means going over the other company's books, looking at the assets, things like that. When buying a house, it means getting it inspected, researching the history, taking a walk around the neighborhood. In many of the lawsuits against Freehoffer and Temple, the judge basically said caveat emptor. Buyer beware."

"I know what it means." As much as I appreciated Mark's help, I resented the translation. It was not the first time that he had talked down to me when discussing a legal issue.

"Sorry. I never assume anything if I'm not talking to another lawyer."

"Tell me again why we're going to see this guy Pepper?" I looked down the highway, searching for the Preston exit so that I could point it out. When we had linked up back in Exile, Mark had insisted that we drive his high-end rental car to the meeting. He had also made me put on a suit and tie.

"He did a lot of business with Temple and Freehoffer over the years, and the folks in Davis said he's a good egg. They've represented him before." He looked down at Dorothea's map. "He might even know what that is."

"You keep referring to Temple and Freehoffer like they were in business together. Didn't they have separate operations?"

"That's a key point. Back in the eighties they played a game where they pretended to be two different entities. They even changed the names of their businesses once or twice. I suspect they played customers off of each other from time to time."

"How's that?"

"If they had a property they wanted to unload, they could pretend to be distinct businesses. One of them would approach a potential buyer and tell him about a good underpriced piece of land, but not arouse suspicion because he wasn't the seller. So Freehoffer might tell a client about some property held by Temple, the client would get interested and ask Freehoffer to broker the deal, and before you knew it a piece of swamp was selling for three times its value."

"That doesn't sound like it would work for too long. Word would get around."

"You know it. They dropped that game in the nineties and merged their companies. Didn't stop them from pulling other tricks, but at least they weren't pretending anymore."

"Why didn't the other developers rat them out? Warn the buyers?"

Mark snorted in a brief spasm, trying not to laugh.

"This guy we're going to see, Mr. Clay Pepper, is probably going to answer that for you." He turned off the highway when I pointed. "But if he doesn't, remember one thing about clubby little businesses like law and real estate."

"What's that?"

"They're clubby little businesses. And the more local they are, the clubbier they are. These guys all live in glass houses, so they don't go telling tales on each other without a good reason."

"Oh, yes," Clay Pepper murmured as he unfolded the West Texas oil company's map. He was in his late sixties or early seventies, and we were seated at his desk in a small office in the Preston business district. Pepper was a large man, not tall and not short and almost completely bald. It was hard to tell what was muscle and what was fat under his business suit, but his voice was deep, strong, and Southern.

"You recognize this?" Mark asked gently. Pepper had been expecting us, and had come out of his office before his buxom secretary could show us in. He greeted us in a loud, friendly voice and insisted that we call him Doc because that was what everyone else reputedly did.

"Oh, no, not this particular piece of hoo-hah, but just the general idea. Look here." He laid a heavy thumb on a rectangle printed on the blue area that represented the Gulf of Mexico. "See that? That's the marker for a possible oil find. You boys would not believe just how many maps like this were kicking around the coast back in the eighties. They found oil in the North Sea, they found it in Alaska, and by God people believed they were gonna find it here."

"Didn't they?" I asked, knowing that various patches of the Gulf are packed with oil rigs.

"Sure, sure, lots of it, too, but not anywhere around here. That's why you needed a map like this one, looking all authentic and such, but the eye-catchin' part was always the plan to develop the coast." He tapped the different portions where the Oswego Oil Company of West Texas had supposedly meant to build. "It's amazing how many people would buy up those parcels without ever finding out if oil had actually been found out there at all. It was a heck of a way to unload coastal property that wasn't moving."

"But wouldn't the buyers try to find out if the map was authentic? At least check and see if there really was an Oswego Oil Company of West Texas?" I asked, as this was the first thing the fact-checker inside me would have done.

"You are one smart Yankee, you know that?" Doc pointed a finger while fixing me with a winning smile. It was impossible not to like him, even knowing that was part of his job. "Sounds crazy, but a lot of folks didn't take the time to do even that. See the part here where it says the map is confidential? You gotta pick the right buyer for something like this, somebody greedy. Once you get the right sort of fella, you don't have to worry about him calling the owners of the map to ask questions. He thinks he's on to something they're keeping secret, and he sure doesn't want to tip his hand."

Pepper stopped talking for a moment, remembering.

"Ya know, I do remember this particular name. That outfit really did exist, a moderate-sized oil concern that got swallowed up by the majors in the nineties. So yeah, if a smart Yankee got suspicious and looked them up, he'd find they did exist and that they were big enough to expand into something like this. And that's as much looking as he'd do before pulling out the old checkbook."

"You sound pretty familiar with this kind of transaction," Mark observed with a smile.

Doc leaned back in his vinyl chair and laughed out loud. The

Davis lawyers had told Mark the man was worth millions, and not to be fooled by the decor. The office was nice without being too nice, with wood paneling, light brown carpet, and a desk that was assembled from a kit.

"You know I am. You're the lawyer, right?" We'd introduced ourselves when we arrived, but Pepper seemed to be making sure. His jovial manner did not dissipate in the least. "That's a lawyer question. And you're right, I am familiar with these transactions, but . . . only as part of the local folklore."

He winked at me and laughed some more.

"Oh, my word, if you boys had been here back in those days. Davis was half its current size, horizontally and vertically, and everywhere you looked there was some kind of building crane. People thought it would keep going forever, but just how was that supposed to happen? Turn the entire Panhandle into Miami–Lauderdale?

"No. So some folks in my business got burned, ended up holding parcels that weren't worth squat. Shoulda known better: There's always the danger that the boom's gonna end just shy of your property. Anyway, that's when the oil rumors started, and the maps followed, and a whole lotta coastline changed hands."

"You bought some of it." I looked up sharply when Mark's words registered. I didn't know everything he'd discovered that morning, but I was pretty sure he was going to get us kicked out of that office without learning a thing about Freehoffer and Temple.

"Done your homework, I'll give you that. My people in Davis told me you were sharp. New York, right?" If Mark had irritated Pepper, it did not show. "Yessir, the doctor sometimes makes a mistake. Particularly in those days. Things were moving awful fast, and if you looked twice you'd end up gettin' left behind. I bought some of that coastland from your friend Freehoffer, in fact."

"It turned out all right for you." Mark was still smiling.

"Oh, more than all right, cowboy. I sure as heck didn't buy into any Oswego Oil Company of West Texas story, but I will confess that I did not recognize Freehoffer was the stalking horse for Temple. They unloaded a bunch of coastal marsh on me, and I had to carry that swamp on my books for years before I got lucky."

He held up his finger again, getting into the story.

"Here's the flip side to worrying about the boom falling short of the land you've staked out. If you can hang on to that property long enough, the world will turn, the boom comes back, and where are they gonna go? Downtown? Of course not. No, they're gonna go right on over to that wet piece of sand owned by their new best friend, Dr. Pepper.

"I made a killing on that land later on." His face darkened minutely, and he actually frowned for an instant. "The only bad part was having every one of my business associates knowing I got tricked. Couldn't take the missus to dinner without being surrounded by people who knew exactly what happened."

"You mean, you saw Freehoffer and Temple socially? Even after that?" I was playing a bad game of catch-up.

"Socially? Frankie boy, the deals are not made in little holes-in-the-wall like this office!" He started laughing again and abruptly turned back to Mark. "You play golf there, Counselor?"

"Tennis."

"No good." Doc shook his head. "You wanna make deals, learn golf. Too many of the folks you wanna rub shoulders with would have a coronary just walking onto a tennis court. So it's golf and dinner, that's where the real stuff happens. And you can't have such a thin skin about your fellow servants of the real estate game, even the ones who bested you, to refuse to break bread with them.

"Heck, we bump into each other at all sorts of places." He leaned back, still smiling, looking straight at Mark. "What's tonight? Thursday? Chamber of Commerce has got a little thing on this evening, how'd you boys like to be my guests? I'll even introduce you to the magical Mr. Brian Temple."

Meeting up with old college buddies can't help but dredge up the past.

I have encountered this same phenomenon with music, where certain songs conjure up vivid memories. I am told I am not alone in this, but I have sometimes wondered if individual people can have the same effect. This seemed to be the case with Mark's presence, but instead of happy visions of our college days I was finding myself assaulted by memories of the bankruptcy.

This might not be surprising, considering Mark's role as my post-bankruptcy negotiator in New York, but it was more involved than that. I was actually experiencing some of the same emotions that had jammed the ugly years of my company's collapse, sensations I had not felt in months. They seemed to alternate between bitter disappointment and deep resentment.

Although those sentiments were usually reserved for my judge and my former partners, they had begun to color Mark's visit. Mark was my best friend in the world, but his obvious success stood out in stark contrast to my current status. Having so little money of my own, I was forced to let him pay for just about everything during his stopover. That evening, contemplating these senseless twinges of envy, I couldn't help noticing I was riding in his high-end rental car because Mark felt my vehicle was too low class for the occasion.

If all that wasn't bad enough, I also suspected that I was projecting some of the resurrected feelings from my bankruptcy onto the current case.

Temple and Freehoffer were the main objects of this illogical enmity, and I at least had the sense to see the reason: They reminded me of my former partners Hammer and Lane. This might seem odd, especially since I had not yet made the acquaintance of Brian Temple and would never meet Andy Freehoffer. However, their reputation for skulduggery was enough to make me see the friendly smile of Frankie Hammer and the calculating smirk of Brad Lane when viewing pictures of Freehoffer and Temple.

I had met Hammer first, having been introduced by a junior member of my company who was fearful of losing his job if we went under. Big and loud, Frankie Hammer had been the picture of a self-made man who needed a place to invest his excess cash. He had been warmly sympathetic about my company's dire straits, and had even thrown in a touching story of his own about the one time he had been forced to fold up a business. By the end of that lunch I was sure I had found the help that would tide my outfit over.

Brad Lane had been Hammer's physical opposite, but no less sympathetic. Tall and thin, he sported a full head of jet-black hair and spoke with a quiet assurance that was downright contagious. He was clearly the details man of the pair, but Tammerlane Group was a family of investment funds and so Hammer and Lane were backed up by an army of accountants, analysts, and lawyers.

I'd been only too happy to let that legion into my shop, and it had not taken them long to find something they could exploit. When my customers had started canceling their business in the face of the worsening economy, I could have held them to mandatory penalties specified in their contracts. Most software development is broken up into phases, with some advance money up-front and the bulk paid as each phase ends. Programmers frequently work several phases ahead, so a company can lose a lot of money if a customer suddenly pulls the plug. That's why cancellation penalties are worked into the contract, and I could have been a real hardhead about collecting that money if I had so chosen.

My thinking had been simple when I had let some of the clients off the hook. They were my customers, they were experiencing bad financial times just as I was, and when those bad times were over they would come back if I treated them well. If I insisted they pay penalty money that they desperately needed to keep their own businesses afloat, they would remember it later and find someone else to design their software. I had also felt a close empathy with the business owners who had sadly told me they could not continue our relationship, because in their eyes I saw the same fear that walked beside me at the time: Their businesses were dying, and they couldn't find a way to save them.

In the end it would have made little difference, as the recession lasted far longer than expected, but you wouldn't think that was the case if you listened to a Tammerlane lawyer. Instead of injecting cash to keep my company alive, they had swiftly moved to have it liquidated. My decision to forgo the cancellation penalties became Exhibit A against me, and in court the smiling Frankie Hammer and the supportive Brad Lane had transformed into hurt, disappointed victims of my ineptitude.

They'd even accused me of the very tactic they'd used to get into my company books: the Bait and Switch. They maintained that I had misrepresented the financial status of my business and that they never would have gotten involved with me had they known the truth.

So those tactics, and the memories stirred up by Mark's visit, were why I associated the dead Freehoffer and his old partner Temple with Hammer and Lane. Freehoffer and Temple had run similar Bait and Switch games on numerous buyers up and down the coast, and I did not find it half as charming as Doc obviously did.

I thought about all this while Mark and I headed to the restaurant where I would see Brian Temple for the first time. As a former business associate of Andy Freehoffer, he was a candidate to be Dorothea's phantom benefactor, the one who insisted on paying her in cash. He resembled Freehoffer enough to pass for him at the bank, and one of his lawyers from the old days was asking suspicious questions in Dorothea's neighborhood.

It was not a big stretch to believe that the cash paid to Dorothea was hush money for some unknown transgression. After all, she had been married to Temple's partner and probably knew a few secrets from the old days. The raid on her safe-deposit box, and the lawyer's quest for friends who might be holding something for her, could be explained as attempts to locate and destroy incriminating evidence. Following so closely on the heels of her accident, they even cast a shadow on the chance nature of her sudden demise.

Despite all that, I recognized that I suspected this total stranger of bank fraud, and maybe even murder, partly because he resembled someone else. In my work, it is not unusual to mentally assemble a case against the first people you interview, but that does not make them guilty. Choosing a favorite suspect early in an investigation can greatly harm a case, and even allow the guilty party to escape. I turned that over in my mind a few times, and decided to give Temple as much benefit of the doubt as I could.

We pulled up outside of Vic's Supper Club, the restaurant where Pepper would meet us, a little after seven.

Vic's was a one-story, red-brick structure that looked like a union hall from the outside. If it weren't for the sign, a lit-glass rectangle suspended over the entrance proclaiming it to be Vic's Supper Club, I would not have known it was a restaurant.

Doc was as good as his word, walking up the sidewalk just as we approached the door. He was arm in arm with his wife, a matronly woman dressed to the nines. Doc had switched from the deceptive department-store clothes he had been wearing during the day into a light green suit that looked quite expensive. His wife wore a long strand of pearls double-looped around her neck, and enough gold to justify an armed guard. Doc had replaced his workday wristwatch with a Rolex, and I was glad Mark had insisted we stay dressed up.

"Here they are, Mabel!" Doc announced loudly even though we'd been in plain sight for several yards. I was about to learn that loud talk was the order of the evening. "Boys, this is my bride, Mabel. Mabel, these are the Yankees I told you about."

I expected Doc Pepper's better half to be the kind of refined woman for which the South is famous, for no other reason than she would have balanced out her husband's personality. I was wrong.

"Hi. I'm Frank Cole. I live over in Exile."

The hand that clasped mine felt strong enough to swing a sledge hammer, and the eyes that bored into me were an interrogator's. She released me almost immediately.

"Pleased to meet you," she said in a demure voice, but I had clearly flunked some sort of preliminary inspection. She had dismissed whatever she saw in my eyes out of hand, and turned to Mark with much greater interest.

"Hello. I'm Mark Ruben, Frank's college buddy and basically a vagrant." I turned and looked at him, surprised by his strange badinage, until I saw what he had seen. Mabel had the senses of a bloodhound, and she smelled Mark's affluence despite his joke. Her smile grew large, and she tilted her head back and laughed.

"Vagrant. I'll bet." She was now almost as loud as Doc, but she turned back to me before it all got too insulting. "Don't mind me, Frank, it's just an old habit from following Doc around all these years. Real estate folk can strike it rich, wear all the fancy clothes and diamonds, but in the end we're just two carnies selling patches of dirt. Isn't that right, sugar?"

She directed this last to her husband, who had stood there beaming throughout this exchange. He didn't answer, merely giving her a peck on the cheek instead, and then motioned us indoors.

The scene inside was a cross between a convention and a wedding reception. Vic's was separated into three function rooms, one a ballroom and the other two presumably much smaller. I didn't see either one of the latter, as Dr. Pepper's crowd was much too large to fit anywhere but the big room.

Most of the floor was covered with round tables set up for parties of six or more. An impressive buffet sat along one side of the room. A vinyl-padded bar ran the length of the back wall, and an expanse of temporary wood flooring suggested there would be dancing later. Some people were sitting and eating, some were going through the line, but the vast majority were standing and shouting at each other. The roar of the crowd drowned out what might have been music coming from speakers overhead, and the lighting was low.

Doc stopped our little group at the door.

"Okay, what you got here is a free-food-meet-and-greet put on by the Chamber of Commerce. The development game's been a little slow around here lately and they're tryin' to jump-start it. Most of the area real estate folks will be here, along with a variety of new fish with money burnin' holes in their pockets. It ain't exactly a building boom, but it's not a bad way to start an evening."

"Mister Pepper!" A mildly intoxicated man in a dark suit came at us from the crowd's periphery. He was a little taller than Pepper, with slightly more hair. Doc stepped up and clasped his outstretched hand.

"That's *Doctor* Pepper, thank you." He growled in fake annoyance. "I didn't go to real estate school to be called 'Mister.' "

The other man began hooting as if that was the funniest thing he'd ever heard, but the Pepper party was on the move and we were carried along. The crowd was a mix of ages, with the men ranging from forty on up and outnumbering the women three to one. Here and there a trophy wife stood dazed next to a loud-talking man conversing with other loud-talking men, but most of the other women were more of Mabel's stripe.

Expensively dressed, they were either participating in the shouted discussions or surveying their surroundings with an appraising eye. I saw one of these scouts steer her still-jawing husband away from one trio and toward another, and finally began to sync up with my surroundings.

That was not a moment too soon, as Doc and Mabel plowed into one of the smaller circles with ferocious intent. They'd clearly been looking for whoever was in that particular group, and I was reminded that they were here on business when Doc looked over his shoulder and suggested Mark and I get a drink. He gave me a meaningful lift of his eyebrows, and a second later I realized he was pointing me in the direction of Brian Temple.

Mark did not survive the voyage to the bar, at least not on the first trip, because someone with Mabel's instincts sensed his financial status and caught him by the elbow. I heard the beginnings of a real estate pitch as I moved away, slightly stung at being passed over for the second time that evening.

That didn't last long, though, as I finally got mistaken for one of the well-heeled just as I was about to break out of the mob. A hand gripped my elbow, and I turned to see a badly overweight man with sandy hair and glasses standing much too close to me.

"Where do I know you from?" he asked, sticking his hand into mine and pumping it once before letting go. The hand on the elbow stayed.

"I've been in the papers," I replied truthfully, and turned to continue my passage to the bar.

"The papers! Which section: Business or the front page?" It was a practiced way of getting a prospect to stop and talk about himself, but I wasn't having any. Like Doc, I was here on business. Besides, as much as it might salve my bruised ego, it wouldn't be fair to exploit this man's ignorance of my poverty.

"The crime section, more than likely." That was the truth as well, as I had been involved in the accidental discharge of a handgun the previous week.

The sandy-haired man began laughing just a bit too loud, and I knew I would have to get rid of him the hard way.

"Actually, I'm here looking for my boss. He forgot to sign a Form Ninety—" That was all it took. His face abruptly fell, and he let go of me as if I had told him I was suffering from a contagious skin disease. I was clearly the hired hand of one of his competitors, and even though I had made up the part about the Form Ninety, it suggested I was not even in The Game. I was some kind of office lackey, not one of the manly combatants in the world of sales, and he wanted no part of me.

"Form Ninety, eh? Yeah, I'm always forgetting to sign those myself. Good luck with that." And he was gone.

The bar area was sparsely populated, and I emerged from the crowd with a clear view of Brian Temple. Many of the outfits in the crowd were bright in color, fitting the age group and the season, but Temple was done up in a sober charcoal-gray suit with faint pin-stripes. He was sitting on a bar stool facing into the room, and would have appeared to be taking in the action if he hadn't been looking straight at me.

I had a solid idea of what I wanted to ask him, so I took this as an opening and stepped up. He looked just like the pictures in his advertisements, with dark hair going gray, strong features, and a tall, fit frame. He beat me to the punch, transferring his drink into his left hand and extending his right.

"Frank Cole. I've wanted to meet you for some time." He said this with a deep, assured voice and a slight twinkle of mirth in his dark eyes.

"You know who I am?" That just came out, but it was a logical question. I quickly guessed that Temple had learned my name from his old lawyer buddy Patterson, but that turned out to be a bit of a stretch.

"Of course I do. You're a local celebrity. Local heroes can really move property." Temple spoke without a trace of an accent, Southern or otherwise, and his eyes never left mine.

"Not exactly a hero," I said, returning the look and wondering whether or not to believe him. Judging from what I'd seen of Doc and Mabel, it was not beyond reason for Temple to keep track of regional personalities in the hope of recruiting them into his practice.

"You've been in the papers. You crashed your car into the courthouse in Bending Palms, as I recall. And from what I hear, the folks in Exile appreciate what you did for that poor dead kid's family."

That first part made me laugh, and he took a sip of his drink while waiting for me to respond.

"Actually, I was hit by another car in *front* of the courthouse. That story gets bigger every time I hear it."

"I'm just joking, of course. I read the real story in the papers. A couple of heavies were driving that car, and they were following you. A little too close, from the sound of things." He tilted his head in a conspiratorial fashion, still smiling. "Amazing how they managed to have that fender-bender right in front of a building crawling with police."

"It was actually the bailiffs who got them." I knew better than to continue this line of conversation, as I had initiated the car accident of which he spoke. "You seem to know a lot about me."

"That's not all I know." He turned and put his glass down on the counter. A young bartender in a black bow tie and red vest stepped right up even though the glass was not empty. "What are you having, Frank?"

"Rum and coke, thank you." It was a drink acceptable anywhere in the Panhandle, according to a PI friend who believes that the wrong drink order can mark you as an outsider. "So what else do you know?"

"I've got some property over in Exile, so I've heard a little bit about your troubles. You really got the shaft, from what I hear."

"That's my opinion." My drink arrived, and Temple dropped a large bill on the bar. He signaled the bartender to keep it, and turned back to me.

"Yep. That's what I think, too." He leaned forward, the preliminaries done. "So when are you going to stop whipping yourself on the sidelines and get back in the game? You're a bright guy, Frank, and you had the backbone to start your own business. I look at you, and I see the entrepreneurial stuff I want in the people who move property for me.

"It's time you dropped this low-rent act you're playing for the court, start making some real money, and get your life going again."

He sounded like a tough-talking version of my girlfriend Beth Ann. His words came across as more of a challenge than an accusation, though, and I felt a momentary competitive thrill. There had been a time, years before, when I had received offers like this at least once a month, and I discovered in that instant that I missed it. Temple's obvious prosperity supported his argument, and it was not the first time that I had considered renouncing my vow of poverty. Regardless of how much of my income would go to Hammer and Lane.

"You don't waste time, do you?"

Temple leaned back and retrieved his glass.

"Hey, it's just an invitation. I hate to see talented people twisting in the wind." He plucked a business card from inside his jacket and handed it to me. "Swing by the office tomorrow and we'll talk more. How's ten sound?"

I dropped him as a suspect then and there, having never met a guilty man who was eager to talk things over with a local investigator. Not even as part of a job interview.

"You're leaving?"

"No real deals are ever made at one of these get-togethers. Lesson one: You want to make money, go get the prospects yourself."

"So why did you come to this?"

"I enjoy watching the competition bump into each other." He tossed back his drink and stood up. He then waved a forefinger airily in the direction of the crowd.

"Remember one thing about that money you owe, Frank. Half

the guys here are paying alimony, half of the others are paying off deals gone bad. They look like paupers to you?"

He shook my hand again and started for the door. I watched him move off, observing that he was in no hurry. I also noticed that I was hearing the roar of the room's conversation for the first time since Temple had started talking.

CHAPTER NINE

Temple's unexpected invitation had a strange effect on me. I knew he was a salesman just like Doc and half the people in the room, and yet I couldn't get his words out of my mind. I had been living in Exile for more than a year, and from what Mark had told me, my life of denial was yielding absolutely no result. My creditors were no closer to settling than they had been at the end of the bankruptcy, and in the meantime life was passing me by.

My own girlfriend felt that way, and perhaps her recent coldness was what gave substance to Temple's offer. Perhaps it was Mark's presence, with its accompanying memories of failure and loss, which made up my mind. And maybe it was just the effect of sitting at the bar, watching all those people conducting business with reckless abandon.

What was it Temple had said? Three-quarters of the people in the room were paying off a debt to somebody, and yet they seemed to be living happy, normal lives. Looking out at that sea of prosperity, I decided then and there to give Temple's offer some serious consideration.

After all, I had considered him a possible suspect only because he'd been in business with Andy Freehoffer and vaguely resembled him. There was nothing concrete about that suspicion, at least nothing as solid as the behavior of the lawyer Patterson. His scavenger hunt through Dorothea's neighborhood, occurring right after someone raided her safe-deposit box, was far more real than Temple's circumstantial association with the case.

Even Patterson was starting to look like a long shot, however. His hesitance to speak with me was not unusual in his profession, and his story about determining the whereabouts of his dead client's property also fit his job. He didn't resemble the fake Freehoffer at the bank, and even seemed comfortable with the lukewarm police investigation that had suddenly sprung up in front of him.

Looking out at the crowd, I had difficulty remembering why I was working an investigation that had failed to interest the police and their hard-nosed assistant DA. Vera had said Dorothea died of an accidental fall, and there was no sign of anyone else having been in her house. Patterson had already shown he wouldn't talk, and so my chances of identifying the safe-deposit impostor looked pretty slim. Temple's offer, on the other hand, was about the only real thing I'd encountered to date.

I stepped down from the bar stool and started moving through the crowd. And this time, when a strange salesman took my arm and began treating me like somebody important, I didn't correct him.

Held up as I was, it took me a long time to find Mark. After several minutes of bumping around in the crowd, it occurred to me that he might have sat down to eat something. I began scanning the tables, and finally spotted him seated with a trio of gray-haired men who were laughing heartily.

He'd been looking for me as well, and motioned me over with a wave. The foursome was off to the side, and had already gone through the buffet line.

"Siddown. I got you a plate," Mark instructed when I got there. "Guys, this is my old college buddy Frank. Frank, this is Ted, Lyle, and Jerry."

I shook hands with Ted, who was an older version of Doc Pepper; Lyle, who was tall and much too thin; and Jerry, who was about average in every way. All three wore the requisite designer suits and lots of gold, and went back to their conversation immediately.

"Yeah, that Dorothea was some looker back in those days, even though she must have been pushing fifty at the time," Ted continued, laughing with the others. They sounded as if they had been partying for a while, but Mark had managed to get them reminiscing about the Freehoffers. He gave me a meaningful look as I picked up a fork and dug in.

"I always said Andy shoulda had her working his front desk instead of that ex-stripper he had as a receptionist. Now what was her name?" Lyle stopped in mid-story and tapped his forehead, as if to nudge it into recall. Getting a closer look at the trio, I saw that they were well into their seventies and maybe even past that. They would have ranked among the ringmasters of this particular gathering back when Andy Freehoffer was peddling phony oil stories.

"Trudy. Tammy. Something like that. Beautiful girl, but I dunno, there was something about that Dorothea. She really livened up the party."

I was not sure how Mark had gotten the old-timers on this topic, but I did get the impression that they knew Dorothea had passed on. It didn't seem to bother them much, but it made me too uncomfortable to start asking more specific questions.

Mark had already prepped the ground, though, and steered them in the right direction.

"Hey, tell Frank what you told me about that crazy Oswego Oil Company scam. That was an amazing story."

The three senior statesmen might not have found it amazing, but they did think it was funny. They began giggling like schoolgirls, and Lyle finally took up the thread.

"Frank, we had a bunch of scam artists roaming the Panhandle back in the eighties, trying to convince people there was oil right offshore. But the best one, hands down, was that Oswego Oil Company fable."

"A lot of people got taken in by that one," Ted intoned in such a mournful way that it made the other two look at him with raised eyebrows. He caught himself a moment later, and responded to their silent accusation. "Hey, not *me*! I'm just saying, if you were going to get taken in, that was the one that would do it. Phony reports, fake building plans, and a real-live oil company that was just far enough away that they didn't hear about it until it was all over.

"And the whole thing was run by one guy, a sharpie who used to work for Oswego as a geologist. That slick kid, what was his name? Cutler? Custer?"

"Carver?"

"Carver! That's him! Good-looking guy, too, if I remember correctly." Ted stopped for a moment, shaking his head as if recalling the antics of a disobedient but beloved pet. Mark gently prodded the group.

"So he was done with this particular game before the folks in West Texas found out about it?"

"That's the whole idea. Get outta town before anybody wises up."

Ted was still reminiscing, and he looked at the other two. "Whaddya suppose ever happened to that kid?"

Despite the alcohol, the frivolity ended with a thud. I saw both Jerry and Lyle giving Ted the tiniest of head shakes.

"Just moved on, I guess," Lyle said, sounding like a stern patriarch ending an off-color conversation at his dinner table.

"Hustlers can't stay in one place too long." Jerry brightened up with a palpable effort. "You remember back when we were kids, and pool halls were the place to be? There was always some ringer comin' down the road, pretending he didn't know a pool cue from a block of chalk, and the next thing you know he's got everybody's money.

"The smart ones were gone the very next day, but the dumb ones hung around. A little later you'd see 'em sporting a mouse under one eye, and that usually got the message across. But if a ringer hung around too long . . . it kinda upset the balance, you know what I mean?"

Even that was too much for Lyle, who decided to end the conversation the old-fashioned way.

"Hey, I need to freshen this up. Come on, you guys, let's hit the bar one last time."

The trio rose as one, made their apologies, and quickly vanished. Mark watched them go.

"Doc pointed this bunch out to me. They've got the dirt on everybody here. Doesn't sound like much, but at least we've got a name to go along with that map."

"They sure clammed up in a hurry, didn't they?"

"Yeah. Makes you wonder if that geologist Carver hung around too long after all."

"They say anything about Temple?"

"Nothing new. Just that he and Freehoffer ran scams on outsiders from time to time, and that Patterson was their lawyer. I saw you talking to Temple over at the bar. What was he like?"

"Not what I expected."

"How so?"

"He offered me a job."

We stayed just a little longer after that. The food was good, and I was still hungry, so I went back through the line just in time to see Doc and Mabel leaving with a large group. From the look of them they were headed somewhere expensive, and I decided that Doc was done with us for the evening.

More wives and girlfriends started appearing around that time. The lights were dimmed even more, the music was turned up, and before long several couples were dancing. Mark had stood to stretch his legs when I came back, so I sat down to finish my meal.

It was a pleasant scene, and I looked up at one point to see Mark's shoulders moving minutely back and forth with the music. I was surprised at how relaxed my lawyer friend looked, and how he had mingled so easily with Jerry, Lyle, and Ted. Though hundreds of miles from New York, he seemed right at home.

We made our way to the door once I had finished eating. It was dark by then, but still warm. The ocean was crashing against some kind of obstacle a block away, making a loud slapping noise when it landed and then hissing its way back out. Mark was doing a modest dance step as we walked toward the car, and I wondered how many drinks Ted, Lyle, and Jerry had gotten into him before I had joined the group.

He stopped on his side of the car and began dancing by himself, one hand on his hip and the other suspended in the air. His eyes were closed, and he was smiling as he gracefully moved his feet in a tight little circle.

"You okay?" I asked with a slight laugh. Our college days were well behind us, and it had been many years since I had seen Mark Ruben even mildly intoxicated.

"I miss my wife," he said without opening his eyes. He continued to dance, and I decided it was time to ask.

"Mark, what are you doing here?"

He opened his eyes and smiled broadly, his feet still moving.

"I told you. Visiting my old college buddy and handling a little business for the firm."

"You've been here almost a week. What's really going on?"

He stopped dancing at that point, letting his hands fall to his sides but still smiling.

"Helping out my buddy with a bank fraud case?"

"No."

He dropped the smile, and nodded his head as if conceding a point in court.

"You're really getting good at this stuff, by the way. The old Frank wouldn't have guessed something else was going on."

"The old Frank would have known, he just wouldn't have asked. What's up?"

He glanced at the pavement, and when he looked up he was wearing a weary grin that I could not place.

"Well, just before I came down here my mentor told me that I'm about to become the youngest partner the firm's ever had." The corners of his mouth stayed up, but it was not the face of a happy man. I congratulated him all the same. It had been a long time since I had heard good news, and I was not going to let whatever was bothering him stop me from celebrating.

"That's outstanding!" I bounded around the front of the car and pumped his hand. "Way to go, Mark! Congratulations! You gonna be on the letterhead?"

"Oh, no, nothing like that. Believe you me, we've got a lot of partners. But it is a big deal, and my mentor wanted to give me some lead time to get used to the idea."

"You can get that house now. The one Miriam's been looking for in secret."

"I suppose so." He dropped back into the uncharacteristic posture of happy helplessness that he'd exhibited a moment before.

"I don't want to seem self-centered, but how does your promotion explain why you're still down here wasting time with me?"

"Actually, it explains everything. I'm not sure I'm ready for this. I'm about to become a father, my wife's looking at houses, and some gray-haired guy is offering me a promotion that's going to map out the next twenty years of my life. Maybe the next fifty."

"So you ran off down here to have an early midlife crisis?"

"Sort of. But I didn't lie to you; I *have* been handling the firm's business these last few days. It's just that, along with those chores, I did some work for me as well."

"And that was?"

"I interviewed with a Tallahassee firm the other day. One of my law school classmates works for them, and he's been after me to come down for years. They asked me to stick around for another interview."

I got to assess this new development while driving back to Exile. It was an unusual reaction for Mark Ruben to shy away from a promotion, but I had experienced something similar myself and thought I recognized the symptoms. It's the same sensation as cold feet at the altar, the mild panic while you're waiting for the love of your life to walk down the aisle. Sometimes we chase things so hard and for so long that we aren't ready when we finally catch them.

I remembered a long moment of hesitation, years earlier, before I began signing the loan documents that initially set me up in business. I had gone to three different banks to get that money, and had built toward that moment since high school, and yet I hesitated. It was a huge commitment for a young man to make, and Mark's response to his approaching partnership sounded familiar.

Familiar or not, I mused, I was not going to let him throw away the rewards of all his hard work just because he was a little intimidated. At the very least, I was not going to let him move next door to me while he was doing it. I might allow him to relive the carefree days of college just a bit longer, but I resolved to have a serious discussion with him sometime in the near future.

That conversation would have to wait, however. Spilling the beans about his career quandary seemed to energize Mark, and he picked up the thread of the investigation once we got back to my place.

"I think your instincts about Temple are probably correct. I doubt he'd volunteer to meet with you if he had something to hide. I also wondered if we weren't jumping to conclusions just because he looks a little like Andy Freehoffer. So let's look at this thing from the very beginning."

I was still stuck on Mark's earlier revelation, but the more I considered it, the more it fit. He'd seemed at home in Exile and the Panhandle because he was honestly considering moving down here. Leery of the promotion that threatened to lock him in for decades of affluence, he had seen this alien corner of the world as a refuge and perhaps even a new beginning.

He'd assured me that Miriam was well aware of his job-hunting, and I considered this my ace in the hole. I somehow could not see Miriam Ruben rearing her first child outside of New York, but then again she might have cast the house-hunting net pretty wide. I set the issue aside as Mark, who was pacing back and forth in my living room, went on.

"Let's say that Temple's not involved, and Patterson is operating on his own. That makes sense, because right now he's the only individual who's actually done something that might connect him to the raid on the safe deposit. The questions he's been asking in the neighborhood sound like the second half of the search for whatever Dorothea was hiding. We were looking at Temple along with him, but only because he was one of Andy Freehoffer's business associates and resembled him enough to be the impostor.

"But Patterson was one of Freehoffer's associates, too, and he probably wouldn't have much trouble finding someone who looked more like Freehoffer than he does." Mark stopped pacing. "What do you think about having Susan get a look at Temple? It would help if we could definitely exclude him as a suspect."

"You were there when I showed her his picture. I don't think Susan's going to be able to exclude anyone for us. And I'm a little leery about putting her up front like that."

"It probably wouldn't make much difference anyway, with the impostor wearing sunglasses and a hat. So back to Patterson. If he's the family lawyer, is there a chance that he already had the passport and the key? Why are we assuming that someone went through Dorothea's house at all?"

"Remember that Patterson brought the police to Dorothea's house on a pretty slim pretext, saying he was supposed to have heard from her and was worried. The police saw Dorothea's purse and keys from the window, and decided to go in because of that, but Wilma told me Dorothea always hid those away when she got home."

"But your new friend the assistant DA said there were no signs of forced entry or that anybody else had been in the house."

"I know. She also says the coroner feels this was an accident. That bothers me, because I just can't accept the idea that Dorothea happened to fall down the stairs the day before the raid on the safe deposit." I went into the kitchen and began heating water for coffee. Mark continued to pace as he talked.

"Let's go with that. Someone wanted to get into that safe-deposit box badly enough to impersonate Andy Freehoffer. Someone was anonymously helping Dorothea pay her bills. Right now I think that all points toward blackmail. Patterson continues the search for Dorothea's valuables after the safe-deposit visit, which suggests that he was the one being blackmailed.

"Even if that's true, it doesn't necessarily make this a murder. How about this: He comes by with the latest payment and finds her dead. He might see this as his big chance to get rid of the evidence she's been holding over him. He knows about the safe-deposit box, so he goes through the place looking for the key."

"That fits, when you remember the map. Dorothea obviously felt it was important, and if she was using it to blackmail somebody, she'd want it protected. That's why she gave it to Wilma."

"Exactly. I don't know why she squirreled away a twenty-year-old draft of something that never happened, but she was clearly afraid someone would take it away from her."

"So you really think it was blackmail? About an old oil scam?"

"That's the part that bothers me. Doc said there were a lot of phony reports being passed around down here twenty years ago. I just don't see that diagram as a prime piece of blackmail material, especially after so many years."

"What if the map was combined with something else? Maybe something that Dorothea kept in her safe deposit? Separately they might not be proof, but together they might paint some kind of picture."

"Maybe. So Patterson wants to get into the safe deposit. He knows he can't pass himself off as Freehoffer, so he gets help from someone who can. The safe deposit doesn't contain what they're looking for, so Patterson puts Dorothea's handbag and keys in plain sight and gets the police.

"He's her lawyer, and he says he's concerned about not hearing from her when he was supposed to. The keys and purse suggest that she's probably inside, but she's not answering the doorbell. The Preston cops told you they know Patterson well, so he expected them to break into the house on his say-so."

"That was probably the plan. It sounds like whoever put the purse in sight didn't know Wilma had Dorothea's spare keys and would let them in."

"They find the body, and the police think Dorothea died by accident. Now Patterson can really go over the place, and when he still doesn't find what he's looking for, he starts asking around the neighborhood."

Mark considered this while pacing. The microwave stopped turning, and I spoke while fixing the coffee.

"Let's back up a little. We know Patterson would have to get someone else to raid the safe deposit. That individual would have been called up on short notice, and might spill his guts if he got caught in the act. Even if he didn't get caught, there's the strong chance that someone at the bank would remember Mr. Freehoffer's visit when they learned about Dorothea's death. If Patterson is Dorothea's lawyer, and she's dead, wouldn't he get access to the box without having to take those chances?"

"Maybe. I'm not familiar with the laws down here, but opening a box after the owner's death can take a while. If Dorothea's accident was ruled to be suspicious, it gets even more dicey. There's a chance that the family lawyer wouldn't be the first one to open that box, or that he might not be allowed to open it alone. Maybe *that's* the chance he didn't want to take."

Mark sipped the coffee and sat down on the sofa. He didn't say anything more, so I went back to my earlier point.

"Here's the problem with just about everything we've said: Way too much coincidence. The bank's safe-deposit area is getting audited. Dorothea accidentally falls down the stairs. And someone with a reason to raid her safe-deposit box finds the body before anyone else. There is no way that all happened by chance."

I had to go to my meeting with Brian Temple the next morning, but Mark and I had uncovered enough new information to keep him busy in my absence.

"Swing by the Exile library and see what you can dig up on this Oswego Oil Company. Ask Mary Beth to help you after you've apologized for the way you behaved the other night. Doc said Oswego was bought out during the nineties, so there should be some kind of news stories about that somewhere. Once you find that, use the information in those articles to search for more recent stuff."

"Shouldn't be hard to do. But why are we looking for a defunct oil company?"

"We aren't. We're looking for the Oswego geologist who was running an oil scam in these parts twenty years ago. I would guess that he was the author of Dorothea's map. If he was, maybe he can explain its significance to us."

"They said his name was Carver, right?" Mark was scratching down notes at the small table in my kitchen.

"Yeah. Write down the name of every Oswego Oil Company official in the news articles covering the company's sale. That's the list of people who might know where this Carver went."

Mark looked at the pad in front of him, and then whistled softly.

"Looking for a guy who blew town twenty years ago. You do many of these in your line of work?"

"This is my first. That's why I gave it to you."

I had another reason for giving the library assignment to Mark. I was honestly intrigued by Temple's offer of employment the night before, and Mark's imminent promotion increased that interest. I know almost nothing about the real estate game, but I easily saw myself shepherding people through the maze of home ownership, doing background checks on the properties, and collecting various court documents. In my mind, it looked a lot like what I'd been doing for the past year.

I also viewed Temple as a potential source of information regarding the case. As Andy Freehoffer's former partner, he might be able to fill in part of the void that was Dorothea Freehoffer. I looked at Temple as a shrewder version of Doc Pepper, and it made sense that a more refined source might have different information.

With all that said, I still couldn't get Temple's parting comment out of my mind. The Panhandle real estate game was full of people

in a debt situation similar to mine who were leading happy, successful lives. That alone was reason enough to hear him out.

Brian Temple clearly did not subscribe to the same school of business thought as Doc Pepper. Whereas Pepper kept his office simple
and low-key, Temple had gone in the opposite direction. His business occupied a suite in a Davis high-rise office building, complete
with security guards in the lobby and a television in the elevator.

The contrast did not end there. Temple's suite ran down a small
carpeted hallway, with offices and meeting rooms on either side once
you got past the receptionist. There was one similarity, in that the
woman working the front desk was just as attractive as Pepper's, but
even this showed a difference. Pepper's secretary was a full-bodied
blonde, friendly but not bright, whereas Temple's was a slim redhead
who sounded educated when she asked who I was.

Temple came out of his office a short distance down the hall when
he heard my name. He was wearing a dark suit similar to the one
from the night before, and unlike Pepper, he wore his Rolex to work.

"Frank! Thanks for stopping by. I'm going to have some coffee.
Would you like some?" He still wore that same confident look, and when
I said yes to the coffee he asked the receptionist to organize it for him.

He then led me down the hallway to his office, a large affair with
a big desk, several chairs, and lots of sun. Color photos of Temple
doing scary things like rock climbing and dirt biking were posted between the windows. The narrow strip of wall behind his desk boasted
various framed licenses alongside awards from numerous business associations. In the far corner a white sheet covered a tall table with a
contoured top, and I guessed it was a landscape model of some place
that Temple meant to develop.

The whole scene screamed real estate, and I was ready for him to continue pitching me a career in the game. Once again I was in for a surprise.

"You sure gave poor Gary Patterson a scare yesterday, I'll tell you that." Temple settled in behind his desk while motioning me into a chair facing him.

So much for the sales pitch.

"I didn't know he had talked to you."

"Of course he did. My old partner's widow died suddenly, so I was one of the first people he called. He wasn't expecting a police investigation at the time, though, and he sure didn't expect to bump into an investigator from Dorothea's bank. He told me all about meeting you."

I was very much aware that Temple was controlling the conversation just as he'd done the night before, but I didn't see any reason to change that. Mark and I might have removed him from the suspect list, but he was edging back toward it with this line of discussion.

"I didn't really talk to him. He clammed up once I identified myself."

"He must have heard the same story I did, the one where you crashed your car into the courthouse. Afraid of you, probably." Temple said this last with a tight-lipped smirk, and I got the momentary impression that he was mocking me. I also realized that he'd lied the previous evening when he'd said he recognized me as a local celebrity. It was more likely that he'd run a background check on me after Patterson reported our brief encounter, and that was where his knowledge of my past came from.

I was used to people hiding things from me, but it did not fit the man I had met the prior evening. At Vic's, Temple had dominated the conversation while focusing it all on me, but here in his office he had voluntarily admitted to recent involvement with Patterson. His explanation for why he had been notified of Dorothea's death was reasonable enough, however, and I still believed that no one connected to a crime would go out of his way to discuss that crime with the people investigating it.

The coffee arrived on a tray, and the receptionist put it on the desk between us. We both leaned in to fix the drinks, and I picked up the conversation where Temple had left it.

"You don't really think Patterson was afraid of me, do you? He struck me as a man who doesn't spook easily, and I only spoke to him for a moment. You two been working together a long time?"

"Oh, Gary and I go way back. There was a time when Andy Freehoffer and I were the whole operation here, and Gary was our only lawyer. Now, I've got so many of 'em I'm not really sure of their names."

"But you still work with Patterson?"

"From time to time. Loyalty's an important thing in this business, Frank. You take me and Andy, for instance. He was the best partner a businessman could ever want. There were times when we were finishing each other's sentences, we were that close. And no matter what happened, we were a team. No matter what trouble came down the way, good economy, bad economy, we stuck together."

He leaned back, stirring his coffee and looking thoughtful.

"Honestly, I haven't found that in anybody else. And believe me I've looked."

I was opening my mouth to ask about his relationship to Dorothea when he changed directions on me again.

"That's why I want you to think about coming on board here, Frank. You're a popular man over in Exile, and people there trust you. You've been through the wringer, too, and I think that counts for a lot. A man who's been run over once or twice has a certain empathy that the clients can sense, and empathy leads to trust. People who trust you will tell their friends to go and see you.

"That's the key to the real estate racket: reputation. Word of mouth. Repeat business. Believe me, you get tagged as a liar or a cheat in this game, and it'll cost you."

That was a little thick for me, so I had to interrupt.

"I'm sorry to have to say this, but I've heard that you and Andy Freehoffer weren't all that careful with your reputations a few years back."

He laughed gently while looking into his coffee, as if we were old-timers reminiscing about indiscretions in a distant past.

"Oh, that Doc. He is never going to forgive me for dropping that parcel on him, no matter how much money he made on it." He looked up suddenly, hoping for some indication that Doc was indeed my source, but I managed to keep a blank look on my face. This seemed to make an impression on him, because he nodded ever so slightly before going on. "Maybe he didn't tell you about that.

"Anyway, yes, it's true, Andy and I were wild young men once, and we did take chances with our good names. But we weren't alone. Those were some crazy times here, with the oil boom in the Gulf, and we weren't the only ones stretching the truth a little.

"But we got away from that once the business was on solid footing. You have to do that if you want to move up, get in on the really big deals." Temple pointed over my shoulder at the covered table I had noticed earlier. "Let me show you what I'm talking about."

He stood up, and we walked toward the model. Getting closer, I began to make out the tops of miniature buildings through the sheet. Temple was reaching for the covering when he suddenly stopped.

"You know, this deal here is happening out in your neck of the woods, so how about I actually show it to you instead? I have to go check that property anyway, so how about you go with me and we'll talk some more? We'll come back here for some lunch afterward, so don't worry about your car. Whaddya say?"

I really do have to learn more about cars. Temple's office building had its own parking garage, and we wheeled out of there in a tiny two-seater that looked like it cost a million dollars. It was a dark gray color that nonetheless shone in the sun, and the convertible roof was a rich black. Temple kept the top up, which was a good thing because he raced off through the streets of Davis and really opened it up on the highway.

"Like it?" he asked once we cleared town.

"Beats my car any day."

"You bet. And every one of my salespeople could afford one of these by the end of their second year with me. Some of them don't go for it, but they could." He glanced over at me. "You could, too."

"I've got some people up north who would want part of that car, remember?"

He laughed in a short, dismissive one-two.

"You've got to drop that mind-set, Frank. Everybody has setbacks. Andy and I came so close to folding one time that we could barely keep the lights turned on. But you can bet that if we had been forced to throw in the towel, we wouldn't have stayed gone."

I'd already heard the pep talk, and took the mentioning of Freehoffer as an opening.

"How'd Dorothea take that? When business wasn't so good?"

"Like a champ. No matter what happened, she was always in Andy's corner." He looked at me again, and then gave that one-two laugh again. "I'm just fooling with you. The truth is I didn't like Dorothea much, and I still think she talked poor Andy into retiring long before he should have.

"You've seen that dump where they were living before Andy died. That's where they ended up when they came back from Miami. Dorothea had some stupid idea about living the high life down south, but Andy hadn't put aside anywhere near enough for that."

He stopped talking to take the exit toward Bending Palms, the town that sits between Davis and Exile. I took the opportunity to nudge him a bit.

"Some of her neighbors said they thought the Freehoffers had money when they moved to Preston."

"*Neighbors?* What do neighbors know about anything?"

He meant for that line to come across as a knee-jerk reaction, and it worked. I was still chuckling when I answered.

"They teach you that in real estate school?"

"No, but they should. I sure teach my people to watch out for the neighbors. You'll lose the sale on a perfectly good house just because the guy next door doesn't like the prospect's looks. He'll tell your customer the area is a war zone, that somebody was murdered in the house you're showing. Heck, he'll tell them he's a convict on parole to mess up your sale. So keep the clients away from the neighbors." This reminded me of the prying Mr. Norbert, and I wondered if Temple might not be right.

He'd gotten me off topic again, so I tried to get back there.

"Most of the folks living near Dorothea wouldn't have minded seeing her move. They didn't like her too much. Did you spend much time with Dorothea after her husband died?"

"Oh, no. I've always blamed her for taking Andy out of the game, and for blowing his money after that. She knew it, too, so when they came back to the Panhandle I think she tried to keep him away from me."

"So you were in contact with him."

"Sure. I tried to talk him into coming back to work, but he wouldn't do it. He said he was out of touch with the business, but I think he was ashamed he'd left in the first place. I think he looked on my offer as a handout."

"So what did they live on?"

"Oh, that Miami foray didn't wipe Andy out; it was just unsustainable. Dorothea had them living beyond their means, but when the money supply got low he convinced her to pull in her horns."

We had passed through the Bending Palms business district by then, and headed down toward the ocean. I noted the jogging trail nearby, having scrutinized it on my first murder case several months before. The houses began showing more space between them, and then vanished altogether just before we reached an undeveloped stretch of the coast.

He pulled the convertible off to the side of the road on a small, densely forested rise. Cars passed frequently, and you could see the ocean if you looked between the trees. Those ended a hundred yards down the sloping road, where a rusty chain-link fence surrounded a large expanse of weeds.

"I have all the land from a mile back, up to just beyond that fenced-in area," Temple announced proudly. He had donned a pair of designer sunglasses, and swept an outstretched hand across the ground he claimed as his own. "When development picks up around here again, it's going to come this way. It'll hop right over Bending Palms, and land right here."

"How do you know that? That it's going to pass Bending Palms?" I was beginning to appreciate his trick with the development model back in his office. He had piqued my curiosity by not showing it to me, leaving me to wonder if it had anything to do with this spot at all. Once again, Brian Temple was in charge of the discussion.

"That's the way it always works. They go for the open spaces first, and then they backfill through the places that weren't open. Yep, I imagine Bending Palms is going to look a lot different in about twenty years." He stared at me through the glasses. "So will Exile."

As much as I had come to expect sudden shifts in his dialogue, this part took me by surprise. Bending Palms was a quiet town, bigger than Exile and a nice buffer zone between my sleepy hamlet and the city of Davis. He was obviously going somewhere, so I let him run.

"You see that abandoned property down there, the one with the chain link around it? It's under the name of one of my old competitors, a man named Ziegler. Somewhere in the middle of those weeds is the foundation that he poured just as the last boom was ending. That was twenty years ago, give or take."

"So what happened?"

"The buyer backed out, and Zig ate the cost. You see, that piece of property really isn't a good spot for anything, not unless you think the rest of the area is going to get developed along with it. So when the buyer figured out that the expansion was over, he pulled the plug.

"The funny part is that Zig had him convinced that I was getting ready to cut down all these trees and build a strip mall. I almost got sued over his stories, but I understood what he was doing." He nodded to himself, and continued in a soft voice. "He sold his whole operation to me about a dozen years ago."

"So how is that land still in his name?"

"Very good, Frank. You're a good listener. When Zig sold out to me, I reorganized my company so that it contained an arm called Ziegler Diversified Properties. The land's under that name, so somebody who doesn't go all the way with their research might not figure out I own that piece of ground."

"A man would have to be careful how he spoke about that property. If he didn't want to risk his reputation."

"Yes, there's always that. It's all in the way you word it. The point is to hide the extent of your holdings when you can. Don't tip your hand."

"You've played that game before."

"That's right. And if you come on board with us, you're going to have to get comfortable with situations like that one. From what I've seen of you, you're a straight-arrow guy. That's fine when you're selling a house to a young couple, which is where I'd have you start. But if you stick around, you're going to be moved up into the big deals fairly quickly. That's where you're going to see people stretching the truth just a bit."

That didn't match his earlier sermon on empathy and trust, and I tried hard to see what he was really getting at. Was he offering to hide my income from my creditors up north if I came on board with him? Or was he just spelling things out for a potential employee who might be thrust into similar ethical quandaries while working for him?

Another thought followed close behind that one: Was he somehow using the jumbled property lines around us to suggest that he was more than a match for anyone investigating him, even if that investigation involved bank fraud and maybe a murder?

The smile popped back onto his face just then, and he clapped me on the arm. It was a signal that the conversation was ending, and meant to point me back to the car.

"Let's get some lunch."

I dropped the suspicion that Temple had been throwing down some sort of gauntlet regarding the Freehoffer case almost as quickly as I had thought of it. His open admission that he'd spoken with Patterson had been a true surprise, but in my opinion it suggested innocence more than guilt. Considered alongside his willingness to meet with me, it just didn't fit my experience of people trying to hide their participation in a serious crime.

I once interviewed an overly helpful suspect who, like Temple, had showered me with extraneous information. He had turned out to be guilty as sin, but every one of his unsolicited disclosures had been meant to cast him in a good light. If Temple was trying to throw me off the scent in a similar fashion, volunteering stories of slightly shady real estate dealings seemed an odd way to do it.

That theme continued through lunch. We went back to Davis and met three of his salespeople at an upscale eatery jammed with a business crowd. He'd explained that he wanted me to meet some of the people who worked for him, but the conversation dealt almost exclusively with the dark underside of the real estate game. The tamest of their many stories involved a roach infestation of a house one of them had been showing.

"So I went to a rental store for a sprayer, spent an hour getting taught how to use it, and took it back there after viewing hours." Jackie, a loud, middle-aged blond gal, was finishing the story. "I looked like some kind of space-age firefighter, between the tank on my back, the rubber suit, and the mask.

"But you better believe every one of those winged discounts was good and dead by the time I was finished airing the place out the next morning. The hard part was vacuuming up all the bodies before the first clients showed up."

The group laughed in the loose way of people who have known each other a long time. Todd, a thirty-year-old black man, took up the thread.

"Yeah, the airing out is the important part, Frank. Bugs are a way of life down here, but you have to know what you're doing. This one guy in another outfit, he noticed a big black ant in a place he was getting ready to show. So he got three or four of those insecticide bombs, set them up in various spots inside the house, pulled the pins, and left. He came back hours later and the place just reeked of the gas, so he went back out and got an armload of scented candles.

"That gas is deadly, but it's also highly explosive, so you're supposed to air the place out before going near it with any kind of fire. Well, he was in a rush, so he set up the first candle and lit it right there in the foyer."

The others couldn't contain themselves at this point, and diners at the tables nearest us began looking over at the ruckus. This had no effect on the Temple crowd, who continued laughing as Todd finished the tale.

"Luckily he'd left the front door open, so the explosion blew him clear of the building and only took off his eyebrows. The place was a total wreck, though. Blew out all the windows, set fires in three rooms, and all because of a single ant."

It was a very chummy atmosphere, and I could not mistake it for anything but a courtship. They all knew each other's anecdotes by heart, and dropped humorous comments so skillfully that the whole scene seemed rehearsed. The sales trio took turns talking, and there was seldom a quiet moment. The last member of the party, a tall, dark-haired fortysomething named Milton, leaned across the table at me when the laughing subsided.

"In case you're wondering, there is no commission when you torch the place," he deadpanned, setting the others off again. I saw a couple of surreptitious glances at wristwatches right about then, and a moment later Temple announced that it was time for his workers to get back on the street.

Temple had been quiet during the meal, and I had stolen a couple of glances at him when the others were telling their tales. He had been the very picture of the munificent host, leaning back and smiling the entire time. The whole scene reminded me of my software company's salad days, when I had been the one taking prospects to lunch.

We chatted a little longer over coffee, and then he walked me to my car. I was parked in a public garage near his building, so he left me at the entrance.

"I'd like to hear from you at the beginning of next week, Frank, if you're interested in signing on. If you've got any more questions about the work, feel free to call.

"I hope you didn't get the wrong impression from my team's little anecdotes. When it comes to stretching the rules, I like to think we're only driving as fast as the traffic around us. Regardless of what you decide, I want to leave you with one idea: When all the other cars on the highway are passing you on the left and the right, and no one is getting a ticket, who's the bad driver?"

I didn't have the slightest idea what he was talking about, and he could tell. He stepped in and shook my hand, and just before he walked off he clarified things just a little.

"When you can answer that question, you'll understand what happened to you and your business up north."

CHAPTER TEN

I had left my cell phone in the car, and there was a message waiting for me. I expected it to be from Mark, but it was a terse order from Gray to call him at once.

"Gray? What's going on?" I asked when he answered.

"Can't talk here. I'll call you back in a couple of minutes." And he hung up.

I don't normally use the phone while driving, but something told me to get on the road back to Exile at once. My cell rang in my hand before I got out of the Davis business district.

"Frank, where have you been?"

Hearing that, I remembered that I had not spoken to Gray since the previous morning. I felt a stab of guilt at having left him working at the bank without so much as an update, but at the same time I did not want to go into a long explanation.

"I had a meeting over in Davis. What's going on?"

"Frank, the place is jumping! Vera came in here this morning with a warrant for that Freehoffer lady's safe-deposit box. I got shooed out the door before I got to hear much, but from what I saw she had a couple of detectives, a couple of state troopers, and Chief Dannon with her."

He stopped to take a breath, giving me time to fully appreciate how badly Vera Cienfuegos had played me. She'd said there was nothing to investigate at Dorothea's, and no connection between her death and the phony Freehoffer. She'd convinced me that the entire thing was about to be dropped, and then run off to whatever judge would authorize her to open that box.

"They grabbed Stan to open the thing, right from behind the counter at Al's Hardware. The poor kid looked like he was going to faint. I guess he's not used to having that much law come at him out of nowhere. You should have seen their cameras, too; puts our stuff to shame. They were all loaded for bear, but what they got was a big blast of nothing."

"It was empty?"

"That's what Stan told me. Not too surprising, when you remember the impostor had the thing all to himself four days ago, but Stan said Vera was a little disappointed."

I could imagine so. She had probably expected it to be empty, but there was always the chance that the impostor, looking for something specific, had disregarded the remaining contents. Gray and I had filled in a lot of blanks using seemingly insignificant items from other boxes, and Vera might have hoped to do the same. Gray continued.

"It sure looks like they're treating this as a full-blown murder. It sound like that to you?"

"Oh, I don't think they're at that stage just yet, unless they've come up with something new since yesterday morning." I felt even more guilty at not keeping him updated, and decided to do that now. "That was when I bumped into Vera outside of Dorothea's house.

She said the coroner hadn't found anything suspicious, and that there were no signs of foul play at the house.

"Mark and I have been talking with some of Freehoffer's old real estate associates, and we met his old partner last night." I stopped talking just then, not because I had to concentrate on my driving, but because I had almost told Gray about the map. With Vera getting warrants to open up safe-deposit boxes, having that item in my possession could be considered obstruction. I had not thought of it that way when she had been insisting that Dorothea's death was an accident, but the search of the safe-deposit box now said otherwise.

"Frank?"

"Sorry, I just lost my train of thought. Are they still there?"

"No, Vera and her crowd cleared out as soon as they got the box open. You should have seen poor Stan. I was sitting in the park waiting for permission to go back inside when he came out. He walked over and practically collapsed on the bench next to me. Took him three tries to light his cigarette."

"He tell you anything else?"

"Nah, just that he was a little spooked when they stormed into Al's and told him he was going with them. I swear the kid thought he was under arrest. They grabbed him so fast that he didn't bring along the gear he needed to replace the lock after it was drilled, so he had to go get it. He told me the box was empty, and then he left."

"Anybody else talk to you?"

"Well, Ollie's about ready for a straitjacket, so I spent the rest of the morning trying to calm him down. And Susan's convinced this has gotten big enough that she's gonna lose her job for sure. Not a happy place."

"Tell her not to worry. We'll figure it out long before they get to punishing anybody." I had no idea why I said that, having only one remaining suspect on my list, but I wanted to help Gray as much as possible. "How's the rest of the job going?"

"Boffo. I started digging at the outdated addresses on the boxes they haven't opened yet, and got lucky with four of them already. The first two were people who moved away, but not far. I searched for their names in an online phone directory and began calling the ones who matched, starting with the closest. I found two of them that way.

"Then I came across a search feature that gives the phone numbers of people who live *around* a certain address. I typed in the outdated information, got the numbers of the box-holder's old neighbors, and began calling them. That took longer, but I crossed off two more. One moved and the other one passed away, but it's all confirmed."

"Gray, I was going to apologize to you for not being there to help, but I think I would have just gotten in your way."

He laughed at that.

"So how is this other thing coming along? Any luck finding out who the impostor was?"

"Still grinding it out. Mark's doing some research over at the library, and I'm going to meet him there."

"Well, when I get it wrapped up down here I'll be free to show you youngsters how it's . . . wait a minute, Emily's waving to me." His voice disappeared for a few seconds, leaving me to wonder where he was calling from. I had been certain he was at the bank, but Emily's presence suggested otherwise.

"Gray, where are you?"

"I'm at the bank. Outside of it, anyway."

"And Emily was waving at you? Did she drive by or something?"

"No, no, she's helping me out with the job. I can't make all these calls and keep ahead of the planning at the same time. I brought her with me this morning, and we are just *racing* through that list."

I was not sure what to make of this. Somehow I could not imagine Emily Toliver obeying Gray's orders the way I had, or even putting up with his chief of staff act for long. I also wondered why I had been so rudely given the boot when it seemed that just anybody could walk in and help out. Remembering how Vera had tricked me the other day made this even harder to stomach.

"Um, Gray, I don't mean to insult Emily, but how come they don't seem to care who works in there, as long as it's not me?"

"Oh, come on, Frank!" He laughed. "How many times we have to explain this? You're a newcomer. Me and Emily, we've been in Exile so long that we're almost as good as the people who were born here."

Mark had taken over a small study room at the library that morning. He had brought a large arrangement of flowers to smooth things over with Mary Beth, and the reference librarian had been helping him all day.

They had covered a lot of ground. The study room was only ten feet by ten feet, with a counter that served as a desk and barely enough space for a chair. Mark had practically wallpapered the place with legal-sized sheets that were tacked up all around. One grouping contained information on the missing geologist Carver, including a grainy printout of an old newspaper article covering his disappearance. Mark had enlarged the photo that had accompanied the article, and a handsome light-haired man smiled at me from the wall.

The rest of the cubicle was adorned with maps. Some were printouts, some were copies of various parts of Dorothea's map, and one was a large road map of the Panhandle. Mark had identified most of the current owners of the land fraudulently marked for lucrative development on Dorothea's diagram, and even some of the previous buyers. He'd drawn that information on the road map, complete with approximate dates of purchase. When he explained his progress, he sounded like a cross between a Supreme Court lawyer and a cop.

"Here was my assumption when I started this morning: For Dorothea's map to have any value as blackmail evidence, *somebody* had to be fooled by that Oswego Oil Company story. At the time, I still didn't see how someone could be blackmailed over land fraud that happened two decades ago, but I approached it from that angle anyway.

"First, I wanted to identify the current owners of the properties marked for development on Dorothea's map. I originally planned to contact each of them and ask who owned that land before them. I figured I could work my way back to who bought those parcels in the eighties, and that talking to those people might reveal why Dorothea was hiding this thing. The whole time, I had one question to answer: What is so important about this map?"

Looking at the walls around me, I was astounded by the progress that Mark and Mary Beth had made in so short a time. Land title searches are not hard, but they usually take place at local courthouses and inside town record vaults. I'd done my share of that kind of grunt work, and could not fathom how Mark had done all this from the library.

"How did you manage to track down so many of the owners?" I asked, pointing at the large map.

"Oh, I've been back and forth on the phone with Doc most of the morning. Guy's got a memory like an elephant. As you can see, he knows the trail of ownership for several of these parcels. He doesn't think anybody got fooled by that Oswego story at the time, but he helped out all the same."

Mark turned to the wall that held the information on Carver, and switched into a more subdued tone.

"Over here is the interesting stuff. David Carver. Geologist for the Oswego Oil Company of West Texas until 1986, when he was fired for misuse of funds. I did that thing you suggested, looking up the Oswego company officers before the place got bought out. One of 'em, a guy named Dempsey, is still working with the outfit that did the buying, and remembers Carver well.

"He'd kinda have to, though. Carver came here in 1987 and began peddling his offshore oil stories, complete with phony Oswego Oil Company reports. When Carver disappeared, his mother thought he still worked for Oswego, and it took them a long time to convince her that the guy had been fired. She sued them over and over, for everything from wrongful termination to wrongful death. This Dempsey, as one of the last Oswego bigwigs left with the merged company, ended up as the answer man every time her lawyers came by. He's not a big fan of Carver's mother.

"She had Carver declared legally dead in the late nineties, but only after a dozen PIs had tried to find him. Guess where the trail always ended?"

"Right here?"

"Exactly." Mark's demeanor became downright somber. "Unless this kid changed his name and moved to a mountain in Tibet, he never left the Panhandle. No activity on his bank account after he disappeared, no use of his credit cards, nothing. The Oswego folks were none too happy about him using their name, and after they got sued by his mother the first time they did some investigating of their own." Mark stopped to let me catch up, but I let him know I was right alongside him.

"That's why Lyle made Ted and Jerry clam up on us last night.

Too many people came through the area asking questions about this kid."

"It's even better than that. Dempsey is convinced that Carver pulled the wrong scam on the wrong people right here in River City. That's why the trail ends here."

"Hung around too long," I said, imitating Jerry from the previous night.

"Upset the balance," Mark added his own Jerry impersonation before turning to one of the legal sheets on the wall. Finding what he wanted, he read the quotation using a Texan accent. "Here's what Dempsey said: 'And they probably fed him to the gators. At least I hope they did.'"

Mark stopped and smiled thinly, but not in appreciation of his little joke voice. Carver had been peddling the very map that Dorothea had hidden with Wilma, and Mark was waiting for me to make the connection.

"I'd say you answered your big question, the one about why a twenty-year-old land fraud map was so important."

"Oh, yeah. I think somebody *did* feed Davy to the gators, or dumped him in the waters over those rich oil fields. Dorothea's blackmail evidence had nothing to do with twenty-year-old land fraud. It was twenty-year-old murder."

Mark's phone rang a short time later. It was the folks in Tallahassee who had interviewed him earlier in the week, and apparently they were ready to get serious. We quickly took down his artwork, and headed back to my place so he could pack.

"I'm going to be gone until Sunday," he said as he zipped up his suit bag. "This is the wining and dining phase. Tonight I'm going to meet the people I'd be working with, and they'll make a final decision tomorrow. I can tell they're going to make an offer, because they want me to attend some kind of social planned for tomorrow night."

"So they'll want an answer by then?" I had not yet found the time to convince Mark to stay in New York, and I think my surprise showed.

"They'll ask, but I already told them I'd want to talk it over with Miriam." He clapped me on the shoulder as if to reassure me. "Don't worry, cowboy. I won't make any snap decisions just because I'm having fun down here."

He was gone just moments after that, leaving me with a large stack of maps that had been tacked to the walls of the Exile Public Library less than an hour before. It was Friday night and, having nothing else to do, I re-created his artwork on my living-room wall. I hadn't gotten a good look at it earlier, and I wanted to ponder what we had learned.

First I put up the large road map, and then I surrounded it with the enlarged segments of Dorothea's diagram. The various copies had gotten mixed up in our hasty departure, and so I had to inspect each one closely before tacking it up near its corresponding location on the road map.

While doing this, I absently looked at the spot between Bending Palms and Exile where Temple had taken me that morning, and my eyes stopped on a faint mark that I had not noticed on the original map. It was a tiny handwritten plus sign, and it sat near the fenced-in property once owned by the unlucky Ziegler.

I unfolded the original and saw that the cross was there as well. The mark was handwritten in blue ink, and I got a chill just looking at it.

My mind fought what my eyes were seeing. I had come away from my two meetings with Temple believing he had nothing to do with this map, but the location of that cross said otherwise. It sat right on the old Ziegler property, the land Temple had gone out of his way to show me.

As if to convince my reluctant brain, a parade of memories flashed before my eyes. Temple sitting at the bar at Vic's, telling me he knew my history because I was a local celebrity. Temple dominating and directing all of our conversations, even when admitting his recent discussions with the lawyer Patterson. Temple looking on while his lackeys joked about the deceitful side of his business.

As if the visuals weren't enough, his parting question from that afternoon rang in my ears: *"When all the other cars on the highway are passing you on the left and the right, and no one is getting a ticket, who's the bad driver?"*

That memory conjured up another image, and I both saw and heard Doc telling us that he'd been duped by Temple and Freehoffer years before.

I dialed the good doctor's cell-phone number.

"What's up there, Frank?" His voice came across with the same eccentric amusement of our first meeting. If he was getting tired of hearing from me and Mark, he wasn't letting it show.

"Hey, Doc, I've got a question about who owns some land near the coast, right about where Bending Palms and Exile come together. It's got a rusted old fence around it, lots of weeds, and an uncompleted building's foundation. I'm told that it went to Temple when a real estate guy named Ziegler went belly up. That sound right?"

"Yeah, old Zig got caught looking the wrong way when the boom ended, sold out to Temple about a dozen years ago. Hang on a second."

I heard his fingers tapping away on a keyboard, and then he came back on the phone.

"This is interesting. Temple bought that parcel back in the late eighties, a few years before Zig went under. That's strange; the boom was long dead by then. It looks like he put it under the name of a 'Ziegler Diversified Properties' when he bought out the rest of Zig's outfit. I guess you can't teach an old dog new tricks after all, huh?"

I was almost too surprised to thank him, and he hung up after wishing me a pleasant evening. I walked back to the map on the wall, actually touching the little cross on the paper. Mark had asked what made this map so special that Dorothea had hidden it, and I believed I now had the complete answer.

The mark on Ziegler's former property was what made the map important, and the people looking for that map had proved it. Andy Freehoffer's old lawyer had risked making himself a suspect in a murder investigation just trying to find out if any of Dorothea's neighbors were holding something for her. A stranger had lied his way into her safe-deposit box, looking for something valuable enough to justify that crime.

The mark sat on a chunk of land purchased by Andy Freehoffer's partner shortly after a geologist named Carver had disappeared in the area. A geologist who had been peddling that very map, along with a con game that had probably gotten him killed. A new building's foundation had been poured on that ground right about the time Carver disappeared, and when the promised building had not been constructed, Temple had bought that land even though it made no sense to do so.

That revelation was closely followed by another that was even more sinister: Temple had taken me to that location on purpose, and then gone out of his way to point at that very spot. He'd lied about the fashion, and the time frame, in which he'd acquired it, but he'd done so in a way that could be easily found out.

What had he said about the gathering at Vic's, the one where no real deals were ever made? *I enjoy watching the competition bump into each other.*

"He's playing with me," I whispered, as if I did not believe my own words.

CHAPTER ELEVEN

With Mark gone to Tallahassee, I decided to run over to Gray's house with my new information. I had meant to get over there anyway, feeling that I had abandoned him and Emily in the box-holder hunt. I also needed to update him on the latest revelations involving Brian Temple, and get his advice on how to proceed.

I took the maps down and put them in a briefcase that I took with me. I was sure that Gray would want to look at these items once I had explained their importance, and I was also unsure of how safe they might be in my house. I was now certain that Temple was involved in the search for Dorothea's hidden keepsakes, and if he was in fact playing with me it was not a stretch to believe he would break into my house.

Or have my house broken into. When I had first seen Temple's picture and observed that he could have been the impostor, I had not known of his wealth and influence. He had plenty of money and lots of loyal people working for him, so he could have found someone else to play the role of Freehoffer. That thought reminded me of Milton, one of the salespeople at the lunch that afternoon. Tall, dark, and middle-aged, Milton could have passed for Freehoffer with just a dusting of gray makeup on his hair. Driving toward Gray's place, I began to wonder if Temple had brought Milton to the gathering just to plant that thought in my head.

Such a gag might fall in line with my suspicion that Temple was playing with me, but I still had one big question that no amount of demented horseplay could answer. Why, if he meant to raid the safe deposit, would Temple have lodged the complaint that had brought so much scrutiny down on the bank in the first place?

"He didn't." Gray was seated on the couch in his living room, his laptop open on the coffee table in front of him. "I don't know who did, but I've been chewing on that very question for some time now. The more I look at the sequence of events when you and I first showed up at the bank, the less it points to the impostor.

"First, the impostor had already been there and gone before we showed up. Whoever got you kicked off the premises did so after Dorothea Freehoffer's safe-deposit box had been raided. There was no reason for the impostor to care if you were working in the bank or not.

"Second, it would be just plain crazy for the impostor to submit a complaint about the slipshod practices in a part of the bank he was hoping to hoodwink. The phony Freehoffer wouldn't have wanted any extra attention on the safe deposit at all. He wanted it just the way it was: disorganized, unsupervised, and basically paralyzed."

He stopped talking and smiled, as if enjoying his wordplay. Emily entered the room just then, carrying a coffee tray and shaking her head.

"You see what I've had to put up with all day? The more of those box-holders we find, the more he talks like that." She set the tray down and began handing out the mugs. Despite the late hour and the events of the day, she did not seem tired.

"Now, let's not forget your contribution, button," Gray drawled in imitation of his wife. "Seriously, Frank, Em came up with an approach we overlooked. I was dead in the water over two of these boxes, until Em thought to call around to the local churches to see if the people we were looking for had been members of a congregation anywhere. One of those got us a forwarding address."

"The other one was a little harder." Emily, ever the perfect hostess, poured my coffee and handed it across. "It was a very common name, and so we found matches all across the country. We did find a local church they used to attend, and luckily it's not one of the bigger denominations. We hoped that they had moved to a state where they could still attend services, and that narrowed the search enough that we found them a dozen phone calls later."

"So how many are left?" I asked, trying to hide my amazement at their ingenuity. I was beginning to doubt that I could have done as well as they had, in what was technically my business.

"Well, the number of unknowns has grown a bit." Gray motioned toward the laptop. "It started out as ten, and we've cleared out nine of those. Three more got added during the week, but we're still digging away at two of those that are starting to look out of reach."

"That's outstanding. When Chief Dannon brought this to me, I told him I wouldn't be able to resolve every single one of them."

"Oh, we haven't given up yet." Gray's voice took on an obstinate tone, and Emily rolled her eyes. "The regulators aren't due until midweek, and I intend to present them a list that is completely up-to-date."

"How is Susan holding up?"

"Oh, she is just a trouper, Frank. She's very concerned about her job, but it hasn't affected her work one iota. They should have put her in charge of that area a long time ago."

That comment jogged my memory.

"Gray, I would like you to ask Susan if she'd reconsider something. She told me last week that someone used to be assigned back there, someone who quit when the audit was announced. She wouldn't give me that employee's name, but I need to talk to whoever it was."

"You mentioned that a while back, and I did discuss it with Susan. She wasn't receptive, so I'm going to need something specific if I ask her again. What have you got?"

"If somebody other than the impostor lodged the original complaint, it's likely that the impostor made his move as a reaction to that. What I mean is, the cleanup probably made him go before he was ready. After all, the impostor does seem to have been winging it just a little: He had the key, but not a driver's license. He used Freehoffer's old passport, but that was what stuck in Susan's mind later. I think the complaint might have rushed someone who was already planning to trick his way into that safe-deposit box."

"And?"

"The impostor knew that Andy Freehoffer was still on the access card. I'm wondering who told him that."

On Saturday, I waited until mid-morning to drive over to Wilma's house. I took a long time driving around the area, scoping it out, before parking two blocks away. I did not really expect the police to be there, but I was still carrying Dorothea's map and was not eager for another chance encounter with Vera Cienfuegos.

There was plenty of reason to believe she might have heard about the map by then. Her sudden descent on the bank the previous day was proof enough that she had a full-bore investigation going, and she seemed thorough enough to have sent police officers through the neighborhood asking questions. Wilma would have been justified in telling those officers that she had given me the map, but apparently that had not happened. I had been home all night, and no one had come knocking.

That didn't rule out the chance that they might talk to Wilma at a later date, however, so I did not call ahead. I had already been threatened with an interference charge, and didn't want to be on record as having asked if the police had been by. I had only one question for Wilma, and hoped to get it answered without discussing the Preston cops at all.

"Oh, those rude young officers came by again yesterday, asking the same stupid questions!" Wilma blurted out when I knocked on her front door. So much for not discussing the police and their investigation. "I told them I didn't know what they were talking about, and just like that they turned around and left. They're *never* going to figure out that I was Dorothea's only friend, and I'm certainly not going to tell them."

I was not sure of that. The Preston police would probably ask Dorothea's other neighbors if the dead woman had any confidants, so it was unlikely that Wilma's special status would go unnoticed for much longer. Wilma's evasiveness, coupled with the map I now held, could very well land me the interference charge Vera had promised the other day. I was not working against Vera or the police, no matter how roughly the assistant DA had handled me, and I also did not want to get Wilma in hot water.

"Wilma, maybe you ought to enlighten them if they come back," I offered slowly, not sure if that would be such a good thing for me.

"Come back? How many times can they ask the same questions?"

"Quite a few. So if they ask if Dorothea gave you anything, go right ahead and tell them about the envelope and the map, and that you gave it to me. Most important, tell them I told you to do that."

"I'll do no such thing! They treated me like the village idiot right from the start, and all because I'm old. Well, how are they ever going to learn not to do that if I pretend it never happened? No. If they want answers from me, they're going to have to start with an apology."

She shifted gears with remarkable ease just then, patting my arm and offering me some tea. We settled into the now-familiar parlor, and I decided to give up on protecting myself from that interference charge. I might try to contact Vera myself a little later, probably through Chief Dannon, but at that moment I still had that question I wanted to ask.

"Wilma, I've been trying to find out who broke into Dorothea's safe-deposit box, and I came across a name I wanted to run by you. Did Dorothea ever mention a David Carver? He might have worked with Andy."

She had just taken a sip of her tea, and from the look on her face I would have guessed it was too hot. Her eyes opened wide, and the fingers holding the cup tensed up noticeably.

"David? You mean that wasn't just a story?"

"What story?"

"I thought she was just exaggerating!" Wilma's lips curled up into an immoral smile, and she began to chuckle. It took her a moment to regain her composure, but it was worth it when she was finally able to talk again.

"I don't know if this is the same man, because she never said his last name, but Dorothea told me there was a Davy many years ago. She'd been married a long time by then, and this Davy was quite sweet on her. She told me she'd had an affair with him, but of course I didn't believe her."

Though completely amazed by this development, I still managed to ask the obvious question.

"Why didn't you believe her?"

"Oh, Mr. Cole!" she scoffed. "We were two old widows swapping stories about our dead husbands. I made up at least two completely imaginary beaus just to keep the conversation interesting. I just assumed she did the same thing."

Before I left, I asked if Dorothea had ever suggested that something bad had happened to Davy. Wilma said no, but also admitted that she had found her neighbor's tale so fanciful that she had never even asked what had ended the relationship. I did not want to upset her, so I kept my quickly hardening suspicions to myself and got out of there.

As I saw it, Dorothea had been receiving cash payments from an unknown source because she had been blackmailing that individual. The map had been part of her blackmail leverage, so she had hidden it with Wilma. The map alone was not exactly proof of a crime, so it was likely that she had something to back it up. That backup might have been in her safe-deposit box, so it stood to reason that whoever was behind the raid on the bank was probably the one being blackmailed.

Assuming that the mark on the map indicated something incriminating, perhaps even the spot where Dorothea's deceased boyfriend Carver was buried, it made sense to believe that her blackmail victim had done the burying. Dorothea's illicit affair with the dead man provided an excellent motive for killing him, but I still could not see how that involved Temple.

I was sure that Temple had meant to show me the spot marked on the map. He might not have known about the map itself, or that I had it, but he had clearly been gauging my reaction. I had not yet noticed the mark at that time, so his little gambit had not paid off. Regardless of his motives, that simple act had put him right back on the suspect list.

But why had he taken me there at all? He had almost completely convinced me that he was not involved, and even the revelation of Dorothea's affair did little to bring him under suspicion. Andy Freehoffer, as the aggrieved husband, could have been expected to visit harm on Carver, but how would that point to Temple?

What was his part in all this? He had spoken highly of Freehoffer as a partner, so perhaps he had helped bury the geologist out of sheer loyalty. Perhaps he had even assisted in the killing. Every real estate man with whom I had spoken had recalled the eighties as a wild time in their circle. Temple and Freehoffer had been much younger then, and had gleefully broken the law in other aspects of their lives. They had grown confident in their ability to trick people, and their lawyer had shown he could extricate them from serious legal tangles. Had that feeling of invulnerability extended to the killing of the man stepping out with Freehoffer's wife?

That line of reasoning suggested a possible explanation for why Temple was playing his little game. Mark had said that the number of lawsuits lodged against Temple had decreased substantially since the early nineties; was it possible that the aging developer had grown bored with his more lawful middle age? Was Temple feeding me clues because the chase had resurrected sensations of excitement and danger, feelings that he missed?

I related to this idea because I was experiencing it myself. Mark's visit, as welcome as it was, had stirred up a host of intense memories.

I had caught myself, every now and then, looking at him and feeling pride in his success right alongside embarrassment at my failure. At times his presence made me feel as if I were still standing in the empty space that had housed my company, long after the movers had taken everything away, and at times that feeling turned into pure resentment. That feeling, I finally saw, had made me consider accepting a job from a man whom I now believed might be a murderer.

Yet another, darker idea came to mind on the heels of that one. Whoever the target of the blackmail was, a decades-old murder was probably the lever for that coercion. Had Dorothea unwittingly rekindled the same fire that had gripped David Carver's murderer so long ago, and had those flames consumed her?

I honestly considered going to see Chief Dannon a little later that day. My discussion with Wilma had left me worried about holding onto the map, largely because I was the only investigator who knew of its existence. Initially fearful that Wilma would tell the police about Dorothea's envelope, I now saw that the Preston cops' callous handling of Dorothea's neighbor had pretty much guaranteed they would never learn of it at all.

I would certainly tell them about the map if I ever determined who had raided the safe-deposit box, but that was starting to look doubtful. So far I had an inconclusive piece of blackmail evidence, a lawyer who wouldn't talk to me, and an overconfident real estate dealer who I suspected of burying a murder victim on the Ziegler property twenty years earlier.

Giving the map to the authorities would greatly aid their investigation, as it would shed light on why someone would want to rifle Dorothea's safe deposit. Even if they dismissed my suspicions about Temple, they were in a position to get information that I could not.

If Dorothea had been extorting money from someone, it was possible she had called that individual on the phone, and that her victim might have called her as well. The police could find that out.

Patterson might have an excuse for speaking with her on the phone, being the family lawyer, but a check on those records could cut both ways. Patterson had told the authorities that he was concerned about Dorothea because she had contacted him about some legal work and then failed to follow up. If he was lying about that, a check on the phone records might prove it. Granted, there are ways around this in the age of the disposable cell phone, but my point is I had no way of conducting such a search myself.

Thinking about Patterson finally convinced me to stay away from the police for at least a little while longer. I had only one reason for my involvement in this investigation, no matter how much Vera annoyed me or Temple mystified me: I was trying to find out who impersonated Freehoffer at the bank. My loyalty was to Susan, whose job seemingly hung in the balance over that very question. Going to the police at this juncture might point them at Patterson or even Temple, but it might not lead to the identity of the phony Freehoffer.

The investigation would not end for me until I knew who had tricked Susan, and had proven that to whoever might want to fire her for that mistake.

Gray called a little later and said Susan had agreed to meet me that afternoon at her place. Though still resistant, she would at least hear me out concerning a meeting with the former employee who had once supervised the safe-deposit area.

Susan's husband was mowing the lawn in front of their house when I rolled up. He cut the motor and shook my hand when I approached him. He was a short, round black man with gray hair, and he did not seem to be sweating in the late-day heat.

"Nice to meet you, Mr. Cole. Sue told me to watch for you. Go right on inside."

"Thank you." I started toward the modest house, but stopped before he started the machine again. "Hey, isn't it a little hot out to be doing this kind of work?"

"Maybe." He looked up at the sky, which was mostly blue just then. "But it's going to rain in just a bit, and I'd have to wait until it dried if I didn't cut it now."

Susan opened the screen door at that point, looking older than I remembered her. Like her husband, she was dressed for yard work in dirt-spotted shorts and an oversized shirt. She took me into the kitchen and gave me a drink of water before listening to my update. I needed to speak with the ex-employee she was shielding, and so I told her everything that I knew.

"Frank, I still don't see what somebody who briefly worked in the safe deposit could tell you," Susan stated when I was done telling her about the map and detailing the strange behavior of Andy Freehoffer's former business associates. She sounded tired, and for the first time I could imagine her forgoing the signature check on the fake Freehoffer just because she had been doing too many things at once.

"Look at it as cause-and-effect. I don't think that the impostor just decided to walk into the bank last Monday on a whim. I think that all the activity around the safe deposit spooked him, and he had to act fast. That's why he only had Andy's passport for an ID. I believe Dorothea was blackmailing somebody, and that it was either the impostor or someone who hired the impostor. Whoever was being blackmailed, I think he believed Dorothea's safe deposit contained the evidence against him."

"I don't see the connection between that and a former employee."

"The impostor knew that Andy Freehoffer's name was still on that access card. How could a stranger find that out without talking to someone familiar with those records?"

She considered that for a moment.

"If Dorothea was blackmailing the impostor, isn't it possible that she told him? It sounds like she had a bad habit of talking when she'd had too many."

That had occurred to me, but I considered it unlikely.

"That's possible, but she was being paid in cash and had almost no visitors. I can't see her tossing back a few stiff ones with someone who obviously wanted to stay in the shadows."

She chewed on that some more, so I went on.

"Susan, I'm not saying this former coworker of yours did anything wrong, at least not intentionally. In my old business there was always somebody from the competition sniffing around, and you'd be amazed at what they could find out from seemingly innocent conversations."

"Frank, I'm going to level with you. The woman who worked in the safe deposit isn't involved in this in any way."

"How do you know that? Is this a close personal friend or something?"

"I can't say we were exactly friends. I was always a little too strict for her." She caught herself, noticing for the first time that she had given me the employee's gender. "Look, she was at the bank for five years, she wasn't the best employee I've ever known, and I think she finally quit when she saw all the extra work that was coming at the safe-deposit area."

"Sue, I have got to talk to her. If she has nothing to do with the impostor, as you say, then this will clear her. But I cannot see someone walking into the bank with a thin disguise, a passport for an ID, and no idea if Dorothea's husband was on the access card."

She smiled weakly at this, and I couldn't tell if I had worn her down or if she had simply stopped trying to make me see reason.

"Okay, I'll set it up. But I have to be there."

"I wouldn't have it any other way."

CHAPTER TWELVE

I waited until dark to go look at the Ziegler property. As predicted by Susan's husband, it was pouring by then.

I had my reasons for visiting an abandoned weed lot in the dead of night in the middle of a rainstorm. Temple maintained that he had come into the ownership of this lot as part of buying out his competitor, but Doc Pepper had then shown that to be false. Temple had purchased the fenced-in parcel during the eighties, not long after supposedly depositing Carver's body there.

It seemed likely that the corpse had been dropped in the bottom of the hole meant for the foundation that Ziegler had been pouring at the time. The rest of the lot was supposed to have been developed shortly after the concrete hardened, so that would have been the only safe place on the property to bury it. Additionally, having a building constructed over the hasty grave would go a long way toward ensuring it was not discovered by accident.

Unfortunately for Temple, the development deal had gone south and the foundation was the only thing that had actually been completed. At that stage, he had a body buried under a useless block of concrete that would be the first thing to go if someone new tried to build something there. So Temple had purchased the land, ensuring such a thing would not happen. When he had bought out Ziegler's operation years later, he had reorganized his holdings to make it look like he'd purchased the dump spot along with Ziegler's other property.

Temple had owned the land for many years, and I believed that somewhere along the way Dorothea had learned about the body. Maybe she had always known. Maybe Andy had told her on his deathbed. Regardless of how she had discovered this secret, someone other than Temple had known about the body. I did not think the man I met would leave a corpse rotting on land he owned when there was an inviting expanse of ocean within eyesight. Particularly when someone else knew about it.

So I suspected that Temple had moved the body, which would have required the demolition of at least part of the foundation. I wanted to confirm this by having a look at it; if the slab was intact there was a chance the body was still down there. Sooner or later I expected a visit from Vera or Chief Dannon concerning Dorothea's map. With that in mind, I wanted to know if the Ziegler property might actually yield up a body before communicating my suspicions to the authorities.

I had planned to park somewhere off the road, which was still well traveled even at that hour. I slowed down as I went downhill toward the Ziegler lot, and saw through the lazy swish of the wipers that the rusted chain-link fence did not have an actual gate. An old mud-and-gravel access road shone in the headlights, and I drove straight onto the lot.

Killing the engine and the lights, I stepped out wearing a dark rain jacket and a black baseball hat. The rain was coming straight down, but there was almost no wind and I quickly moved through the knee-high weeds toward the compound's center. If any heavy equipment had worked this site in the last few years, there was no evidence of it.

I was far enough from the road to risk a flashlight by then, and began moving the beam back and forth as I walked. I found the foundation less than a minute later. It had not been large, and I would have guessed it was meant for a gas station or perhaps a convenience store before the deal was canceled. Even so, it made a nice pile of chopped-up stone, broken up by some kind of blade many years before and swept off to the back of the lot.

The dirt beneath the spot had settled over time, and it was impossible to tell if the machine that had ripped up the concrete had then set to digging for the prize hidden beneath. I walked across the depression, trying to see if there might be anything of interest in what remained. Twisted tendrils of reinforcing metal poked up from the pile of broken rock, and weeds sprouted through the cracks.

The wind picked up a bit just then, and a flickering movement caught my eye. Almost exactly in the middle of the muddy rectangle where the foundation had sat, a single reinforcing rod stuck up like a finger. A piece of red paper fluttered on the rusted flagpole at waist height, and I wondered how it had survived the elements for all that time as I approached.

I got my answer when I reached out and stopped the tag's movement. The string that secured it to the rebar was white and new, and so was the tag. Someone had thoughtfully laminated the small piece of red paper, but even so it was obvious that it had been placed there recently. The digging might have occurred long ago, but the tag was quite new.

I turned it over, at first unwilling to believe what I was seeing. On both sides, written in large script with a black marker, were the letters "RIP."

For the second time in as many days, I announced to an empty space that Brian Temple was playing with my mind.

Mark called while I was toweling myself off at home. I considered his sudden recall to Tallahassee to have been quite fortuitous, in that it had occurred just before I saw the mark on Dorothea's map. That alone made the map a significant item in Vera's investigation of Dorothea's death, and I was glad that my friend the attorney did not know about it. It was one thing for me to get hauled in for interference, but it was quite another for Mark.

I tried to keep him in the dark, focusing on Susan's promise to introduce me to the former bank employee, but it didn't work. He had been focused on the map just before he left, and his questions quickly established that there had been some progress in that area. I suggested that he might not want to know what I had learned, but he didn't accept that either and so I filled him in.

"That is just plain amazing," he said when I finished telling him of the red tag at the Ziegler property. "And you're right; he is playing with you. That 'RIP' notation means nothing in itself, so even if you take it to the police they aren't going to accept your conclusion that Temple put it there.

"And even if they do, it proves nothing. He dug the place up years ago, so whatever was under that foundation is long gone. You don't suppose Dorothea knew that, do you? That map becomes pretty slim blackmail material if the body's not there anymore."

"I thought about that. This fits what we were talking about the other day, the idea that there was more evidence than just the map. The solid stuff must have been in the safe deposit."

"Maybe. I've been thinking this whole thing over, and I had an idea about that. What if there really wasn't any solid evidence? What if the map was all there was? It wouldn't be the first time that someone threatened to reveal something they couldn't actually prove."

"I sure hope not. From the way Temple's been taunting me, he doesn't seem like the kind of guy you'd want to bluff."

"Speaking of that, do you think he knows about the map?"

"I doubt it. No one—Patterson, Vera, or the police—seems to know that Wilma was holding it for Dorothea. I think Temple was just trying to gauge my reaction when he took me out there on Friday, maybe find out how much I knew."

"So the tag was just some throwaway joke, then. If you figured out that he bought the land earlier than he said he had, you might go out there and see it. If not, it was just a marker with some letters in a vacant lot. That guy's not even a little bit worried, is he?"

"I'm afraid not. But I think I'm going to find something out when I talk to Susan's friend tomorrow. She worked in the safe deposit just before the complaint was lodged, and if Temple was sniffing around for information he might have spoken with her. He found out that Andy Freehoffer was still on the access card somehow, and if this lady can identify him, it should be enough to take to the police."

"Don't do anything until we talk. I'll be back around mid-afternoon, and I want to go over what you've got before you talk to the cops."

"I was thinking about that, too. Maybe you ought to stay up there until after I've spoken to Dannon. There's no reason for you to get dragged into this."

"As if it's not going to come out when they start asking you questions. Besides, I worked hard on this thing and I want to be there when you try to explain it to Vera. That's not going to be easy, you know."

"That's what I mean. Can you afford to get in trouble right about now?"

"Me? I'm just your helper. Besides, I've got a great new job offer here in Florida and a promotion waiting for me up in New York. I don't think I've got much to worry about."

"So they made you an offer?"

"Yep. The money's not what I'd be making up in NYC, but the benefits are better and of course they were pushing the locale as family-friendly. I was hoping they'd do that."

"Why?"

"So I could tell them I had to talk it over with the missus."

"You are one conniving lawyer man, aren't you?"

"That's another reason you want me with you when you talk to the authorities. Call me as soon as you're done with Susan's friend, even if it leads nowhere. We'll meet up after that and decide on what to do next."

Susan was a churchgoer, as am I, and so that was how Sunday began. Susan's attendance lasted almost until lunch, so I picked her up at her place just after noon. She was still wearing her Sunday best, which was a peach-colored dress with a wide-brimmed straw hat. I was wearing my lightest suit and dreading the heat. The rain had ended just before dawn, and the sun was high in a deep blue Panhandle sky.

She gave me directions after we pulled away, and we headed for Bending Palms, the town just to the west of Exile. I did not press her for the former employee's name, but she gave it to me without being asked.

"Her name is Imogene Crandall. We called her Midge. Not a bad employee, but she required a lot of supervision. I felt she was the type that would goof off if you didn't watch her."

"The safe-deposit area seems a bad place to put someone like that."

"I told Ollie not to put her back there. She didn't get a darn thing done, and was always whining about being all alone. That's what you're going to find out when you talk to her. She quit because she didn't like being all alone in the safe-deposit area all day."

"I don't doubt it. But I really need to know if someone was asking questions about the Freehoffer box before the complaint was registered. I think that the complaint forced the impostor to speed up his plans, and that he had been scoping out the safe-deposit area long before he made his move."

We pulled up outside a tiny white house in a middle-class section of Bending Palms, and Susan led the way to the door. Midge Crandall met us before we could knock, and invited us in from the midday heat. She was a slightly chubby redhead with a very pretty face, and I would have guessed her age at around forty.

"Susan has said some very nice things about you, Mr. Cole," Midge began once we were seated in her living room. Her place was so small that it reminded me of my own. "I do hope you can find out who that impostor was."

"Well, that's why we're here." I removed a copy of Temple's picture from my briefcase and showed it to her. "Have you ever seen this man before?"

She gave the picture a close once-over, and then shook her head.

"I don't think so. But he does have a pretty common-looking face. Maybe I met him and didn't know it." I suspected this observation was Midge's way of letting Susan off the hook for having been fooled by a man fitting Freehoffer's description.

"All right. How long did you work in the safe-deposit area?"

"Oh, just a little over six weeks. I really hated it. The lighting is awful, and I was all alone. I had people to chat with when I worked as a teller, but not back there."

"Did anyone ever approach you to ask about how the safe-deposit area was run? Ask you where the access cards were kept, maybe?"

"No, I can't say anyone did. New customers always had some kind of question, is that what you're asking about?"

"It could be." I had wondered if Temple might have gained access to the safe-deposit signature cards by posing as a new customer or even renting a box. "The questions I'm interested in would have concerned who had access to what box, particularly Dorothea Freehoffer's."

"No, no one asked any questions like that. I've wracked my brains ever since Susan called, trying to remember if anyone asked about that box, but honestly I had never heard the name Freehoffer in my life until Sue called."

I was beginning to get that feeling, the one where your team is far behind and the game clock is running out. It seemed Susan had been right about this being a dead end. I didn't want to be unkind, but I did have one last question. Midge had quit just after the complaint was lodged against the safe deposit, and that had never sat level for me.

"Midge, can you tell me why you left the bank?"

I half expected her to get defensive at that, so her reaction was a little unexpected. A silly smile cracked her lips, and she blushed straight down into her dress. I glanced over at Susan, and was pleased to see that she found this response as odd as I did.

"Did I say something funny?" I smiled, trying to keep it light, but I needn't have bothered. Midge made one last effort to contain herself, and then gave up entirely.

"Oh, Ollie said it's all right to tell people now, so I'm just going to say it!" For a moment there she looked like a ten-year-old about to share a very big secret. "Ollie and I are seeing each other, and he just couldn't get used to the idea of dating an employee. Said it looked wrong, silly man."

"Wait a minute." Susan leaned forward in her seat. "You told me you left because Ollie put you in the safe deposit."

"I know. He did. That was my cover story! We agreed I would stop working at the bank, and he didn't want anyone guessing why, so he put me in the back so I would have an excuse for quitting."

My PI friends tell me that people lie for the most astounding reasons, and I have found this to be true in my work as a fact-checker. Even so, no lie I had encountered to date was as outlandishly motivated as this one. Susan had disregarded any connection between Midge and the original complaint against the bank because she believed she knew why the redhead had quit. Although the truth proved her to be half right, Susan did not seem thrilled about it.

"Why, that devious old dog. And here I thought I knew everything that went on in that bank."

We wished Midge good luck with her new relationship before getting back on the road. The whole episode had taken less than half an hour, and I got the impression that Susan was even more disappointed in the interview than I was, though for different reasons. As for me, I had earnestly hoped for some kind of confirmation that the impostor had been planning his escapade before the complaint was filed, and so this was a letdown.

"Susan, can you talk to the other tellers for me? Ask around to see if anybody was trying to sniff out information about the Freehoffer box before the impostor showed up?"

"Frank, I grilled everyone in the bank as soon as I found out that Andy Freehoffer was dead. No one remembers being asked anything about that box."

I shook my head, trying to reorient my thinking now that my big lead had turned out to be nothing. Mark had said that it was time to tell the police what we knew, but now we were going to have to do that with very little evidence and a whole lot of supposition.

That was when Susan asked the question I should have been asking right from the start.

"Frank, you said that lawyer—"

"Patterson."

"That this Patterson was the one who brought the police to Mrs. Freehoffer's house the day after the impostor came to the bank."

"Right."

"And Patterson was walking around the neighborhood trying to find out where she might have stashed her valuables."

"Yes."

"And that was after he'd been inside Mrs. Freehoffer's house long enough to start inventorying her belongings?"

"Right again."

"Well, why didn't he call the bank? I left those messages on her machine, and we never heard from him."

CHAPTER THIRTEEN

I now felt I had found something that would make Patterson talk to me, and I called Mark just after dropping Susan off.

"That's right, she left at least two messages on Dorothea's phone machine after Patterson had gained access to the house, and he still hasn't contacted the bank. Doesn't exactly fit the picture of a lawyer trying to locate his deceased client's assets, does it?"

"Amazing." Mark was already on the road back to Exile. "You know, I never understood his involvement, right from the start. No lawyer I know would expose himself the way this guy has. He's the only face that anybody can connect with the hunt for Dorothea's valuables, and he got the police to open up her house on pretty flimsy reasons. But now we've finally got a big question to ask him."

"Exactly. When he walked away from me the other day I had nothing I could use to make him stop, but this is a question he's got to answer. And if he won't, then we're headed straight to the Preston police with everything we know."

"Oh, he'll talk to us." Mark sounded strangely confident, and I waited for him to explain his optimism. "Think about it: He didn't return Susan's phone calls because he knew the safe-deposit box had already been emptied. So that probably means he's working with Temple. If that's the case, why would he let himself become the only face from the old days that's been seen around that neighborhood? I understand loyalty up to a point, but he's really hung himself out to dry here just for an old business buddy."

"What do you mean?"

"It's so simple I'm surprised I didn't think of it earlier. There's only one reason Patterson would be taking the chances he's taken here: He was in on Carver's disappearance. He's got just as much to lose as Temple does. That's why he was trying so hard to find out what Dorothea was holding, and where it was hidden."

"I'm not going to speak with either one of you."

Patterson said this from behind the screen door of his simple two-story house in Preston. Mark and I had formulated a basic plan for getting him to talk, and had headed out to his place just as the sun was setting.

"That's fine. Maybe you'd like to do some reading instead." Mark sounded bored as he uttered his lines, and even managed to look detached when he held up a color copy of Dorothea's map. We had folded it so the Ziegler property was in the dead center, and I had added a stick-on arrow in case Dorothea's mark wasn't easy to see.

Patterson was dressed in a baggy set of khaki pants and an oversized shirt that didn't hide his belly. He matched Mark's disinterest when he glanced at the map, and looked at us without giving any indication that it scared him.

"And that is . . . what?"

"Told you," I quipped to Mark as if I had won a bet. I smiled at Patterson and started back down the short walkway toward the street.

We were parked several doors down, and had watched his house for a while to make sure he was home.

"Hang on a second," Mark called after me. He turned back to Patterson. "Maybe you don't recognize this, so I'll tell you what it is. Dorothea Freehoffer gave this map to a friend to hold for her, and the friend gave it to us. See that little X mark? Your old friend Temple took my buddy here out to look at that exact spot just the other day."

I walked back up to the door. "Nice place, looks like somebody tried to build something there about twenty years ago. Even had a foundation, but somebody dug it up for some reason."

"Get out of here," Patterson burst out gruffly, reaching to shut the door while shaking his head as if we were two escaped lunatics. Mark had not expected to crack him with the map, so he was ready with his next line.

"Just one thing, Mr. Patterson, before we go see the police. Why didn't you return the phone messages left by Dorothea's bank?"

The door stopped moving when Patterson heard that one, and for the first time he actually showed a sign of concern. Our little gambit with the map had gotten him wondering just what his buddy Brian was up to, but the question about the phone messages was just the kind of thing that the police would want to know.

"Now hold on. I was trying to determine if any of Dorothea's property had been borrowed or stolen. That was the first step in assessing her estate. Anything in her name at that bank was secure right where it was. I just didn't get around to them yet."

We had reached the end of our prepared lines, so it was just as well that he had started talking. Even so, I turned to Mark as if Patterson weren't even there.

"Oh, I don't know if I buy that one. Those messages asked Dorothea to call back regarding an issue with her safe-deposit box. I would have expected her lawyer, the guy trying to assess her estate, to return a call like that."

Mark chimed in softly, "I'm a lawyer. I would have returned those calls."

The gears in Patterson's head were already spinning. Mark and I had hoped to prod him into recognizing that he was the public face of whatever sinister forces were at work here, and it seemed to be working.

Patterson had first appeared in this scheme when he summoned the police to Dorothea's house, and he'd followed that entrance with a visit to every one of the neighbors. He'd had access to Dorothea's house right up until the police had begun to investigate her death in earnest. The Preston cops had then canvassed the neighborhood, and even though they'd been rebuffed by Wilma it was likely they had asked Patterson a few questions as well. By now he probably saw what Mark had seen: Temple was well hidden in the shadows while he, Patterson, was heavily exposed.

Even so, he knew better than to say anything in the presence of two witnesses. He looked back and forth between us, as if trying to choose, but Mark knocked that idea right out of his head.

"But maybe we're just plain wrong. I'm sure he's telling us the truth, and he just got busy. So let's take our map and our questions down to the Preston police station and see what they make of it." He looked up at Patterson, without making a move to leave. "Of course, when we're done with that, the police are going to take a very close look at the phone records between you and Dorothy Freehoffer. How do you think those'll match up with that crazy lie you told about having arranged to meet with her?"

Patterson's mouth swung open slowly, and he exhaled a weak breath of air that was just loud enough to be heard. He pushed the screen door open with a defeated sweep of his arm, and motioned us inside.

"A couple of Preston detectives already talked to me." Patterson spoke slowly, as if he'd already considered a conversation like this one. "They didn't read me my rights, but they're digging away at this thing. I figured they'd be back by now."

"They will be. And you have to decide who they're going to listen to. You or Temple." I was seeing Mark's professional face just then, and so I let him talk. Judging from Patterson's body language, he was ready to throw in the towel.

Even so, I stayed standing while Mark and Patterson sat facing each other in his living room. This was where my work with private investigators gave me an advantage over Mark; I had been warned about the too-friendly suspect who takes you inside his house and then comes up with a gun. Although he was still well below my normal weight and not exactly a street fighter, I was watching the fat man closely and hoping he believed I was armed.

"Why wouldn't they listen to me? Brian brought me in on this thing just to ask a few questions."

"Was that after he went to the safe deposit?"

"Of course. If he'd found anything in that box, he might have left me out of this completely." He sighed and looked at the floor. "Lord, I wish he had."

So the box had been empty, forcing Temple to recruit some help for a more extensive search. He'd contacted his old buddy and asked him to use his cover as the Freehoffer family lawyer to go look through the house. He'd put Dorothea's handbag in plain sight to help Patterson convince the police to break in, and probably told him to check around the neighborhood, too.

"Did he kill Dorothea?" Mark resumed.

"No!" Patterson came back to life just then. "She'd called him up and told him some nutty story about her bank opening all the safe-deposit boxes, and how she was going to just sit back and let them open hers unless he came up with more money. He told me she'd been blackmailing him ever since Andy died. He went to see her, and there she was at the bottom of the stairs. So he went through the place, found the key, and decided to try and pass himself off as Andy."

I tried to keep my jaw from dropping. If this was true, Temple had basically winged it the entire way. All my suspicions about a well-conceived plan, accelerated by the complaint at the bank, went out the window.

"Wait a minute." I stepped a little closer. "How did he know Andy Freehoffer was still on the access card? And that a passport would be good enough for identification?"

Both Patterson and Mark looked at me as if I were a child interrupting the grown-ups. Patterson answered first.

"You've met Brian. The guy could talk his way into Fort Knox. I didn't ask, but believe me he didn't *have* to know anything about how that place operated. Access card or no access card, if he had the key, he was in."

"So Dorothea was blackmailing him over Carver." Mark tried to get Patterson back on track, now that my outburst had subsided.

"Yeah. Brian and Andy buried him right where that X is on your map."

"But you helped." Patterson looked ready to debate that, but

Mark didn't let him get started. "That's the only sane explanation for your getting involved in this. You wouldn't stick your neck out this far, bringing the police to Dorothea's house and then asking all those questions, if it wasn't already on the chopping block. So what was it? You were there when it happened, or you just helped get rid of him?"

I'd learned a few things about asking questions in my time as an investigator, and Mark's corporate background was starting to show. He was answering some of his own questions even as he asked them, but luckily Patterson was too beaten to play any games.

"I swear I only helped get rid of him." He looked up at me, and then back at Mark. "I didn't even know the kid was stepping out with Dorothea. Nobody did. Not that I would have cared."

He suddenly got animated, half rising from his seat.

"You had to *be there*! Those were some wild times. The money was flowing, the deals were stacking up, and more than a few of us were sniffing the Happy Dust if you get my meaning. It was one long party, girls everywhere, so who cared if somebody was running around?"

"Somebody did," I offered.

"Yeah, somebody did." He got quiet just then, but we let him decide when to continue. "Brian and Dorothea were always at each other's throats, fighting over who was going to tell Andy what to do. I bet it was the best day in Brian's life when he found out Dorothea was cheating with Carver.

"I don't know exactly when he told Andy, but you can bet it didn't take him long. Anyway, there was this one party, over at the Davis yacht club when it was nothing more than a boat launch. That was back when you could have a bonfire on the beach without filing an environmental impact statement. Must have been fifty people drifting in and out, all the nice cars pulled up near the sand with the lights on and the music blasting.

"I was pretty loaded when it began to break up, so I decided to catch a few winks in my car before heading home. The next thing I know, Brian's tapping on the glass and telling me to open the trunk. It must've been three in the morning. The bonfire was almost dead, nobody was around anymore, and they dragged that kid right across the sand to my car."

He stopped, shutting his eyes as if to block out the memory.

"Why'd they involve you?"

"That's easy. Andy and Brian owned these flashy two-seaters, the ones with no trunk space at all. I was still a step or two behind them in the money department, so I was driving this old four-door. They'd wrapped him up in a blanket, so I asked who it was."

"Let me get this straight." Regardless of how much I wanted him to keep talking, his story had started to sound too much like a gangster movie. "Two of your clients dragged a dead body up to your car, getting ready to put him in your trunk, and the only thing you could ask was who it was?"

"Two of my clients? They were my *only* clients! If it weren't for them I would have been pumping gas for a living! Besides, I'd been covering their butts for years by then, and they never lost a single case when I was their lawyer. It was second nature to help them.

"And you know something else? I knew it was Carver before they told me. Know why? Because somebody was going to do it sooner or later. That kid was the dirtiest little double-crosser you ever met. I never trusted him even for a minute, and I kept telling Brian and Andy to get away from him. But they wouldn't listen to me, and all because that kid was laying the golden eggs. Man, did I loathe that guy. I used to sit up nights wondering when he was going to get my meal tickets sent to jail. I was glad he was gone. I still am.

"So I asked who it was, and Brian told me the kid had been two-timing Andy with Dorothea. Andy was going through a Tough Guy phase at the time, carrying around this shiny little pocket automatic that he was always waving around. I put two and two together and asked where we were headed."

"The Ziegler property."

"Brian had land right next to it, so he knew they were going to pour that foundation the very next day. It was way off the beaten path, not like it is now, and all we had to do was bury him in the bottom of the hole they'd already dug. The three of us watched the concrete go in from up on Brian's property, sitting on the hood of my car and drinking beers.

"That's when Andy told me he didn't shoot the kid. Brian was answering nature's call, and Andy leaned over and said he didn't do it. Brian had told him about Carver and his wife, and they'd agreed to take the kid aside and shoot him. They told Carver they had a new deal to discuss, and walked off down the beach to a deserted spot. The kid began begging for his life when he realized what was happening, and Andy told me he didn't have the heart to do it.

"So he said Brian just walked up, took the gun out of his hand, and shot Carver in the head. That's why Brian was paying Dorothea off. She said she had the gun, that Andy had written up a description of what happened before he died, and that she'd take the whole thing to the authorities if he didn't pay her."

"There was supposed to be a gun in the safe deposit?" Mark asked with a concerned look on his face.

"Not just any gun. *The* gun."

"You sure it wasn't there?"

"What do you mean?"

"I mean, you've got to be crazy to believe that Temple found Dorothea dead. She was blackmailing him, she had just upped the demands, and somehow she accidentally fell down the steps?"

"The police said the coroner ruled it as an accident."

"So Temple got lucky with the way he tossed her."

"So what if he did?"

Mark shook his head in disgust.

"What kind of lawyer are you? The only face that anybody connects with Dorothea's accident is yours. Temple's been in the background this whole time. You helped bury the body, you already said you hated Carver, the blackmail was paid in cash, put it together, will you?

"If that gun was in the safe deposit, Temple's got it. He knows the police are digging into this, so he needs to make them stop. And what would make them do that better than the lawyer who was asking the questions, the one who was Andy Freehoffer's buddy, dead in his house holding the pistol that Freehoffer used to wave around?

"Heck, they wouldn't even need a suicide note."

"That's nonsense. Brian dumped Carver's body out at sea years ago, so the gun's got no significance. And if they can't trace the cash to Brian, the guy who actually paid it, how could they trace it to me? Killing me wouldn't stop this thing."

Mark leaned forward with a blank look on his face.

"Keep on talking. Maybe you'll even convince yourself one of these days. But here's one thing you've missed: There's no way that Temple could have known the coroner would rule Dorothea's death an accident. He had to assume the police would treat this as a homicide. So, did he try to hide the body, like he did with Carver? No. He went to the safe deposit, almost guaranteeing that somebody would investigate Dorothea's death. And just supposing he told you the truth, and the box was empty, what did he do then?

"Go back and get rid of the body? No again. Instead, he called you. He didn't know the coroner would rule this was an accident, but he called you anyway. Later, he fed clues to my buddy here when he saw we weren't letting this one go. He meant for you to take the rap here, right from the start."

At the time, I considered Mark's impromptu suggestion that Patterson's life was in danger to be a bit overblown. Patterson didn't think so, however, and he quietly agreed to accompany us to the Preston police headquarters. I thought it would have made little difference if he had refused, believing the police would have rounded him up after we spoke to them, but that was only until we got outside.

Temple was coming up the walk when we came out the door. It was the first time I had seen him without a tie on, but what really struck me was the darkness of his clothing. He was wearing black trousers, black training sneakers, and a blue windbreaker. The windbreaker had a hood that he could have quickly pulled up over his head as a disguise, and his hands were both inside the pockets of the baggy jacket. The whole scene brought Mark's observations about Andy Freehoffer's missing pistol to mind.

It was quite late by then, and the street was deserted. I was in the lead, and for the briefest moment thought I detected a wild light in Temple's eyes. This was the same man who had intentionally dropped clues in front of me, and one of the lawyers following behind me knew him as a cold-blooded killer. There was a long moment, standing there, when I believed he had made the decision to take out the gun and start blasting.

"Hold it," I said in a voice that was surprisingly firm. I had wrestled someone for a handgun a little more than a week before, and had no desire to try it again. "They might believe one dead lawyer inside the house, but three dead bodies on the lawn? No way they'll buy that."

The words were a continuation of Mark's argument, but they struck a chord with Temple nonetheless. He turned his head slightly, as if hearing a far-off noise and trying to determine its origin, and then relaxed. A slight smile slipped onto his lips.

"People have been buying things from me all my life, Frank. I don't think there's anything I couldn't sell." He looked past me. "You sounded a little stressed on the phone, Gary. I thought I'd come by and check on you. Everything all right?"

Patterson looked ready to faint. If he hadn't felt threatened earlier, he sure did now. Mark was standing directly in front of him with a cold look on his face, and I saw that Patterson's hand was gripping his shoulder. Even so, Temple's old friend managed to speak to him.

"It's over, Brian. They know everything."

I half expected that statement to restart Temple's internal argument over whether or not to shoot all three of us, but it had the opposite effect. Temple smiled broadly, as if he'd just received good news.

"I don't know what you're talking about, Gary. Where are you and your new friends going?"

"To the police," Mark answered, still staring Temple down. "They're expecting us. Now why don't you get out of the way?"

Temple gave a shrug and took both hands out of his pockets. He held them open a little away from his sides, and stepped onto the grass to let us go by. I stayed where I was while Mark walked Patterson to the car.

I waited until I heard the engine start, and then quickly walked away. Temple was still smiling when I turned my back, and just before I got in the car he called my name.

"Hey, Frank! Remember, I expect to hear from you about that job. Call me in the morning."

CHAPTER FOURTEEN

Once we put a few blocks between us and Temple, Mark suggested that I call Chief Dannon. I was still focused on the wraith back on Patterson's lawn, and at first did not understand what Mark was getting at. That was when I remembered we had discussed this prior to visiting Patterson. We were about to present the Preston cops with a major suspect in an investigation they were running, and it might help to have a police officer they knew and respected speak up for us before we got there. Despite Mark's lie to Temple back on the lawn, no one knew we were on our way.

Chief Dannon was asleep when I called, but he was used to getting shaken out of bed and quickly grasped our situation. He promised to call the Preston police station just after getting off the phone with me.

Preston is a bigger town than Exile or Bending Palms, but it is by no means a city. They do have real detectives on the Preston force, though, and one of them was talking to the desk sergeant when we walked in. Mark had suggested that Patterson do the talking, largely because the local cops knew him, and also because he was there to confess. That was how my college roommate and I ended up in the lobby of the Preston police station early on a Monday morning while a man who had buried a murder victim twenty years earlier spoke for the three of us.

The aforementioned detective came out from behind the desk once Patterson was done talking. He was a slim, fortyish man in light trousers and a white civilian shirt who introduced himself as Detective Al Melvin. He had spoken with Chief Dannon just a few minutes earlier, and had immediately called Vera after that conversation had ended. He suggested that Mark and I take a seat in the lobby.

He took Patterson by the arm and walked him through a door that presumably led to an interrogation room. The place got very quiet right about then, and Mark and I exchanged glances of surprise and confusion. We had been prepared to be treated as possible suspects ourselves, and even with Dannon's phone call we had not expected to be handled this loosely. I felt like a cabdriver who has just been asked to wait with the meter running.

The lobby had a few chairs, and so we sat down. Mark had suggested that we watch our words once we got to the station, so neither of us said a thing. The desk sergeant, a tall, balding man in a khaki uniform, finally broke the silence.

"You guys want some coffee?"

Things did not stay quiet for long. The Preston police chief, a short, stocky man named Waters, came through the doors first. He was dressed in the blue Preston police uniform and had found the time to shave. He conferred briefly with the desk sergeant, a whispered conversation that seemed to focus on what Mark and I were doing in the lobby. The desk sergeant's answer was too low to hear, but Chief

Waters apparently did not like it. He abruptly shook his head as if dismissing a bad thought, and without another word went through the door that had consumed Patterson twenty minutes earlier.

A couple of middle-aged men in civilian clothes entered the station a short time later. They were unshaven but awake, and gave us the long look as they passed by on their way into the building's back offices. I was starting to enjoy the fuss and confusion we had created when Vera came through the double-glass doors. Her hair was hastily piled on top of her head, but otherwise she looked remarkably composed for someone who had probably been roused from a sound sleep to learn that one of her investigations had been solved by an amateur. She glared at me without a word, and disappeared into the station's interior.

Things got quiet again, and Mark finally decided to break the monotony. He kept his voice low, in case the desk sergeant was listening.

"You know, you really stepped up back there. On Patterson's lawn when Temple showed up. Your PI friends teach you that?"

"I couldn't think of anything else to do. I was sure he was going to take out a gun and start blasting."

"That's what I thought, too." Mark went quiet for a moment, and then spoke with just a touch of excitement in his voice. "I gotta tell you, I am having a lot of fun down here."

I had feared this would be his reaction, and that it would affect the Ruben family's possible relocation to the Panhandle. It was time for us to have that little conversation.

"Enjoy it while it lasts. As far as I'm concerned, this case is closed and it's time for you to go back to NYC."

"I've got a job offer down here."

"You've got a promotion up there."

"I've got a baby on the way, and there are some nice wide-open spaces down here."

"That baby's parents are two native New Yorkers, and there's plenty of open space in the suburbs."

"I'm looking for something new."

"No you're not." I turned to look him square in the eye. "You're a little intimidated by the corner office, that's all. I know the feeling. When the banks finally approved the loan I needed to start my business, I almost didn't sign the papers. I'd been chasing them for over a year, and at that moment I almost turned around and ran away.

"It was just fear of the unknown, nothing more. And no matter how it turned out in the end, one of the best things I ever did was take the plunge and start that business. As for you, you're about to get the thing you've been working toward your entire life, and I'm not going to have you living next door when you realize you walked away from it."

We both went quiet again for a full minute. I was beginning to wonder if I'd gone too far when Mark spoke.

"We weren't going to move next door to you. We would have lived in Tallahassee, close enough to the office for me to ride a bike to work." I didn't reply to that, noting the tense of the verbs he was using. "You were the one who was going to have to move."

"Me? Why would I move?"

"I told Miriam you'd be on call all day every day as a babysitter. It's the only reason she even considered coming down here. Exile's too far away from Tallahassee for that, so you would have had to move."

"Mark Ruben. Youngest partner in the history of the firm."

"Looks that way, doesn't it? Now that my oldest friend in the world says he doesn't want me next door."

"I'll move next door to you someday. Count on it."

Chief Dannon arrived just after that, dressed in the gray uniform of the Exile police. Like Chief Waters, he had managed to shave and was greeted in a familiar fashion by the desk sergeant. He waved at us before asking the khaki-clad officer a few questions, and then walked over.

"He confessed?"

"The Preston police had already talked to him earlier, so they should get most of the credit," Mark answered in a voice loud enough for the desk man to hear. "But yeah, he told us everything."

"So this Patterson killed the woman who was renting the safe-deposit box?"

Mark and I exchanged glances. We had assumed, ever since Vera's surprise search at the bank in Exile, that she and the Preston police had been conducting a wide-ranging investigation. Suspicion of Temple just seemed to go along with that assumption, and their earlier decision to let Patterson sweat awhile at home suggested that they believed he was not in this alone.

Chief Dannon's question knocked all of that into a cocked hat. For a smug instant I imagined Vera sitting in a Preston interrogation room with Patterson, hearing of the magical Brian Temple for the very first time, but that image didn't last long. Chief Dannon might have been with Vera and the troops when they searched Dorothea's safe-deposit box, but perhaps they had neglected to keep him informed after that. Over in Exile he was the chief, but that did not necessarily entitle him to a blow-by-blow report on a Preston police investigation. At any rate, Chief Dannon was in the dark about what had brought an impostor to the bank in his town, and he deserved to know what was going on.

I motioned to the seat next to mine.

"Have a seat, Chief. This gets pretty confusing."

I did not know the half of it. We sat outside for another hour before someone asked for Chief Dannon, and he disappeared behind the lobby door just like the others. A short time later a Preston police officer came out and asked if we had Dorothea's map in our possession.

Mark went to the car to get it, and the cop asked me a couple of basic questions while we waited. He wanted to know if Wilma had given me anything more than the map, or if Dorothea had told her to do anything with it if something happened to her. I said no to both inquiries, and he took the map and its original envelope through the door.

Some official-looking people in suits arrived at the station just after that, which prompted Mark to speak.

"Those last folks, the ones in the suits, I bet they're some of Vera's colleagues. Maybe even her superiors."

"Think they're here to work up the charges?"

"I sure hope so. I've been going over what Patterson told us in my head while we've been sitting here, and the more I consider it the more circumstantial it becomes. I'm not a criminal lawyer, but there are a few things here that are starting to bother me.

"Patterson didn't see Carver get killed. And Freehoffer, the guy who told him Temple did it, is dead. The body's not out at the Ziegler property anymore, and . . ." He trailed off for a second, and then he spoke in a quiet, urgent voice. "Hey, did Patterson ever say he actually *saw* the body? He said it was wrapped in a blanket. If he didn't see enough of the body to definitely say it was Carver, Temple's lawyer could do just about anything with that. He could even say it was just a gag and there wasn't a body at all."

My stomach began tightening up on me. That was why this was taking so long. Patterson was in there spilling everything he knew, but the people from the state attorney's office were having a hard time finding anything solid. Mark's question jogged my memory, and I gave him an answer I did not like.

"Freehoffer told him that Temple shot Carver in the head. Freehoffer wouldn't have had to tell him that if Patterson had looked at the body and recognized it as Carver. Would he?"

"It depends. Patterson thinks they used Freehoffer's gun, and that sounds like some kind of small caliber pocket gun. Some of those don't make too much of a—"

The door opened, and the official-looking guys swept by as if they had somewhere to be. They didn't look terribly unhappy, so I tried to convince myself that they were arranging for the speedy arrest of Brian Temple.

The door opened just after they left, and Dannon came out wearing a somber expression. We stood while he walked over to us.

"Good job, guys. As usual, the lawyers are making this a lot more complicated than it has to be." He caught himself, and dropped a hand on Mark's shoulder while chuckling quietly. "Sorry, Mark, I meant government lawyers.

"Anyway, it looks like they're going to question Temple at some point, but they've got a few more things to iron out first. Vera's very concerned that the case boils down to Patterson's word against Temple's."

"Speak of the devil," Mark said in a normal voice when the door opened yet again. Vera followed two Preston police officers into the lobby and walked toward us with a bemused smile.

"Well done, Frank. Well done." She spoke in a soft, pleased voice, but I didn't buy her act for a minute. "Thanks to you, our investigation is completely blown. Do you know that there isn't a single phone call connecting Brian Temple to Dorothea Freehoffer? Incoming, outgoing, you name it."

So she had known of the magical Brian Temple before that night. She must have had people pulling phone records for quite some time, to have such an accurate picture of the communication between Dorothea and Temple. Or the lack thereof.

"That doesn't prove a thing. Ever heard of a cell phone?" Mark's voice took on a spiteful edge, and he slipped between Dannon and me to get right in Vera's face. She didn't back off at all, and it swiftly became apparent that someone had told her Mark Ruben was a lawyer. She gave me a malicious glance before responding with the same line I'd used a few days before.

"Where'd you get your law degree? If I can't *prove* it, it didn't happen. Dorothea called Temple's office the Friday before she died, but the call only lasted a minute. There's no proof she even got through to him. A short time later someone called her house on a disposable cell phone, so guess what? I may know in my heart that it was Temple, and that during that conversation Dorothea gave him the demand that made him decide to kill her, but I can't prove it."

Although Mark was only inches from her, Vera had kept her voice calm and level. She sounded like a mother patiently explaining something simple to a wayward child.

"So Dorothea's death is now considered a murder?" I interjected in a neutral tone, trying to imitate her.

"What did I just say? I *know* it was a murder, but there's no proof.

The medical examiner found no evidence of foul play. Me, I think she was thrown down those stairs, but without a witness or a confession she died by accident. There are no signs of forced entry, nothing's missing, and there are no prints that we can't explain. Exactly what I told you three days ago."

"If Dorothea called Temple's office, someone must have taken that call. Would the receptionist be able to tell us if Temple spoke to her?" I offered.

"As of yesterday, maybe. But that was before you two told Temple you were taking his lawyer to the police. You see, we sent a couple of detectives to talk to Patterson, and they said he was close to cracking. We were hoping he'd finally see his predicament and give us a call, but without Temple knowing about it. But that's all gone now. As of right now, Temple's had hours to get his story together, and all thanks to our amateur sleuths."

Something strange happened then. Perhaps Mark's visit had stirred up one bankruptcy memory too many, perhaps Vera simply reminded me of all the legal people who had called me names up north, and maybe I was just tired. Vera's last comments, the ones about hoping Patterson would crack without Temple knowing it, brought back the image of Temple in the dark clothes, and I knew what to say. I stepped between Mark and the chief and let it out.

"Oh, lady, you are so full of it." I caught both Mark's and Dannon's surprised looks, but I was in full swing and that wasn't going to stop me. "You were waiting for Patterson to crack? And we ruined it? If it weren't for me and Mark, that guy would be *dead* right now. Temple came to his place to *kill* him, and your case would have ended right there. You've got a witness only because of us."

I felt Mark's hand on my upper arm, and it was not making a suggestion. I didn't even look at him, staring instead into Vera's cold calm eyes and wondering why she wasn't responding. I didn't get to think about that for long, as the desk sergeant called over to her and said she was wanted in the back.

Vera shook her head as if realizing she had been arguing with an idiot, and went back inside without another word. I tugged my arm away from Mark once she was gone, and took a few steps around the lobby. My heart was pounding, but it felt good.

"Chief?" Mark asked behind me.

"Yes, Mark."

"Why hasn't anyone taken a statement from Frank and me?"

Chief Dannon took some time to explain that the Preston police were a bit leery of any official connection with our investigation. He believed they wanted to portray us as little more than the guys who drove Patterson to the station. They felt we could not provide them with anything that Patterson had not, and I was happy to let them take that approach.

I lived in the area and was perfectly happy to answer whatever questions might come up, but I wanted Mark to be free of this thing. With the issue of his possible relocation to the Panhandle settled, I did not want to see Mark forced to come back to testify in a case that truly did not involve him.

Dannon made sure we were free to go, and the desk sergeant waved us a cheery good-bye as we left. The sun was almost up when we stepped outside, and Dannon stopped short once the doors closed behind us. Both Mark and I turned to see what he was going to say.

"Frank, can I give you a little insight here? Vera Cienfuegos is not only the sharpest graduate of Exile High, but she's also our best actress. Juries eat out of her hands, and on a good day she can spin a judge around in a circle. And she never does, or says, anything without a reason."

"You mean she was acting in there?"

"She did it to you once before," Mark said, as if thinking it over. "She had you thinking nobody was investigating this at all."

"Is that what she's doing?" I asked this of the chief, but he simply shrugged. It was plain to see that he was not going to share anything official, but we were spared the effort of attempting to pry it out of him.

The station doors opened, and Vera stepped out into the light. She was completely relaxed as she walked up, as if my earlier explosion had never occurred. An explosion that had garnered no response from her whatsoever.

"Frank, I just got off the phone with a Wilma Gibson who says she knows you."

"She's Dorothea's neighbor." Studying her bland, directed manner, I felt a slight tinge of embarrassment at my earlier eruption.

"Yes," she replied sweetly. "I have a couple of important questions for her, and she says she won't speak to anyone but you."

"She felt the local police insulted her on the morning when they found the body."

"That's what she said, but she agreed to speak with me if you were present. She's waiting at her house right now."

"All right."

"Chief, would you mind giving Frank and me a lift over there?" This request caught Dannon off guard.

"Actually, Vera, I'm here only because Chief Waters and I are buddies. I'd be seriously overstepping—"

"Chief, I don't want to take my car because then I would have to make small talk with Frank. If you're worried about jurisdiction, you don't have to come inside with us."

"Can I come along?" Mark asked, the suggestion of a smile forming on his lips. Vera and I both answered him at the same time.

"No."

CHAPTER FIFTEEN

Vera and the chief exchanged updates on their mutual acquaintances in Exile while we rode. As for me, I sat in the back of the chief's car congratulating myself for being kind to Wilma at the outset of the investigation. I felt certain that Vera resented this special relationship, and that she'd restrained herself back at the station only because she knew she might have to ask for my help. I intended to rub it in once we got to Wilma's.

Even so, I hoped this side trip would not take long. I had sent Mark back to Exile with instructions to get his things together for the return flight to New York. Regardless of Chief Dannon's assurances, I wanted to get Mark out of the picture as soon as possible. Judging from what both he and Vera had said about the value of Patterson's story, I was beginning to believe that this case was not yet closed.

Wilma greeted us at her front door, and the smell of fresh coffee rose from her kitchen. As promised, Chief Dannon stayed in the car. Vera had assured him that the interview would take only a few minutes, but I doubted that. Wilma had dominated all of the previous conversations I'd had with her, and even if she didn't dominate this one, Vera had a lot of catching up to do.

Or so I thought. We had barely settled into the parlor with some much-needed coffee when the assistant state attorney asked the biggest question of the case so far.

"Wilma, can you describe for me just how Dorothea asked you to hold that envelope for her?"

"Certainly, dear." Wilma had been so polite at the door that I had to wonder if she was not yet awake. Now I could see she was on her best behavior, and I imagined she hoped to show the pretty young prosecutor what a little politeness can get you. "Actually, it's rather funny.

"Dorothea and I exchanged house keys quite some time ago, and I think she thought I wasn't home that day. She came across the back-yard one Sunday morning, at a time when I'm usually at church, and was letting herself in when I surprised her.

"I was feeling poorly, and so I was sitting here reading my Bible when I heard her at the back door. Well, she looked as if she were go-ing to die of fright! I asked her what she wanted, and she said she was hoping I would hold that envelope for her."

I tried very hard not to show my absolute mortification. I was the only one Wilma had been willing to talk to, and the very man she had given the map, and yet I had not asked this most obvious question.

By itself the map was worthless, but I had always supposed that Dorothea's true blackmail materials had been in her safe-deposit box. Even if that was true, I should have explored the circumstances under which Dorothea gave Wilma the envelope instead of becom-ing distracted by it. Especially when there was no note accompany-ing the map, and Dorothea had given Wilma no instructions about what to do with it if something happened to her.

Vera continued with her questions, serenely hammering nails into the coffin lid of my investigative competence.

"Did she explain why she brought it over at a time when you weren't likely to be here?"

"Oh, yes. She said she didn't want to forget to give it to me, and that she meant to drop it off and come back later to tell me what it was." In my mind I could see a surprised Dorothea, madly trying to think up an excuse for why she was in her neighbor's supposedly vacant house. Her answer hadn't been a good one, but it had worked all the same.

If I had only thought to ask the questions Vera was posing, I would have discovered that Dorothea had not meant to give the envelope to Wilma at all. She had intended to hide it inside Wilma's house, probably right alongside her other, more effective blackmail evidence. With her own set of keys, she had been trying to turn her neighbor's home into a giant safe-deposit box that she could access at any time.

Mark and I had guessed that Dorothea had decided to give Wilma the map so she could retrieve it at all hours. We had also surmised that the map was only one part of more coercive materials. We just hadn't gone the extra step of determining if that additional evidence was also hidden with Wilma, without her knowledge.

I was catching up to Vera, but way too late. According to Patterson, Temple believed Andy had given Dorothea some kind of deathbed confession regarding Carver's disappearance. Learning of the map's existence only that morning, Vera had not accepted the idea that Dorothea would go to the trouble of hiding such a worthless piece of evidence with her neighbor. Not by itself, anyway.

"Wilma, did Dorothea suggest a hiding place for the envelope?" I watched in outright admiration as Vera closed in.

"Why, yes she did. How did you know?"

"Just a guess." Vera reached out and patted Wilma's knee before turning to look at me. "I just remembered. Frank here has someplace he needs to be. Would it be all right if he got going?"

Vera walked me out onto the stoop, but only because she had to make a phone call beyond Wilma's hearing. I stood there feeling used while she called Chief Waters and asked him to get some people out there right away. She snapped the phone's cover shut with authority, and then stared at me as if I shouldn't be there.

"You asked Chief Dannon to drive us out here so I'd have a ride back to Exile," I said accusingly.

"Oh, no, I told the truth about that," she responded with a sincere shake of her head. "I really didn't want to exchange pleasantries with you on the ride over here. But yes, I also wanted a way to get rid of you if my hunch played out."

"You could at least thank me for paving the way with Wilma."

"Well thank you, Frank!" She let her voice take on an enchanted, girllike quality, and then dropped it just as quickly. "You've caused me a lot of trouble, hanging on to that map as long as you did. I'd say you owed me this."

"I've got a question. You obviously think Dorothea hid some more evidence in Wilma's house, but you only found out about the map this morning. What tipped you off?"

"You already know. Patterson told you the same thing he told me. He said that Temple was being blackmailed with something more concrete than that silly map. He thinks it's a statement from Freehoffer describing what happened to David Carver. That might not be great evidence, but it sure will connect Temple to all this if it matches Patterson's description of events.

"You remember the officer who asked you for the map at the station? I prepped him to ask you if there had been anything else along with it when Wilma gave it to you, any special instructions if something happened to Dorothea. You said no, and I put two and two together.

"Dorothea had no friends except Wilma. She didn't include a note with the map, or tell Wilma what to do in the event of her death. So it looks like she was simply hiding it. If she wanted to have her evidence where she could get at it on short notice, the safe deposit was out. Honestly, I think that safe-deposit box was empty, just like Patterson says. I think Dorothea used it as a red herring so no one would think to go looking anywhere else. She'd hidden the map here, so it made sense to come out and ask a few questions."

She didn't need to say the rest, the part where she classified those questions as something that any seasoned investigator would have asked. It must have shown on my face, because she did take a little pity on me at that point.

"If it makes you feel any better, I've been looking for Dorothea's second stash for days. Patterson's little question-and-answer trip through the neighborhood told me the safe-deposit box didn't hold everything he was looking for, so I just widened the net. I've had people showing Dorothea's photograph at every safe deposit and self-storage place for a hundred miles around."

Chief Waters rolled up with a car full of Preston detectives at that point, and Vera's business face came back on. Chief Dannon had been leaning against his car, and he playfully raised his hands when the Preston police approached.

"Hey, I'm just the prosecutor's driver on this one. I didn't even go inside."

"You're welcome to come with us if you bring your toolbox," Waters replied, clearly one of Dannon's friends. "Sounds like Vera's got a little carpentry work for us in there."

"I may." Vera spoke with easy authority, and the older men stopped in front of her. "I might have found some of the blackmail evidence that Mrs. Freehoffer was using. It looks like she hid it in here. I didn't want to play around with the chain of custody, so I haven't seen anything just yet. If the stuff's not where I think it is, we may have to do a little rooting around."

They passed me without so much as a nod, and Vera stopped them at the door.

"The owner's cooperating nicely, and I want to keep it that way, so let me do the talking."

The door closed behind them, and I went down the walk to the chief.

"Wanna stick around and see what happens?"

"Nah. I think I've been shown up enough for one day. Let's get out of here."

The ride back was pretty quiet. Dannon and I can usually find something to talk about, but I was chewing over the events of the last few hours. I wondered what Temple was doing just then, knowing that Patterson had gone to the authorities. If he had any sense at all, he was barricaded somewhere with a few good lawyers.

I still wondered just what kind of a case Vera had inherited from us. She had admitted on Wilma's front stoop that even a written description of David Carver's murder wasn't going to be worth much in court. Back at the station, Mark had pointed out that the evidence against Temple was all circumstantial, and even before then we had noted how much Temple had managed to stay in the shadows.

Perhaps that was why Vera had been so pleased. She had focused on Patterson's canvass of Dorothea's neighborhood right from the start, and that had yielded nothing. She had interpreted Patterson's door-to-door act as a sign that the safe-deposit impostor had not found what he was looking for, and then launched a search of her own. She'd sent people looking for any place where Dorothea might have hidden whatever it was that Patterson was seeking. That quest had radiated to every commercial lock-up for one hundred miles only because the local police had alienated Dorothea's back-door neighbor.

Vera hadn't sat on her hands while that was in progress. She'd secured a court order granting her access to Dorothea's safe-deposit box, and kept that maneuver secret until it actually happened. She'd convinced me that there was no official investigation while her people had been showing Dorothea's picture to every self-storage outfit in the region.

When all those efforts had produced exactly nothing, she had decided to turn up the heat on her only identifiable suspect. Her detectives had visited the hapless Patterson just to scare him into seeing how exposed he was, a move that suggested Vera believed someone else was pulling his strings all along. At the very least it acknowledged the involvement of someone who did not look like Patterson, the impostor from the bank.

She must have done a back flip when Patterson told her about the map, and yet another when he mentioned Temple's belief that a written confession from Andy Freehoffer existed somewhere. All those gymnastics had led her back to Wilma's place, with the question that I should have asked days before.

"Chief, it looks like Dorothea hid more than a map with Wilma. You're familiar with this case; would a written confession by a conspirator in a twenty-year-old murder be enough to convict somebody?"

"Oh, I doubt it. But that Patterson character was pointing pretty hard at his pal Temple, so anything that brings Temple in for questioning is worth something."

"How so?"

"This Temple's got money, right? He'll have a pretty big lawyer with him when he comes in, but that doesn't make him bulletproof. In a lot of cases a good lawyer will calculate the odds and get his client to agree to a plea deal."

"I've spent some time with Temple these last few days. He's as cool as they come. I swear he was dangling clues in front of me, even when I didn't consider him a suspect. It was like he thought it was a game. Somehow I don't see him pleading guilty."

"You may be right. At this point the medical examiner has no evidence that Mrs. Freehoffer's death was anything but an accident. Even Patterson believes she fell down those stairs."

"The guy's completely under Temple's spell. Twenty years ago he helped bury a murder victim on Temple's say-so. Just last week he believed Temple when he said he'd found the woman who was blackmailing him dead in her house. He still believes that, even though Temple showed up at his place last night dressed up like some kind of ninja."

"I'm sure Vera's going to lean on that point. Way too many crazy things happened for that to have been an accident. And if she's found the thing that the other two were looking for, who knows what leverage that will give her?"

We fell silent for a while, and before long we were back in Exile. Chief spoke again once we were close to my house.

"Frank, I hope you see that you accomplished what you set out to do here. You wanted to know who tricked Susan into opening that safe-deposit box, and you did that. Who cares if Vera gets the credit, or even if, God forbid, this one doesn't go to trial? It doesn't change the fact that you figured it out."

Observations like that are why Denny Dannon is the father figure for the entire town of Exile.

"Thanks, Chief." I let out a small chuckle, feeling the mood lifting. "I mean that. I'd almost forgotten why I started this one."

"You really are a lot like her, you know."

"Who? Susan?"

"No, although you and Susan do share the same hard head. No, I mean Vera. You're both sharp, you both ask intelligent questions, and neither one of you knows when to let go. Once you've had a little time to think about this, ask yourself this question: What prosecutor in her right mind would pursue a homicide that the coroner says is an accident, and a decades-old murder with no body and no witnesses?"

Mark left for the airport just before noon. He doubted he'd have to return to make a statement, because he'd decided on his own that the case would never go to trial.

"Nah, Temple's not going to plea to anything. Look at the way he behaved while you were chasing him. Nobody who actually thinks he's in real jeopardy would have done the things he did. He knows this would be one bear of a case to prove, even with Patterson spilling his guts."

"You don't suppose Temple was just using me to set him up, do you? If Patterson killed himself before the police questioned him, everything you and I discovered would have been used to explain why. Is it possible that Temple meant to tip somebody off all along, and it just happened to be me?"

"Maybe. But you know what I really think? I think Patterson was right about what makes Temple tick. He thinks he can sell people on just about anything. I bet Temple never expected anybody to look into this, and that he made Patterson the front man only as a precaution. When we showed up at that meet-and-greet with Doc, you can bet he realized that somebody *was* looking into this."

"Well, it's out of my hands now. And good riddance."

"Your chief was right, though. We did solve it. No matter what Vera does with this, we found out who the impostor was."

We were standing outside near his rental car, and there didn't seem to be much left to say after that. I hugged him hard, but was surprised to find myself choking up.

"Now get out of here. I'm glad you're not taking that job; you don't belong here any more than I do."

I meant it as a joke, but it had an unexpected effect on him. He cocked his head slightly to the side and narrowed his eyes as if trying to recognize me.

"You think so, huh? That you don't belong here? Well, you tell me: Who else would Chief Dannon have gone to when he needed help with the bank? Yeah, I know you and he are friends, but I didn't hear any other names bandied about when he asked for your help. And what about Susan? She'd only known you a few days, but she didn't go to Gray when she was in trouble. She came to you.

"And speaking of Gray, do you know the real reason he doesn't like me?"

"He holds you responsible for my being here."

"Yes, in a way he does. And maybe even he doesn't know the real reason. But the truth is he doesn't like me because he's afraid I'll straighten things out up north and then you'll go home."

That was just too much for me, following on Dannon's comments of that morning, so I deflected it.

"Well, we both know he's wrong about that."

"Hey. Get yourself a better lawyer."

We hugged again, and he was gone.

Mark's parting words reminded me that I had promised to help Gray finish up the safe-deposit job. With the investigation into Brian Temple out of my hands, I figured it was time to catch up with Gray, if for no other reason than it might provide Emily some relief from her obsessive husband.

I called Gray at the bank just after Mark left, and filled him in on the latest developments regarding the safe-deposit impostor.

"That's great news, Frank. Susan will be so pleased . . . am I allowed to tell her?"

"You know, I really hadn't given that much thought. How's this sound: I'll come down and tell her what I can. That way if Vera objects, she'll just be a little madder at me and not someone entirely new."

"Yeeaah . . ." Gray's voice drifted for a moment, as if he were distracted by something. "Sure. We're a little busy right now, but you can come by later. Why don't you meet me in the park, say just after one?"

It sounded like I was still persona non grata at the bank, but somehow that didn't sting very much anymore. Gray had tracked down just about every outdated or unknown client involved with the safe-deposit area, and the auditors weren't due for two more days. A seat on a park bench sounded all right, and so I showed up a little early.

If I had stuck to Gray's schedule, I would have missed one of the most exciting police arrests in the history of Exile. It was around twelve-thirty, and I had just sat down on a bench facing the bank when its front door popped open.

I say it popped because it is not accurate to say it flew. Someone pushed the glass door hard from the inside, and it certainly did swing open, but no one came out at first and the door quickly swung shut again.

It was a lovely day, and there were a lot people heading out to lunch or coming back, so I should not be faulted for not noting the nearby presence of Chief Dannon. I half stood when the bank's door opened again, and this time it stayed that way. It was propped open by the assistant locksmith from Al's Hardware, a young man named Stan whom I had met just a week before.

Stan was holding a large canvas bag in both arms, and seemed stuck in the doorway. His left leg was hung up on something, and he jerked it forward only with the greatest effort. I was having a hard time seeing just what was impeding his progress when he finally broke free. Whatever had been anchoring him was left behind in the bank, but Stan tripped and almost fell when he tried to go down the stone steps.

Quite a few people saw what happened next, but I still have trouble believing my own eyes. Like some leather-capped football player from a forgotten age, Gray Toliver barreled through the doors and leaped on the younger man's back. Stan had been bent over at the time, and so their combined weight sent them both rolling down the remaining steps to the sidewalk.

I took one step in their direction, but a black hand landed on my shoulder and Denny Dannon swept past me at a fast walk.

"I've got it, Frank," he advised in a much deeper voice than normal, and I watched him half cross the street toward the struggling men. I say he half crossed because he stopped in the middle of the thoroughfare and pointed a commanding index finger at Gray and Stan. He never even reached for his gun.

"Hold it right there." He didn't shout, but I swear his voice boomed across the town square. Stan had been trying to heave Gray off of his chest when Dannon spoke, and the blond man reacted like a trained dog. He looked up at the chief, closed his eyes as if in pain, and then sagged back. He raised his hands over his head to show they were empty, and I realized that this was not the first time Stan the assistant locksmith had been spoken to by a police officer.

Gray stopped moving as well, and I saw that he was collapsed across Stan's torso. The bank door opened again, and Susan came rushing through and down the stairs. We both reached Gray at about the same time, and the chief simply stood there glowering at Stan until we rolled Gray off.

Gray was breathing heavily, but it became clear after a moment that he was all right. His cheeks stood out as a dark red against the whiteness of his hair, but he was simply winded. His face wore a mad mask of enjoyment, and he grabbed my shirtfront while Dannon started cuffing Stan.

"Did you see it?" he demanded. "Did you see it? I *got* him!"

I looked over at Stan, and saw that the large canvas bag he had been carrying had come open. It was jammed with stacks of large-denomination bills, and I didn't have to guess where it came from.

Gray reached out and took Susan's hand.

"We got him, Sue. We got him."

CHAPTER SIXTEEN

Susan explained things to me once the ambulance had taken Gray to the hospital. I thought he looked fine, but Susan wasn't taking any chances and so off he went. I was standing on the sidewalk, expecting to see Emily Toliver somewhere in the crowd, when Susan came up.

"Who you looking for, sweet pea?" she asked in the calm, confident voice that I remembered from a week before.

"Gray's wife. Wasn't she helping him down here?"

"I just called her. The safe-deposit work's all done, so she wasn't here today." Susan looked around her, and then took me by the arm. Quite a crowd had formed outside the bank, and newspeople were arriving, so she led me across the street into the park.

"Listen, Frank, the official story here is that Gray happened to notice Stan doing something wrong in the safe-deposit area and called Chief Dannon. Don't go asking any questions, and everything will be fine."

"It'll be fine if you tell me what happened."

"Glad to. I owe you for putting a face on Mr. Freehoffer's

impostor. Here's what happened: Gray never believed that the impostor wrote the original complaint. He kept questioning how you got booted off the job, how it was a second complaint that did it, and how you'd only been working on this for a couple of days when it happened. When Vera and the police came here with their warrant, Gray noticed that Stan was about ready to jump out of his skin."

That all fell into place smoothly, in light of what Stan had been carrying when Gray had tackled him. Recently hired as a locksmith by the business that serviced the bank, he'd written the original complaint because it would get him into the safe-deposit area. I did not know which box he'd opened to get hold of all that cash, but he had probably hoped to do it at a time when he was unobserved. I had ruined that plan by insisting that every action inside the vault was recorded, and that nonbank employees be supervised as well. Stan's original complaint had gotten him inside the vault, and his second grievance had gotten me out of his hair.

"The only time that Stan had been alone in the vault was just after Vera had him drill open Dorothea's safe-deposit box. She'd grabbed him so fast that he didn't have all the tools he'd need to replace the lock. He went back and got his things, and he was allowed in there alone, because he was replacing the lock on a box that had been emptied.

"Gray suspected him by then, and so we cooked up a little test. We identified all the owners a couple of days ago, so Anna and Vicki weren't working in back anymore. We had one last box for Stan to drill, and so we called him over this morning.

"Sure enough, he told us he'd forgotten one of the tools he'd need to replace the lock. He left for a few minutes and came back, and by then I had finished inventorying the box. We left Stan alone in there, just like the other time when he'd forgotten one of his tools. Gray had set up a spy camera in the vault and was watching from his office, and Stan went straight for one of the big boxes. He popped it open like it wasn't even locked.

"Gray called Chief Dannon once he had that on tape, but Stan was a lot quicker than we thought he'd be. He had that bag ready, and just up-ended the box into it. He left his tools right there and walked out with that sack of money toot-sweet. He was at the front door when Gray caught up with him."

I could easily see the hard-bitten old chief petty officer deciding to take matters into his own hands at that point. Stan had been trying to get away from him when I first saw the front door pop open. Apparently Gray had wrapped his arms around Stan's ankle and it had taken the younger man several tries to shake him off.

"You got it all on tape?"

"Yes we did, but only because Gray was experimenting with a remote method for taping future inventories. It was meant as a backup to the up-close taping." She rattled that off as if she'd rehearsed it, and I finally understood her admonition not to ask questions. Gray's tape, and Susan's sudden absence from the vault, might sound a little like entrapment to the wrong ears.

"Do you have any idea whose money that was?"

"We're checking the records now, but it looks like an alias. The box is all paid up, as you might imagine, but that was a powerful stack of money in there. I would guess that some criminal bigwig just lost his rainy-day fund."

It was a beautiful day out, not too hot, and I had not yet eaten lunch. I picked up a burger and fries at the Exile Diner and took a seat at one of the picnic tables on the town's main square.

The scene in front of the bank kept me entertained for close to an hour, with television crews taping their coverage of the day's events. I even saw Ollie out front being interviewed at one point, and for once the guy didn't look like he was coming apart at the seams.

Chief Dannon walked by on his way back to the bank just as I was getting done with my meal, and he stopped to give me a friendly update.

"Yeah, old Stan there has a bit of a record. No wonder he could land that locksmith job; he's been breaking and entering since he was fifteen. He told us who all that money belonged to, and I was just going to tell Ollie. It was an emergency fund for a big-league criminal who Stan knew in prison."

"You can't tell anybody anything these days." Dannon smiled at that, and I decided not to ask just how the chief had come to be standing outside the bank when Gray had "noticed" Stan's unusual behavior in the vault.

"Hey, Vera called to tell me she interviewed Temple a little while ago. He brought his lawyer along, but he didn't refuse to talk. And boy does it sound like he had all the answers. He's barely connected to Mrs. Freehoffer, and nobody's ever seen him near her house. He explained his phone conversations with Patterson as just being two buddies who used to work with the widow's husband.

"The medical examiner still says she died by accident, and Patterson didn't even witness the other murder twenty years ago, so it looks like this one's not going to trial. Sorry."

"Did they find anything hidden in Wilma's house?"

"Oh, yes, I forgot. It was a signed confession from Andy Freehoffer about his role in the murder of David Carver. It backs up what Patterson said about Temple actually pulling the trigger, but with no body and no living witness it's not much. Vera sounded like she wanted to go for it anyway with the evidence they have, but I think her boss said no."

"Mark said it wasn't much of a case, even if they did find some sort of confession. You should meet this Temple, Chief. Patterson's right; the guy could talk his way into Fort Knox."

"I know the type. Even so, trial or no trial, you found out who tricked Susan into opening that safe-deposit box. And in a way, you were the one who caught Stan."

"How so?"

"You straightened out Ollie and Susan about watching the people in the vault. Stan admitted he sent in both complaints, by the way. He says he could have stolen the money easily if you hadn't come along and made Susan tighten things up. So I say you caught him."

"Thanks, Chief."

"Nada." He started walking away, but turned after just a few steps. "Hey, you planning to go back up north, with your buddy Mark?"

"Now how could I do that, Chief?" I raised both hands as if hoping to catch raindrops in my palms. "I mean, things around here are getting downright interesting."